# Memoirs of the Life, Character, and Writings, of Sir Matthew Hale

by John Bickerton Williams (Sir.)

Address:
HardPress
8345 NW 66TH ST #2561
MIAMI FL 33166-2626
USA
Email: info@hardpress.net

# Memoirs of the life, character, and writings of Sir Matthew Hale ...

John Bickerton Williams

35.
41 6.

35.
41 6.

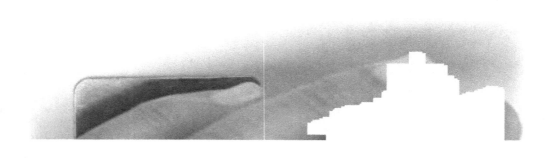

35.

41 6.

Drawn by W. Wilson from the original Painting in the possession of R. Hale Blagden Hale Esq? Engraved by H. Meyer

Mathew Hale. 17 July 1674

# MEMOIRS

## OF THE

## LIFE, CHARACTER, AND WRITINGS,

### OF

# SIR MATTHEW HALE,

#### KNIGHT,

𝕷𝖔𝖗𝖉 𝕮𝖍𝖎𝖊𝖋 𝕵𝖚𝖘𝖙𝖎𝖈𝖊 𝖔𝖋 𝕰𝖓𝖌𝖑𝖆𝖓𝖉.

### BY

## J. B. WILLIAMS, ESQ. LL.D. F.S.A.

## LONDON:

## JACKSON AND WALFORD,

#### 18, ST. PAUL'S CHURCH-YARD.

#### M DCCC XXXV.

*416.*

CLAY, PRINTER, BREAD-STREET-HILL,
DOCTORS'-COMMONS.

TO THE

# REVEREND THOMAS CHALMERS, D. D.

PROFESSOR OF THEOLOGY

IN THE UNIVERSITY OF EDINBURGH,

THIS VOLUME IS INSCRIBED,

AS A MEMORIAL OF FRIENDSHIP

AND ESTEEM,

BY

THE AUTHOR.

# PREFACE.

How carefully soever the catalogue of laymen, which embellishes the Church, is perused, it would be difficult to select from it, an individual more distinguished than Sir Matthew Hale. To *his* memory, as well as Hooker's,[1] even " princes, and the most learned of the nation, have paid reverence."

The lavish praises bestowed upon him may, in part, be attributed to the relics of his own industry ; and, in part, to the fragrant memorial of his virtues, by Bishop Burnet : a memorial

---

[1] " His memory deserves the same honour as St. Simplicius ; for kings and chief magistrates, throughout the learned world, do honour themselves, by wearing of S.S. in memory of the name of St. Simplicius, and in acknowledgment of his eminent justice." Short account of Hale, in " The ancient and present State of Gloucestershire," by Sir Robert Atkyns, p. 208. fol. 1712.

which not only registered facts, but appealed to survivors for their accuracy, while the Judge was fresh in their recollection; and which, though prepared without personal knowledge, was no "dry, and withered branch of composition." It was translated by Louis Dumesnil into French:[2] in the list of books recommended by Dr. Johnson,[3] it is the only piece of biography mentioned: and the venerated Wilberforce, numbers it among those lives of eminent Christians, which are most practically useful.[4]

An abridgement of it speedily appeared, from the pen of the Rev. Samuel Clark:[5] it was reduced yet more, in the Biographia Britannica; in Tomes's Biographical Collections; in Middleton's Biographia Evangelica; in the General Biography of Dr. Aikin, and others; and the invaluable Dictionary of my lamented friend, the late Mr. Chalmers. The whole was reprinted, not long since, by the Rev. Dr. Wordsworth,[6] now Master of Trinity College, Cambridge.

Other editions might be noticed, but three only are deserving of particular mention. Two of them were edited by the late Mr. Knox, of Dublin, and

[2] In the year 1688, and published at Amsterdam.
[3] Life by Boswell, vol. v. p. 195. 12mo. 1811.
[4] Practical View, c. 7. s. 2.    [5] Fol. 1683.
[6] Eccles. Biog. 8vo. 1810. vol. vi. pp. 1—106.

the other by a distinguished prelate.[7] As, however, the latter copy embraces both Mr. Knox's *Prefaces*, that alone will be used in the following pages.

A life of Hale was written by Mr. Serjeant Runnington, preliminary to his edition of the " History of the Common Law;"[8] and, by the Venerable Archdeacon Wrangham, in his British Plutarch; in each case, with great taste, and elegance: but neither of those sketches, made any approach to a reprint of the Memoir by Burnet; and they were too brief to interfere with that now adventured. A writer in the " Gallery of Portraits," published by the Society for Diffusing Useful Knowledge, has pointed out the imperfect condition of *all* the accounts of Hale; Burnet's, as too partial and panegyrical;[9] and the rest, as not sufficiently minute.

That the eminent individual in question, has a strong, if not a peculiar, claim to regard, will, it is thought, be admitted: for, independently of the

---

[7] Lives, Characters, and an Address to Posterity, by Gilbert Burnet, D.D. Lord Bishop of Sarum; with the two Prefaces to the Dublin edition, edited, with an Introduction and Notes, by John Jebb, D.D. F.R.S. Bishop of Limerick, Ardfert, Aghadoe. 8vo. 1833.

Bishop Jebb recommended the Life of Hale, by Burnet, in his Primary Charge, p. 13.

[8] 8vo. 1779. In a subsequent edition, he much enlarged the Memoir. [9] No. XIX. p. 76.

natural, and acquired, endowments which have rendered him famous; and, independently of public attachment to a portion, at least, of his writings, evinced by their constant sale;[10] he, like his devout contemporary, De Renty, was no "retired, or cloistered person."[11] He was one who, besides discharging the ordinary duties of domestic life, occupied several exalted stations; and filled all of them, so as to rivet attention; to extort applause, even from enemies. Opposition, when it arose against him, was borne down by the weight of his character: so resplendent, in short, were his excellencies, that, to this day, if an instance of *singular* virtue and uprightness, especially in the legal profession, is to be adduced, the mind turns as instantly to Lord Hale, as the needle to the pole. He contributed more, by his example,[12] to remove those vulgar errors which once were entertained, and are still not extinct, respecting professional men, than any argument could have effected. It was by conversation with him, and with Selden, that the prejudices cherished by

[10] Some of his Letters have been embodied in an elegant little volume, entitled "Practical Wisdom," or the Manual of Life, the Counsels of Eminent Men to their Children. 12mo. 1824.

[11] The Holy Life of Monsieur De Renty, Chancellor to Louis XIII. 12mo. 1658.

[12] Mr. Hayley styles him the "blameless Sir Matthew Hale; the favourite model of integrity." Life of Milton, p. 129. 4to. 1796. 2d edition.

Archbishop Usher, against lawyers, were banished.[13]

There will be some danger, lest the ensuing narrative, viewed as an illustration of practical Christianity, should produce amazement, rather than emulation ; but such a misuse, alike unfavourable to personal advantage, and dishonouring to God, is to be vigilantly avoided. It should be deeply impressed upon the reader, that the most prominent features in the moral image of Hale—his " delight in the law of the Lord ;" his patient, and faithful diligence, as a member of society ; his studiousness of peace ; his urbanity and seriousness ; his self-denial ; his freedom from ambition ;— identified, as they are, with personal religion, are qualities *never* set forth in the Bible, as wonderful, or rare ; but as essential, and ordinary lineaments of the christian character. It is, therefore, evident, that the acquisition of the " same mind," the doing of the " same things," is, in the case of every individual, no less a duty ; no less indispensable to felicity ; no less necessary to the divine glory ; than in the case of Hale, and the countless host of believers.

Upon the life, by Burnet, the Memoir before us,

[13] See Hale's Histor. Plac. Cor. vol. i. Pref. p. vi. fol. 1736. and *post*, p. 131.

as to its basis, rests: but the arrangement is entirely new; and the whole increased, from the "Notes" of Baxter and Stephens; the Judge's own manuscripts; and every other accessible source.

The *facts* have been thoroughly examined; and, as much as possible, attended to, chronologically.

In addition to this, the labours of others, in the same department, have been freely used. When any thing not noticed by Burnet is introduced, the authority is quoted: but the Bishop's work is seldom formally referred to; every circumstance in it, connected with the Judge, being avowedly retained.

It is not improbable, that some persons may, for a moment, feel surprised, if not offended, that the *style* of that standard book should have been abandoned: and the feeling is entitled to sympathy. At the same time it must be observed, that it appeared impossible to give it entire, and use, as it seemed desirable to use them, the materials which will be found in the present volume. For, had the Bishop's narrative been reprinted, the new matter must have been exhibited separately; which would have seriously affected the arrangement; and occasioned, too, in addition to other awkwardnesses, intolerable repetitions. Beside which, (to make no allusions, by way of shelter, to the criticisms of

Pope, or Swift, upon Burnet as a writer; nor yet to the observations of Mr. Stephens,[14]) it may be anticipated that the offence, if it be such, will appear the more venial, when it is recollected, that the admirers of the beautiful Memoir alluded to, have the easiest possible means of gratification : numerous copies are to be obtained, particularly the one recently edited by Bishop Jebb; and as *that* edition contains the other " Lives " Burnet wrote, and wrote so well, the expectation is justified, that the supply will continue to be unfailing.

While, for purposes of verification, the collected edition of our author's writings, " moral and religious," published in the year 1805, under the superintendence of the Rev. T. Thirlwall, M.A.[15] has been employed ; the *title* of each " Contemplation" is, also, given, in order that any other edition may, the more readily, be consulted.

The introduction of his Lordship's Will ; the account furnished of his numerous publications ; and the notice taken of them (with unfeigned diffidence), will not, it is hoped, be considered superfluous.

The parenthetical explanation just given, is applicable, and I wish it applied, to the whole work. Nor can I, with Mr. Serjeant Runnington,

---

[14] See *post*, p. 390.  [15] In 2 vols. 8vo.

on an occasion somewhat similar, help saying, that
it is " dismissed—with fear and trembling." For,
in spite of every effort, and attention studiously
vigilant and sedulous, imperfections will present
themselves; quite sufficient, if it were not for the
estimate commonly made in such cases, to induce
an appeal to the reader's candour, and indulgence.
It may be mentioned, however, without any apology, that the undertaking has been strictly that
of an amateur; that it has been prosecuted under
the pressure of duties, rendering more than occasional progress impracticable; confining, indeed, in
a great measure, recreative engagements like that
before us, to moments abridged from sleep.

In the " Notes," some regard has been paid to
illustration; and, unless I am deceived, without
unnecessary minuteness. That service might have
been greatly extended, and in a manner gratifying
to the curious; especially in relation to philosophical subjects; the times; Sir Matthew's official
conduct; and the use, moreover, he occasionally
made, by alteration, of other writers: an instance
of the latter occurs at page 75, in reference to one
of the sayings of Plautus.

All attempts to furnish a *complete* pedigree of the
Judge's family and representatives, have failed; an
acknowledgment made with the more regret, because had it not been so, Burnet's fond and

accurate anticipations—that " in after-times," it would " be reckoned no small honour to be descended [16] from" Lord Hale—might have been fully met; as well as that " reckoning up " of his Lordship's " issue," which the good Bishop commenced," [17] best continued, and displayed. The pedigree Mr. Thirlwall framed, was limited to the eldest son of Sir Matthew, and *his* descendants. [18]

To my esteemed friend, Joshua Wilson, Esq., Barrister at Law, Highbury-place, London, I am afresh indebted, for the use of books out of his well-furnished library; and also, for the liberal communication of an authentic transcript of Lord Hale's " History, and Analysis of the Common Law."

By the kind assistance of Sir Henry Ellis, and the obliging librarians of the British Museum, I

[16] Life, p. 184. 12mo. 1682.
The Rev. Robert Uvedale, M.A., Vicar of Fotherby, near Louth, Lincolnshire, in a letter with which, with unsolicited kindness, he favoured me, states, that " Mary, second daughter of Edward Stephens, Esq. of Cherrington, Gloucestershire, by his wife Mary, eldest daughter of Sir Mathew Hale, married the Rev. Robert Uvedale, LL.D. Rector of Orpington, in Kent. Dr. Uvedale," he adds, " who was my great grandfather, died in 1722, aged 80, and his wife, in 1740, aged 84. Rachel, eldest daughter of Mr. Stephens, married the Rev. Robert Bull, (son of Bishop Bull), Prebendary of Gloucester, and Rector of Tortworth, in Gloucestershire.—See Nelson's Life of Bishop Bull, p. 476."
[17] See *post*, p. 160.
[18] Works, vol. i. p. 193.

was enabled to acquire, with facility, all the information to be gained in that splendid depository, as well from the Hargrave Collection of Lord Hale's papers, as from not a few printed volumes, and uncommon pamphlets.

The politeness of the Librarian of Lincoln's Inn, in whose care are the valuable MSS. bequeathed by Lord Hale ; as also the ready acquiescence of the Benchers in my wish to transcribe the catalogue, demand most grateful acknowledgment.

The name, likewise, of my friend, Joseph Blower, Esq., of Lincoln's Inn Fields, is entitled to particular mention ; not only for offices of kindness, rendered in person, but for the willing use of his time and influence, for the promotion of my object. Through him, too, I obtained an introduction to the possessor of the Judge's private MSS. and various relics—Robert Hale Blagden Hale, Esq., of Cottles, near Melksham, in Wiltshire. The obliging readiness of that gentleman to further, by all the information within his power, the present undertaking ; his permission to copy the very fine family picture[19] of the Judge, in his possession ; his

---

[19] An excellent full-length portrait of Sir Matthew Hale, is in the possession of the Right Honourable the Lord Kenyon, at Gredington, in Flintshire.

A list of the various engraved portraits of Sir Matthew, may be seen in Granger's Biog. Hist. vol. v. pp. 119, 120. 8vo. 1824: and in Walpole's Anecdotes of Painting, &c. by Dallaway, vol. v.

communication of the MS. for the *fac-simile* of the hand-writing; and his cordial liberality, in reference to the whole of those unrivalled treasures which he possesses, — have laid me under the deepest obligations; for, although the selections made, from the rich and unique MSS. alluded to, owing to their nature, and the studied compression of the following account, not to mention his Lordship's wishes respecting them, are comparatively few, they have imparted, with respect to some statements, a degree of confidence, which could not, in their absence, have been felt: they have shed a light upon Hale's own course, as well as the period in which he lived: and, by supplying a guide to his opinions, both of men and things, have given to the work a value, it could no otherwise have possessed.

Miss Hale must permit me to express my cordial thanks, for the trouble she so handsomely took, in furnishing the drawing of the armorial bearings, which is engraved at the foot of the portrait.

It would have been pleasant, to have enlarged upon various subjects *collateral* to the following pages; to have dwelt upon themes of general

pp. 114, 203, 301. A copy of the portrait in Lincoln's Inn Library, is given by Mr. Lodge, in his Illustrious Heads. fol. ed. No. XX.; and by the Society for Diffusing Useful Knowledge, in the number of their " Gallery," already quoted.

history; upon a few, at least, of the coincidences observable between times past and the present; upon the importance of contemplating exalted lawyers as models;[20] and upon some of those lessons which naturally suggest themselves, in " this our age" especially, from such a picture of wisdom, moderation, and piety as is here delineated. For various reasons, however, topics of this description have been left, in the main, to the

---

[20] See Letters on the Study and Practice of the Law, by John Raithby, Esq., 2d ed. 1816. Particularly pp. 17—26, &c., and 144.

I cannot, notwithstanding the risk of too long a " note," refrain from placing before the reader, a single extract from an able " Review" of pamphlets on the abuse of charities, in the Christian Observer.

" Of law," says Hooker, " there can be no less acknowledged than that her seat is the bosom of God, her voice the harmony of the world. All things in heaven and earth do her homage, the very least as feeling her care, and the greatest as not exempted from her power; both angels and men, and creatures of what condition soever, though each in different sort and manner, yet all, with uniform consent, admiring her as the mother of their peace, and joy."—" If such be the parent, what might we not expect from her peculiar children, from those who catch the lessons of truth and wisdom from her lips, and live in the beams of her presence? We might, surely, expect them to be men of orthodox opinions, and correct practice, and large hearts, and charitable tempers. We might expect no longer to be driven back to the days of *Sir Matthew Hale*, for an example of the highest legal eminence, combined with the deepest, and most striking piety. We might expect, that his honoured mantle would fall on many of his successors; and that a vast proportion of them would be seeking that ' bosom of God,' which is the tranquil and eternal seat, not only of the fundamental principles of their profession, but of their hopes, their triumph, and their unchanging happiness."—Vol. xvii. pp. 816, 817.

reader. The inspired writers rarely did more, in narrative, than communicate the simple facts : *they* stirred men up to the praise of HIM, " from whom every good and perfect gift proceedeth ;" while with motives, and inferences, and circumstances, not essential to the story, they seldom interfered.

Although the notice, at any length, of the *advantages* of biographical records, would be foreign from my design, it may not, nevertheless, be amiss to glance at the *tendency* of them, just so far as to remark, the directness of their bearing upon another world : their adaptation to cure those fallacious views of life, which all are prone to cherish. They have, indeed, a voice—loud, significant, and salutary ; not unlike that of the Apocalyptic angel, when the Apostle saw him " stand upon the sea, and upon the earth, and lift up his hand to heaven, and sware by Him that liveth for ever and ever, that there should be time no longer."

Were that voice only *heard ;* had but memorials, like the one before us, their legitimate effect ; were mankind, commencing merely with Lord Hale's birth, as an era from which to calculate, to place, in steady view, the multitudes who, *since* that date, in spite of rank, and vigour, and vivacity,

and wealth, have, as he has done, " passed away ;"
and to connect with the computation, the assurance
—that a similar event must happen to every living
person ; how speedy, and entire would be the
change, in their character, opinions, and habits!
Instead of the *shortness* of time, furnishing, after
the fashion of the Epicureans, an argument for
sensuality, and indifference, would there not be
one universal supplication ?—" *So teach us to
number our days, that we may apply our hearts
unto* WISDOM."

JOHN BICKERTON WILLIAMS.

THE CRESCENT, SHREWSBURY,
    *March* 4, 1835.

# CONTENTS.

## CHAPTER I.

## CHAPTER II.

## CHAPTER III.

## CHAPTER IV.

### A. D. 1648 TO A. D. 1653.

## CHAPTER V.

### A. D. 1653 TO A. D. 1660.

## CHAPTER VI.

### A. D. 1660.

## CHAPTER VII.

### A. D. 1660 TO A. D. 1662.

# CHAPTER VIII.

### A. D. 1662 TO A. D. 1666.

# CHAPTER IX.

### A. D. 1666 TO A. D. 1671.

# CHAPTER X.

### A. D. 1671 TO A. D. 1676.

# CHAPTER XI.

### A. D. 1676 TO HIS DEATH, A. D. 1676-7.

## CHAPTER XII.

### HIS HABITS AND CHARACTER.

## CHAPTER XIII.

### SOME ACCOUNT OF HIS GENIUS, LEARNING, AND WRITINGS.

PAGE

---

ERRATA.

Page 6, note, *for* ' Note E E,' *read* ' Note GG.'
 105, line 13, *after* ' Happy,' *insert* ' would it have been.'
 123, ... 4, *after* ' all,' *insert* ' of.'
 159, ... 4, from bottom, *for* ' 1676,' *read* ' 1677.'
 161, ... 21, *for* ' Alderley,' *read* ' Adderley.'
 325, ... 14, *for* ' occupation,' *read* ' occupations.'

" THE last year of my abode at Acton, I had the happiness of a neighbour, whom I cannot easily praise above his worth—SIR MATTHEW HALE, Lord Chief Baron of the Exchequer—whom all the judges and lawyers of England admired for his skill in law, and for his justice ; and scholars honoured for his learning ; and I highly valued for his sincerity, mortification, self-denial, humility, conscientiousness, and his close fidelity in friendship."

R. BAXTER.

―――――――

" IMMORTAL HALE ! for deep discernment praised,
    And sound integrity, not more than famed
    For sanctity of manners undefiled."

COWPER.

# MEMOIRS

### OF

# SIR MATTHEW HALE.

---

## CHAPTER I.

### FROM HIS BIRTH, A.D. 1609, TO A.D. 1629.

MATTHEW, the only child of Robert Hale, Esq.,
by Joan, daughter of Matthew Poyntz, of Alderley,
in the county of Gloucester, Esq., was born at
Alderley, November 1, 1609.

His mother was a scion of the "noble" family
of Poyntz, of Acton; but his grandfather, Robert
Hale, of Wotton-under-Edge, in Gloucestershire,
like many of his progenitors, was a clothier: eminent, however, in his line; affluent also; and
" rich in good works."

The father of our author was trained to the bar,
and became a member of Lincoln's Inn; but early
in life was embarrassed by scruples respecting the
phraseology used in pleadings.

It is in vain to conjecture the *extent* of his difficulties; and equally impossible to estimate, with

B

accuracy, their character; but the direction contained in his will—that his son should follow the law—appearing so entirely to negative the fact of their continued influence, they would seem, independently of other reasons, to have been unfounded. That they, at one period, operated forcibly upon his own mind, may, nevertheless, be concluded from the circumstance, that, in consequence of them, he early abandoned his profession,[1] and with it the only means in his power of increasing the paternal inheritance, already, nominally at least, reduced by a disposition eminently benevolent. He not only liberally dispensed his alms in his lifetime, but at his decease charged his small estate (about 100*l.* a year) with a perpetual annuity of 20*l.* in favour of the poor of Wotton: an act of kindness well approved of by his son, and afterwards confirmed by him, with some addition ; and with this regulation also, that it should be distributed among such poor housekeepers only as lived without parochial relief.

Before young Hale attained his fifth year, both his parents were removed by death. The God of Orphans, however, "took him up;" and after some opposition from Mr. Thomas Poyntz, his mother's brother, he was committed to the care of one of his near kinsmen, Anthony Kingscot, of Kingscot, Esq. That gentleman being puritanically inclined, and intending his young charge for a divine,

[1] Some judicious remarks upon Mr. Hale's conduct occur in Edgeworth's Essays on Professional Education, ch. vi. p. 348. 4to. 1809.

bestowed upon his education correspondent care, a circumstance which seems to have provoked Anthony Wood's wrath ; for, noticing Sir Matthew's grammar-learning, he remarks, that it was obtained at Wotton-under-Edge ; " not in the free school, but under one Mr. Staunton, the scandalous vicar."[2]

Of Hale's early years nothing further is known, than that, while at school, he had the reputation of being an extraordinary proficient in learning ; and that, before he was seventeen, he removed to Magdalen Hall, Oxford.

His college tutor was the Rev. Obadiah Sedgwick ; Burnet merely mentions it : the editor of Hale's " Moral and Religious Works "[3] does more ; and having, in a note, endeavoured, very obviously, by extracts from the " Athenæ Oxonienses," to degrade Mr. Sedgwick, it is necessary to remark, that if the union of piety, and learning, and wealth, *could* have formed a shield against those surly prejudices which chastised even Dr. South for his wit, it would have protected Sedgwick. But, the circumstance of Sedgwick being a Puritan, roused Wood's malignity to the utmost ; he, therefore, regarded and represented him as, on account of his politics, he did the father and tutor of John Locke, as fanatical. Sedgwick, after all, notwithstanding some blemishes, was a man of distinguished excellence :[4] were nothing more known of him than that he was chaplain to the renowned

[2] Ath. Oxon. vol. iii. p. 1090. 4to. 1817.
[3] *Ut supra*. It is pleasant to notice, that Dr. Wordsworth, in his Ecclesiastical Biography, has not followed Mr. Thirlwall's example.
[4] See Brook's Lives of the Puritans, vol. iii. p. 295.

Lord Vere, of Tilbury, and Hale's tutor, his memory would be sufficiently embalmed.

While at Oxford, Hale became so enamoured of stage entertainments, as almost wholly to forsake his studies : the gravity of his deportment, for which he had been remarkable, was abandoned ; a fondness for dress succeeded ; and he delighted much in company. It is said, however, and it furnishes no slight encomium upon his education, that, although addicted to many youthful vanities, he preserved his purity and great probity of mind.

Scarcely were the bonds of early discipline thus slackened, than he gave full scope to his constitutional vigour ; and the attractions of gymnastic exercises became so dominant, as to threaten an entire disregard of the charms of literature. In proof of the proficiency he made in fencing, the following incident has been mentioned, and it demands attention, as direct evidence of his good-nature, and as an illustration also of that abhorrence which seems to be involved in the due hatred of flattery. One of his instructors persisting that he could teach him no more, Hale regarded the assertion as insincere ; and, to prove it, promised the flatterer, who was his tenant, the house he lived in if he could hit him a blow upon the head. As might have been expected, the master succeeded ; and so satisfied was the chivalrous youth with the discovery, that, in spite of the indiscreet nature of the engagement, he freely performed it.

By no unnatural transition, Mr. Hale's thoughts were now, for a time, turned to military affairs ;

and his tutor, Sedgwick, having engaged to attend
Lord Vere to the Low Countries, he determined
to accompany him " to trail a pike" in the army of
the Prince of Orange. The resolution was unex-
pectedly, but very happily, frustrated.

Circumstances connected with a law-suit, which
involved part of his estate, led him to London, and
brought him into the society of his counsel, Mr.
(afterwards Serjeant) Glanville.[5] That eminent
man, struck with his client's clearness of intellect,
solid judgment, and other indications favourable to
legal studies, recommended them to his attention.
At first the subject was irksome, for Mr. Hale
felt an aversion to lawyers ; he regarded them as
a barbarous race ; and as unfit for any thing beyond their own profession. The learned serjeant's
prudence and candour, nevertheless, ultimately
prevailed ; and that entire change in the pursuits
of his young acquaintance, which he so much desired, was effected. It seems necessary to remark
here, that *before* the period just alluded to, the
good effects of Hale's early discipline had begun
once more to appear ; reflection upon past indo-
lence and vanity had produced considerable regret ;
and, under a conviction often alluded to in his
writings, how much the one and the other had
arisen from inordinate attachment to plays, he had
resolved, on quitting college for the metropolis,
never to enter a theatre ; a resolution which, in
the letter of advice to his grandchildren,[6] hereafter
quoted, he tells us he faithfully kept.

[5] See Note A.　　　　　[6] See Chap. XIII. *post.*

# CHAPTER II.

A.D. 1629, TO HIS CALL TO THE BAR.

On the 8th of November, 1629, Mr. Hale was admitted a student of Lincoln's Inn; and under the deepest impression of time already *lost*, he at once brought to bear upon his books the whole energy of his powerful mind. So intense was his ardour, that difficulties only stimulated him to exertion: for a while[1] he studied at the rate of sixteen hours a day; and not only threw aside his gay attire, but sunk, unhappily, into the opposite extreme. So unlike a gentleman did he become in his personal appearance, as actually, on one occasion, to be impressed for the king's service.

His retreat from vain company was more gradual: not, in fact, till he was driven to it by a sad, though to him felicitous,[2] occurrence. Having joined some young men in a convivial party out of town, one of their number, notwithstanding all Mr. Hale's efforts to prevent it, indulged in wine to such a degree, as to become insensible; and, at length, apparently dead. Mr.

---

[1] Burnet says *for many years:* but that statement appears to have been too unqualified. See *post.* Note E E.

[2] Note B.

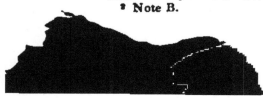

Hale retired to another room; and having shut the door, prayed to Him "-who seeth in secret," that his friend might be restored, and that the countenance given by himself to such excess might be pardoned. He vowed also against the indulgence in such companionship in future, and that he would not even drink a health. His friend recovered, and the vow was performed, occasionally to the inconvenience and reproach of its framer; for, in after days, when drinking the "*King's Health*" was deemed a distinguishing mark of loyalty, Mr. Hale was sometimes uncivilly treated because of his refusal to observe the ceremony.

That change being now wrought which made virtuous attainments thenceforth the main objects of his desire and effort, he was well able to endure both the opposition and the scorn of men: his late associates were forsaken without regret; and he industriously divided his time between the sacred occupations of piety, professional duties, and general science. So uniform was he in the former, as during six-and-thirty years not to have failed once in going to church on the Lord's-day: he made the observation, when his attendance was first interrupted by an ague; and he reflected upon the circumstance with grateful acknowledgments for God's great goodness.

It is uncertain at what time he composed that interesting summary of "Rules," which, though intended merely for private use, has been scarcely less admired than Jeremy Taylor's elaborate Treatise on "Holy Living;" but, following the path marked out by Bishop Burnet, it will be best perused in this connexion. Any disposition the reader may feel for criticism, will yield, it may be hoped, to those inspiring traces which it reveals of devout elevation; to that earnest seriousness which ought to characterize all such as, fully alive to present evils, are intent upon the momentous concerns of eternity.

### MORNING.

I. To lift up the heart to God, in thankfulness, for renewing my life.

II. To renew my covenant with God in Christ: 1. By renewed acts of faith, receiving Christ, and rejoicing in the height of that relation. 2. Resolution of being one of his people, doing him allegiance.

III. Adoration and prayer.

IV. Setting a watch over my own infirmities and passions, over the snares laid in our way. *Perimus licitis.*

### DAY EMPLOYMENT.

There must be an employment—two kinds :—

I. Our ordinary calling, to serve God in it. It is a service to Christ, though never so mean, Coloss. iii. Here, faithfulness, diligence, cheerfulness. Not to overlay myself with more business than I can bear.

II. Our spiritual employments. Mingle somewhat of God's immediate service in this day.

### REFRESHMENTS.

I. Meat and drink, moderation, seasoned with somewhat of God.

II. Recreation : 1. Not our business.  2. Suitable.  No games, if given to covetousness or passion.

### IF ALONE.

I. Beware of wandering, vain, lustful, thoughts; fly from thyself, rather than entertain these.

II. Let thy solitary thoughts be profitable; view the evidences of thy salvation, the state of thy soul, the coming of Christ, thy own mortality; it will make thee humble and watchful.

### COMPANY.

Do good to them.  Use God's name reverently. Beware of leaving an ill impression of ill example. Receive good from them, if more knowing.

### EVENING.

Cast up the accounts of the day.  If aught amiss, beg pardon.  Gather resolution of more vigilance.  If well, bless the mercy and grace of God that hath supported thee.

-------

Mr. Hale's habits soon attracted the attention of Sir William Noy, afterwards Attorney General. That distinguished man, whom James Howell's facetious statements [3] have rendered additionally

[3] Familiar Letters, vol. i. p. 261.  12mo. 1655.

celebrated, often called upon him, directed his reading, and occasioned him, by his kindness, the appellation of *Young* Noy.

It was his happiness to obtain, likewise, the notice and friendship of the immortal Selden; of Mr. Vaughan, afterwards Lord Chief Justice of the Common Pleas; and of " the most reverend, learned, humble, and pious"[4] Dr. Usher, the Lord Primate of Ireland. Under the eye and patronage of these renowned individuals, he prosecuted his studies with increased enthusiasm and diligence. He kept the hours of the hall in term time, and seldom put himself out of commons during the vacation.

He took nothing upon trust; and, like his friend the Attorney General, was unwearied in searching records:[5] he made collections, moreover, out of the books he read, and, mingling them with his own observations, digested them into a common-place-book: a plan of procedure which, whatever objection may be urged against it, as sometimes managed, has had the sanction, and been recommended by the example, of not a few of the most illustrious men. The volume referred to now enriches the Library of Lincoln's Inn. One of the Judges who borrowed it from its compiler, declared that, although composed before Mr. Hale was called to the bar, no lawyer in England could have done it better.

Having surmounted the difficulties of his pro-

[4] Richard Baxter, p. 206. fol. 1696.
[5] Familiar Letters, *ut supra*.

fession, he at once extended his inquiries. The civil law,[6] arithmetic, some branches of the mathematics, and natural philosophy, medicine, anatomy, surgery, ancient history, and chronology, and, especially, divinity, were severally subjected to the most inquisitive investigation. So great was his mental vigour, that he regarded philosophical and mathematical pursuits as *diversions*—in which, when weary with studying law or theology, he found recreation.

As his studious pains and exemplary deportment, as well as the patronage he received, were known, it is not surprising that he should have become the theme of applauding conversation : and that he was spoken of, as likely to *rise*. A draper, with whom, in bargaining for a " new suit," he differed about the price, told him he should have the cloth for nothing, if he would promise him 100*l*. when Lord Chief Justice of England. The offer was of course declined, but the draper lived to see his customer advanced to that high dignity.

[6] See Note C.

# CHAPTER III.

In what year Mr. Hale was called to the bar, is doubtful; nor can it, because of the imperfect state of the earlier records of Lincoln's Inn, be ascertained. It was certainly not long prior to the commencement of those unhappy feuds, from which there was no refuge, and which issued, as is well known, in results the most disastrous and solemn. For some time before the general agitation reached its climax, it had been no easy matter for a man either to preserve his integrity, or to live securely. But then the difficulty was increased a thousand fold; and few more keenly felt it, or deplored it with a deeper sorrow, than the subject of this biographical record. In his " Discourse of Religion[1]," to mention no other of his writings, there is, in spite of the feverish excitement which so universally prevailed, the calmest, and, on that account, the most affecting reference to the subject; he seems to have been charmed by the almost universal perturbation into " quiet thoughts," — just as Walton eloquently

[1] Works, vol. i. p. 306.

supposed some persons to be affected by a recital of the " spiritual conflicts" of George Herbert.

Having observed, in the " Life of Pomponius Atticus," how a season of uncommon distraction was spent by him, not merely free from danger, but without the least blemish to his character, nay, with universal esteem, Mr. Hale selected him [2] as his pattern: and observing that, besides those virtues which are necessary to all men, and at all times, there were two things to which that Roman citizen was particularly indebted; the one, engaging in no faction, and meddling in no public business; and the other, a constant favouring and relieving those that were lowest,—he determined to guide himself by the same rules.

The high reputation he had at this comparatively early period of his history attained, is demonstrated by the extent and magnitude of his practice. Burnet says, that he was one of the counsel assigned to the Earl of Strafford on his arraignment in the year 1640: though it has been accurately noticed by Mr. Sergeant Runnington,[3] that there is no evidence of it from the " trial" itself. There were, however, such allusions made by Hale in another case of treason, where he *was* engaged, as confirm the bishop's assertion,[4] and upon which, in conjunction with that testimony, the reader may, it is thought, rely.

[2] See Note D.
[3] Life of Sir M. Hale, prefixed to the History of the Common Law, p. 5; and see Hargrave's State Trials, vol. i. p. 759.
[4] State Trials, vol. ii. p. 160.

Whether Hale took any part in the loyal offer of services which was now made by the members of the inns of court, it is impossible to affirm. The probability is, that he did. But whether it were so or not, his loyalty is no more a matter of correct doubt than whether he preferred the Church of England to any other section of Christendom. Wood, obviously with a view to make him, if possible, *dis*loyal, stated that, in 1643, he took " the covenant," and appeared several times, as he had often been informed, with other lay persons, among the assembly of divines.[5] But this representation rests upon no other testimony. Burnet is silent ; nor is it mentioned by Roger North. Without, therefore, denying or admitting it, and without attempting to justify the test itself, which, *as* a test, appears unjustifiable, and, according to Baxter, who took it and repented, " a snare," also, " to the conscience ;" still its leading feature was well calculated to make a deep impression upon such a mind as Hale's. Its avowed design, as to England and Ireland, was " a reformation of religion in doctrine, worship, discipline, and government, according to the word of God, and the example of the best reformed churches."[6]

On the supposition, for a moment, that Wood's account is correct, it will not be amiss for those who feel more inclined to censure than approve, to " take " (the counsel is Mr. Thirlwall's) " a sober and dispassionate survey of the times and circum-

[5] Ath. Oxon. vol. iii. p. 1091.  [6] See Note E.

stances in which the subscription was called for.
If," observes that reverend gentleman, "he refused,
he was deprived of the privilege of exercising his
profession, in which he was advancing to fortune
and celebrity by rapid strides. He could not,
therefore, be disposed to take his measures without
revolving in his mind the very serious alternative
which was presented to his choice. He was not
unwilling to abridge the prerogative of the king,
and reconcile it with the liberties of the people ;
he could feel no difficulty in joining with parliament to a limited extent ; and whilst they still
proclaimed their allegiance to the king, and respect
for his person and authority, he consoled himself
with the prospect of an amicable adjustment between the crown and parliament, and the establishment of a constitution that would balance the
just rights of the king with the inalienable privileges of the subject. Of this the covenant afforded
a satisfactory pledge. He saw in it an express
acknowledgment of the sovereign's rights, and the
elements of national peace and concord. His love
for his country, loyalty to the king, and attachment
to a free constitution, would dispose him to give
the most favourable construction to an instrument
which, apparently, led to such important and happy
consequences. The mere form and outward struc-
ture of the Church, always appeared to him an
object of a secondary nature."[7]

Mr. Hale, it is worthy of remark, had no
scruples about the doctrine of " divine right," in

[7] Works, vol. i. p. 130.

reference to any "form of government;"[8] a fact sufficient, in the absence of every thing else, to account for his taking "the covenant," if such were really the case.

"It is incumbent," he writes, "upon him that *affirms* a divine right, to prove these two things— That some determinate form of government is of divine institution; and, that the form for which he contends, is *that* form which *is* so. For, if he doth only the former, and not the latter, his second assertion contradicts and destroys his first assertion; for it were ridiculous to say there is a form of government of divine institution, and yet he knows not what it is. We will, therefore, suppose the assertion to be of episcopal, or presbyterial, or congregational government; and of all, or any of these, *we* say there is *no* evidence of such divine institution.

"Although the primitive practice, since the apostles' times, seems to be episcopal, yet, since the reformation from the papacy, many churches, sound in their professions of the truth, have used a presbyterial form of government, being most consistent with the constitution of the time and places of such reformation, as the French, the Dutch, the Swiss, the Genevan, and others; and it were hard to censure either the one or the other for schism, or an apostasy from an indispensable institution, when, doubtless, they were the true churches of Christ, who might, on all hands, challenge an

* Orig. MS.

interest in that promise of his, ' that he would be with them to the end of the world.'

" Under both forms, men of singular piety, learning, and soundness in the truth, have been brought forth, to the honour and glory of God, and the profession of the christian religion.

" Every man must needs agree, that these external forms are but in order to a greater end ; the shell, or the corners of badger skins, to the tabernacle ; the mint and cummin, in comparison of the true and real kingdom of Christ in the soul ; such as, without the latter, are but empty shells and forms; and the latter, as it may be, and hath been, without this external formality, so it is infinitely beyond it, and therefore, certainly, the disputes and controversies about these external forms of government can no way countervail the neglect of that inward, powerful, and sovereign kingdom of Christ in his church and people, by his Spirit subduing the heart to a willing obedience to his sceptre and will.

" It is most apparent, that the affixing of the seal of the King of heaven to any form of government, without a commission from him, is a presumption and crime of a high nature, and such as is derogatory to his glory and truth, in a very high degree ; and therefore men had need be careful how they coin their own conjectures and imaginations, or it may be their own designs, interests, and affectation of power, with the stamp of a divine authority ; and so much the rather, because, if detected of falsity (as it is impossible for all the claims of the several pretenders to be true), the damage that comes to religion thereby is scarcely reparable.

" The several claims of divine authority, in the several pretenders to ecclesiastical government, under differing shapes, namely, the papal, the prelatical, the presbyterian, the congregational, and the controversies concerning them, have been the great instruments of disquietude in Christendom; the great scandal of religion; the great breaker of christian charity amongst the professors of the same Christ; the great occasion of effusion of christian blood, and embroiling of states and kingdoms in civil wars; the great upholders of tyranny over the consciences of men, in points dogmatical and practical, upheld to maintain the credit and infallibility of their cause; and which is worse, if it may be worse than all the rest, the canker that hath eaten out the heart and life of true religion, Christianity, and the power of godliness in the hearts and lives of men, and overthrown the true kingdom of Christ when the pretence is to establish it; so that, if the Son of God should now come to judgment, and should look for faith, humility, self-denial, heavenly-mindedness, charity, gentleness, contempt of the world, waiting for his second appearing to judgment, and the fruit of the seeds which his divine doctrine and Spirit hath sowed amongst mankind; instead thereof, nothing but factions, policies for establishing power and greatness in the ministers, with uncharitableness, tearing one another for the earth, and the things of the earth; and all religion turned into nothing but professions of distrust, forms of governments, and zeal for that, and new hard names and titles of pontifical, prelatical, presbyterial, and such words of distinction and dissemination. Surely we have great cause to fear that the envious man hath sown the seeds that produce this kind of crop, who, if the true power and efficacy of that inward kingdom of Christ be laid aside, cares not what new names be taken up, under what pretences soever, so they banish peace and goodness from the world."[9]

Such being his recorded sentiments, the observation made by Mr. Thirlwall becomes additionally important. " Neither the letter nor the spirit of the covenant, forced upon Mr. Hale a subscription to unscriptural articles of faith, nor even prescribed the use of the Common Prayer, and the Liturgy of the Church of England. Though it was not without a degree of violence to his conscience, he renounced the jurisdiction of the bishop; yet he could discover, engrafted upon the *primitive* constitution, superadditions of human policy, which moderated, in a considerable degree, his admiration of its excellency and purity. But, in examining this article of the covenant more critically, his mind found a further relief from observing, that the ' extirpation of prelacy' was connected with, and qualified by, a subsequent sentence, which was evidently inserted for the purpose of removing the scruples, and satisfying the consciences, of the moderate Churchman."[10]

[9] Hale, Orig. MS.          [10] Works, vol. i. pp. 130, 131.

Hale, no doubt, well knew what had passed upon the topic last mentioned in the Westminster synod; and that the phraseology of the covenant, too, was altered prior to its being offered for signature by the nation, so as to meet the objections started, during the debate, by those venerable men, who declared their judgment to be for the *ancient*, moderate episcopacy. Nor could he have been a stranger to the tender made of it to the House of Lords, with this public explication— that by the word "prelacy," and to which extirpation was attached, was not meant *all* episcopacy, but only the form there described."[11] Hence, in all probability, it was, that so many of the *clergy* took the covenant. Some of them filled dignified situations after the Restoration; and it does not appear that any of them were questioned respecting their conduct.

Mr. Lodge pronounces the league a "vile compact;" but he asserts, that it was presently enthusiastically subscribed by the *entire population* of the capital and its vicinity; and, before the lapse of many weeks, by that of nearly the whole of the kingdom.[12]

It is not unworthy of observation, that Monk himself, "the great instaurator," was included in the statement just made. *He* took the covenant, and, what is more, accepted a commission under Cromwell against the Scots. But neither the one circumstance, nor the other, prevented the king's

[11] See Reliq. Baxter, p. 48, &c.
[12] Illustrious Portraits. Life of Charles the First.

confidence in him, nor at all hindered a reverend
vindicator from asserting his claims, because of
eminent services, to the ready celebration of " undoubted virtues." [13]

And surely the claim, were it even more certain
than it is, that he was in the same condemnation,[14]
may be made with equal force, and for the same
reason, on behalf of Lord Hale. His " eminent
services," and his " virtues," are as little questionable as those of Monk ; and his title to a
favourable construction is, to the full, as good. It
was Hale himself, and men of the same description,
who aided Monk in the accomplishment of the
" Restoration ;" an event, indeed, " which," although
*he* almost exclusively acquired the honour, " it was
impossible to prevent." [15]

In 1644, on the arraignment of Archbishop
Laud, Mr. Hale was assigned one of his counsel ;
a fact, with other occurrences yet to be mentioned,
which, whether the covenant was taken by him or
not, completely weakens the force of Wood's statement. As the senior, Mr. Hern led upon the
trial, and ably contended, that nothing which
" his Grace had either said, or done, was treason
by any known established law of the kingdom."
The argument has been fully reported ;[16] and, on
the authority of Lord Chancellor Finch, it is to

[13] See Dr. Skinner's Life of the Duke of Albemarle, with a
Preface, by the Rev. William Webster, M. A. 8vo. 1723.
[14] See Note F.
[15] Stuart on the Government of England, p. 30.
[16] The State Trials, p. 938.

to assert the fact;" and the other, "it may be presumed," he adds, "would have scarcely passed it over without some remark."

In this representation, it seems to have escaped the critic, that the notice taken of Hale by both those authors appeared *subsequently* to Burnet's Memoir; and that, as both wrote with a view of detracting from, and with the most marked hostility to, Hale's reputation, their silence, instead of impeaching the bishop's testimony, confirms it. If Hale had *not* been assigned counsel to the king, the keen inquisitors referred to, would gladly have seized so fine an opportunity for contradiction.

It is easy to perceive from Mr. Thirlwall's observations, that, notwithstanding the avowal he makes of a high and laudable admiration of Hale, his eyes, at the time he wrote, were dazzled with the astonishing talents and acquirements so often ascribed to Charles! The king, it may be remembered, though no lawyer professed, claimed the knowledge of " as much *law* as any gentleman in England."[23] Perhaps Mr. Thirlwall was acquainted with that circumstance; and, if so, it is the more intelligible how his imagination was seduced into the conjecture, that no lawyer was applied to. But did it not occur to him, that how much soever such a view of the matter may savour of respect for the " blessed martyr," it pays the very poorest compliment to his understanding? The silence of Mr. D'Israeli

[23] State Trials, vol. i. p. 988; and Mr. Amos has noticed it in one of the notes which enrich his elaborate edition of Fortescue de Laudibus Legum Angliæ, p. 18. 8vo. 1825.

upon the point, whose zealous concern for the monarch's glory would prevent inattention to any circumstance, however trifling, that could increase it, may fairly be presumed to betoken such an opinion. Indeed, there is some difficulty in imagining the amount of ignorance, conceit, and presumption, necessary to produce in any individual, how illustrious soever, a disregard to self-interest so entire, as the notion now under consideration supposes.

But why, it may be asked, any surmisings or suspicions at all upon the subject, especially at this period of time? Why an effort to exhibit, not indeed " negative evidence," but unsupported hypothesis; and that in the face of direct assertion, never before doubted? If the intention were to " honour the king," it surely was mistaken zeal: if to refute the bishop, hypercritical absurdity could scarcely be more glaring.

It ought not to be forgotten here, how very expressly Burnet, in the preface to his Life of Hale, alludes to the *authentic sources*[24] whence his information was derived; and he then adds, " I am under no temptation of saying any thing but what I am persuaded is exactly true; for where there is so much exact truth to be told, it were an inexcusable fault to corrupt that, or prejudice the reader against it, by the mixture of falsehoods with it."

Mr. Hargrave, whose erudition and accuracy are

[24] One of these, and there could not be better, is hereafter specified—Robert Gibbons, Esq.

C

well known, so far from doubting whether Hale enjoyed the distinction thus questioned, adopts the bishop's statement : [25] and another acute and able lawyer, Mr. Serjeant Runnington, not only echoes it, but conjectures, with the greatest probability, that Hale furnished " the objections which Charles so pointedly applied."[26]

[25] See Note G.  [26] See Note H.

# CHAPTER IV.

## FROM A.D. 1648 TO A.D. 1653.

No sooner was the sentence against King Charles executed, than the regal office was formally abolished by—if the relics of the parliament, ludicrously styled the Rump, deserve to be so designated — the House of Commons. A free commonwealth was for the present declared to be the form of government. The coin was stamped on one side with the arms of England, between a laurel and a palm, with this inscription,—" The Commonwealth of England ;" and on the other, with a cross and a harp, having this motto,—" God with us ;" whence arose the witty observation, that God and the Commonwealth were not both on a side.[1]

In addition to these alterations, the oaths of allegiance and supremacy were abolished, and a new one appointed, called the Engagement, obliging those who complied to be true and faithful to the Commonwealth of England, without a king, or house of lords. Such as refused the oath were declared incapable of holding any place, or office

---

[1] Neale's History, vol. iv. pp. 1, 2. 8vo. 1822.

of trust; *without* the engagement, says Baxter, who was its invincible opponent, no man could have the benefit of suing another at law; a regulation, he drily notices, adapted to keep men a little from contention, and to mar the lawyer's trade.[2]

Hale, at this early period of his history, had made progress in those " Pleas of the Crown," upon which his fame, as a lawyer, materially rests; but the distressing circumstances of the country obliged him, for a season, to lay them aside. To prevent their falling into ill hands, he hid them behind the wainscotting of his study, not, however, without observing—and there is a melancholy tone of loyalty, not to say of tender and almost prophetic anticipation, in the language—that there would be no more occasion for them until the king should be restored to his right.

To detail the incessant changes, severities, and commotions, of the eventful period to which we have arrived, would be foreign from the present design. Suffice it to observe, therefore, that, as well to maintain the new regimen, as to strike terror into the cavaliers, and to check every movement of the royalists, the rigour and resolution of those who guided the helm were terribly conspicuous. The Duke of Hamilton, the Earl of Holland, and the Lords Capel and Craven, were early brought to trial, as enemies of the Commonwealth. For each of them Mr. Hale appeared as counsel. The elaborateness, as well as the length

[2] Reliq. Baxter, p. 46.

of his speech, in the former of these cases, has been specially noticed;[3] and such was the power of his argumentation in the latter, that the attorney-general threatened him for appearing against the government. To whom he answered, that he was pleading in defence of those laws which they declared they would maintain and preserve; that he was doing his duty to his client; and that he was not to be daunted with threatenings.

The time *when* Hale took the Engagement does not appear, though the fact of his having done so is certain: he publicly avowed it on the trial of Christopher Love;[4] and it may be noticed, in passing, that, as in January 1651, he was appointed, by the parliament, one of the committee for considering the reformation of the law,[5] it must have been prior to that undertaking. How much modern senators have been indebted to the results of that appointment has never yet been stated; but an examination of the subject would discover obligations of no ordinary magnitude.

It is observable that Burnet takes no notice of the Engagement, any more than of the law-reform commission. The probability is, that he regarded the compliance as no reflection either upon Mr. Hale's character or principles. Nothing can be

---

[3] State Trials, vol. ii. p. 5. The plea framed by Hale, is printed in Burnet's Memoirs of the Dukes of Hamilton, fol. 1676.

[4] See the State Trials, vol. ii. p. 159.

[5] Works by Thirlwall, vol. i. p. 140. See Whitelock's Memorials, pp. 520, 521, fol. 1732.

plainer than that Hale himself so viewed the matter; as scarcely implying, to borrow the suitable phraseology of an able modern historian, more than such an expression of a purpose to live peaceably and inoffensively under *the present administration*,[6] as is ordinarily required by all governments.[7]

Mr. Thirlwall, nevertheless, expresses himself much at a loss for reasons to exculpate Hale from the charge of pusillanimity, selfishness, or versatility of principle ;[8] a thing the more surprising, since he acknowledges that the uniform tenor, and general complexion, of Hale's whole history, his character, his acknowledged reputation for learning, integrity, and piety, and his own statements, all forbid the supposition that he was *not* a loyal and patriotic man, strictly conscientious, as well as eminently wise, and tremblingly alive to the sanctity of an oath ; one that, rather than wound the peace of his conscience, would have submitted to the bitterest privations.[9]

In fact, the question before us, like all others of a similar nature, will, of necessity, be differently viewed by different persons. Violent politicians will indulge their theories, and nothing can prevent them from censuring or commending accordingly : while others, more moderate and impartial, will, in the absence of accurate know-

---

[6] One of the tracts published at that period, is entitled "A Persuasive to a mutual Compliance under the present Government." 4to. 1652.

[7] See Note I.    [8] Hale's Works, vol. i. p. 138.
Works, vol. i. p. 139.   See Note J.

ledge of the governing reasons and motives, not only be slow to pronounce an *unfavourable* judgment, but will give such men as Hale credit for acting, amidst such pressing difficulties as a civil war creates, according to the genuine dictates of conscience. They will associate the decision of Hale, for instance, with numerous influences; with the avowed pattern of his conduct—Pomponius Atticus—who anxiously endeavoured after " tranquillity in difficult and troublous times," and to " steer himself between the rocks of contesting factions without shipwreck ;"[10] with that regard to the welfare of the community, which marked him " as a friend to human nature, and mankind in general ;"[11] with his notions of obedience to existing authority, which his manuscripts show to have extended very far, even as to things *indifferent* in matters sacred ; and with the current and popular opinion, not to mention the example of multitudes around him, who were men of the truest patriotism, and distinguished alike for their piety, their talents, and their learning. Even Archbishop Sancroft, in the deservedly popular tract which he wrote *against* the then prevailing party, admits that something is to be conceded to the place, and time, and person; and exhibits those distinctions which are obvious to impartial reflection, so as fully to meet Hale's case.[12]

Dr. Johnson has noticed Dryden as the pane-

---

[10] Works, vol. i. p. 467.  [11] Ib. vol. i. p. 465.
[12] Modern Policies, 12mo. 1652.  Principle VI.

gyrist of the "usurpation," *and* "of his most
sacred majesty King Charles the Second," happily
restored ; but he adds, with characteristic good
sense, "if he changed, he changed with the nation,"
so that "the reproach of inconstancy produced
neither hatred nor disgrace."[13]

Sir Michael Foster, in his observations on
some passages in the writings of Hale, relative
to the principles on which the revolution was
founded, noticed his having taken the Engagement, "when of high rank at the bar." He
remarked, also, that, *in the sense of those who
imposed* it,[14] it was plainly an engagement for
abolishing kingly government, at least for sup-
porting the abolition of it ; but he adds, and
the observation goes a great way, with regard to
those who took it, it might, upon the principles
of Sir Henry Vane's case, have been easily improved into an overt act of treason against
King Charles the Second.[15] Now this we know
was *not* done. Nay, Hale himself, immediately
after the monarch's restoration, was not only no
object of court censure, but was elevated, as we
shall presently see, to one of the highest law
offices ; a proof, if any were wanting, that those
severe censures, in which a partial view of the

[13] Works, vol. ix. p. 281. 12mo. 1816.
[14] The Government admitted men to take it in their own sense.
See Harris's Life of Charles II. vol. i. p. 58 ; 8vo. 1766.
[15] Report of some proceedings on the Commission for Trial of
the Rebels in the year 1746, and of other Crown Cases ; to which
were added, Discourses upon a few branches of the Crown Law.
p. 402. fol. 1762.

question before us, if not settled prejudices, have led some to indulge, might have been spared.

The arraignment by Cromwell's council, of the young and unfortunate Christopher Love, for treason, has already been alluded to. As a minister of the Presbyterian church, popular and generally beloved, the excitement produced by the occurrence was considerable. The trial commenced June 20th, 1651; and the "plea against the charge and evidence" was entrusted to Mr. Hale. His efforts proved unsuccessful, and Love was beheaded; but it is impossible to peruse the narrative of the judicial proceedings,[16] which continued six days, without admiring the acuteness of Hale, his caution, and his solicitude, as well as his great energy and skill. In the "Clear and Necessary Vindication of Mr. Love's Principles and Practices,"[17] a tract written by himself only fourteen days before his death, he notices the ability displayed by his counsel; and, as if peculiarly struck with it, attributes it to "divine assistance."[18]

Upon all occasions, Mr. Hale discharged his professional duties with distinguished learning, fidelity, and courage; so much so that he was, as we have seen, employed in many of the leading cases where the accused were obnoxious to the government—that government to which his own submission was professed. Nor was he satisfied with mere professional exertions; he often relieved the necessities of those for whom he was retained, and, considering the danger of the time, in a

[16] Quarto, 1652.    [17] Ibid. 1651.    [18] Vindication, p. 42.

manner no less prudent than charitable. He frequently deposited considerable sums with a gentleman of the king's party, who knew their wants, leaving the distribution, not merely to his discretion, but with an injunction of silence as to whence it came; and a prohibition, likewise, as to any account to whom it was given.

On the 25th day of January, 1653, Hale was by writ created a serjeant at law.[19]

It can be no matter of surprise, that he should have attracted the notice of Cromwell, the sagacity of that extraordinary person being in nothing more apparent than in the selection of his chief officers. It was remarked by Thurloe, that his master " sought out men for places, and not places for men."[20] The splendid talents, acquirements, and tried worth of some of them, inspired the pen of Milton. But the immortal bard's powerful delineation [21] has been too long admired to render more than the merest allusion to it necessary.

The Protector's installation happened on the 16th December, 1653. The patents of those judges he chose to continue were renewed as on a demise of the crown, but only one *new* judge was made, and that was Hale,[22] and he was reluctant to accept the proffered dignity. Being pressed by Cromwell for the reason, he at last stated, that

[19] See Note K.     [20] Life of Dr. Owen, by Mr. Orme, p. 137.
[21] Second Defence of the People of England. Prose Works, vol. vi. pp. 433—440. 8vo. 1806.
[22] Godwin, vol. iv. p. 25, &c. See also the Perfect Politician, or Life of Cromwell, by J. S. 1660. 8vo. p. 355.

he was not satisfied with the lawfulness of his authority. Cromwell replied, that since he had possession of the government, he was resolved to keep it, and would not be argued out of it ; that, nevertheless, it was his desire to rule according to the laws of the land, for which purpose he had selected *him ;* and that if not permitted to govern by red gowns, he would do it by red coats.[23]

The difficulty Hale felt has been ascribed by Burnet to his perception of "a snare," and to scruples respecting the lawfulness of taking a commission from usurpers, "having never made any declaration in acknowledgment of their authority;" a statement obviously incorrect, and only to be accounted for from the bishop's ignorance that Hale took the Engagement ; or from his forgetfulness of the fact. The silence observed by him in the Life respecting it has been noticed.

Let the real cause, however, of Hale's objections to the wishes of the court have been what it may: whether, in spite of what he had already done, scruples connected with the ruling powers, or the distinction he perceived between the administration of civil and *criminal* law ; or, a reluctance to abridge, by more public occupations, the little time he could command for literary enjoyments ; or, which is not improbable, an unwillingness to exchange his thriving and lucrative practice for the toil and uncertainty of the judgment-seat ; the obstacles *were* effectually

[23] See Hale's Histor. Plac. Cor. by Emlyn, vol. i. pref. p. ii. fol. 1736.

removed: he arrived at the conclusion that, as it was absolutely necessary to have justice and property at all times upheld, it was no sin to take a commission from those whom he regarded as usurpers.

To the bringing about of this important result several eminent royalists in his own profession were instrumental, particularly Sir Orlando Bridgman, and Sir Geoffrey Palmer; and he was much influenced also by Dr. Henchman, and Dr. Sheldon, who afterwards filled the sees of London and Canterbury.

The honourable and matchless Edmund Burke, having alluded with admiration to Cromwell's wisdom in selecting the dispensers of justice, instanced the case of Lord Hale; and added, that "in the appointment, he gave to that age, and to all posterity, the most brilliant example of sincere and fervent piety, exact justice, and profound jurisprudence." [24]

[24] Letter to a Member of the National Assembly. Works, vol. vi. p. 16.   8vo. 1801.

# CHAPTER V.

HALE is known to have felt a strong objection to being engaged in the trial of common felonies: in a measure, he overcame the difficulty; but with offences against the State he never *would* meddle, believing that, in some instances, the acts themselves might be warrantable, and that the putting of men to death on account of them would be murder.

Accordingly, for a time, he presided as well on the Crown side as at Nisi Prius; but his scruples returning, he refused, after the second or third circuit, to try criminals: such, indeed, upon some occasions, had been his conduct, as to make his determination rather welcome than otherwise to the government.

Not long after he was made a judge, a trial took place before him at Lincoln under the following circumstances. An inhabitant of that city, who had been of the king's party, being met by a soldier of the garrison in the fields, with a fowling-piece on his shoulder, was accused of disobeying the protector's order—that no such persons should carry arms. A conflict ensued, and the soldier was well beaten and conquered. So soon as he recovered sufficiently to reach the town, he made his case known to one of his comrades, and prevailed upon him to accompany him, that, together, they might avenge the injury. When their victim approached, the gun was again demanded; it was refused; and, while struggling with one of the soldiers, the other inflicted a mortal blow by thrusting his sword through the man's body. The melancholy catastrophe happening at the time of the assizes, both the soldiers were at once arraigned. No evidence being given against the one of previous malice, *he* was found guilty of manslaughter, but the other was convicted of murder. Colonel Whaley, who commanded the garrison, urged vehemently that the man was killed for disobeying the protector's order, and that the soldier merely discharged his duty. Hale, however, paid as little attention to his reasons as his threats, and not only pronounced sentence of death, but ordered execution to follow so quickly as to prevent the possibility of a reprieve.

In another case, where the protector (being interested) had ordered a jury returned, Hale took occasion to display the illegality of the procedure: he showed, from the statute book, that all juries were to be returned by the sheriff, or his lawful officer; he likewise dismissed the jury, without trying the cause. Cromwell angrily told him he was not fit to be a judge. Hale answered that it was very true.[1]

[1] An................................of Cromwell, p. 452. 8vo. 1762.

To some Anabaptists, who rushed into a church, and violently disturbed a congregation while receiving the sacrament, he remarked, how intolerable it was for such as claimed and advocated liberty of conscience, to interrupt others in their worship, especially when it had the sanction of the law, and he determined that the law should take its due order in this case; but the evil-doers found that support from certain officers and magistrates which actually defeated his proceedings.

There can be no doubt, that occurrences like these greatly influenced him in forming the resolution which has been mentioned,[2] and which he soon carried into full effect. The trial of the honourable Colonel John Penruddock coming on at Exeter[3] during vacation, gave him the desired opportunity. Hale was at his country house at Alderley, and a messenger being sent to require his assistance, he not only refused to go, but alleged that the four terms, and two circuits, ought to suffice; that the small interval between them was little enough for his private affairs. He thought it unnecessary to speak more clearly, though, if urged to it, he would not have been afraid of doing so. Mr. Roscoe has observed, reasonably enough, that it would perhaps have been more honourable, if, notwithstanding the disgust which the injustice of the proceedings alluded to occasioned, he had still persevered honestly and

[2] Page 37.  [3] State Trials, vol. ii. p. 261.

impartially to administer the criminal laws of his country.[4]

In the year 1654, the return of Cromwell's second parliament, Mr. Hale was chosen one of the five knights of the shire for the county of Gloucester.[5] At that time there was no House of Lords, so that his station as a judge formed no hindrance. The honour was, however, entirely unsought, and the most pressing importunity was necessary to obtain his acceptance of it. He was elected free ; and, in spite of great expenditure on the part of another candidate, by a large majority. The Earl of Berkeley defrayed the charges of his entertainment on the day of election, and girt him with his own sword.

There were two parties now in vigorous activity, who, being actuated by the most opposite principles, and bent upon projects of the most obnoxious character, rendered the duties of a statesman unusually difficult. The one contended for the wild schemes of the fifth monarchy enthusiasts ; the other, intent upon personal aggrandizement, availed themselves of the unsettled state of public affairs, and the fears of the sober-minded, to attempt, at every hazard, the increase of their own fortunes.

Between both Mr. Hale steered a middle course ;

[4] Lives of eminent Lawyers, p. 68.
[5] The members ret... Hale,
John How... Hist.
of Eng...

aiming, as much as possible, to make parliamentary movements the hindrance of mischief, when the doing of much practical good seemed hopeless. When a proposal was made in the House of Commons to destroy all the records in the Tower, and to settle the nation on a new basis, he pointed out the madness of the proposition, its injustice, and the evils that would follow from it; and he did it with such clearness, and strength of reason, as to confound its fanatical originators.

Nor was that all: on the fourth day when the question was discussed, whether the House should approve of the system of government by a single person and a parliament, and it was resolved that they should form themselves into a committee of the whole House, Mr. Hale submitted an expedient, by which he hoped to reconcile all parties. He proposed, " That the legislative authority should be affirmed to be in the parliament of the people of England, and a single person qualified with such instructions as that assembly should authorise, in the manner suggested by the republicans. But, to render this palatable to the executive magistrate, and practicable under the circumstances, he recommended that the military power, for the present, should be unequivocally given to the protector; and that, to avoid the perpetuity of parliament, and other exorbitancies in the claims of supremacy, that officer should be allowed such a co-ordination as might serve for a check in these points." With this suggestion the republicans seemed inclined to close.[6]

It was in the midst of these anxieties for the public welfare, that he was called to mourn the loss of his friend, the illustrious Selden. That extraordinary man expired on the 30th October, 1654. Grotius styled him the "Glory of England;" but, because he opposed ecclesiastical tyranny, neither the greatness of his soul, nor his conscientious attachment to the Church of England, could shield him from severe reflections. Many reported, that, in reality, he was an infidel, and inclined to the opinion of Hobbs. But Hale often stated to Mr. Baxter, that he was a "resolved, serious Christian;" that he was much averse to Hobbs' errors ; and that he had seen him openly oppose the unbeliever so earnestly, as either to depart from him, or drive him out of the room. Selden appointed the judge one of his executors. Hale cherished the highest regard for his memory, and kept his picture ever near him.[7]

Out of respect more especially to Hale and Vaughan, as well as the deceased, the venerable Usher, who at that time had left off " preaching in great congregations," delivered the funeral sermon at the Temple church, where Selden was buried.[8]

The parliamentary career of Hale was short ; though probably not more so than was quite pleasant to himself. The alienation of mind manifest

[6] Godwin, vol. iv. pp. 118, 119.
[7] Baxter's additional Notes. Hale's Works, vol. i. p. 112.
[8] Life of Usher, by Parr, p. 74. fol. 1686.

in many of the members as it respected the existing administration—their constant dissensions, and the tendency of their whole proceedings, alarmed the protector; and, within five months, brought about a dissolution. Nor was another parliament summoned before September, 1656; of that Mr. Hale was not, though the reason is unknown, a member.

After the inauguration, which took place the following year, Cromwell constructed an assembly which was to perform the functions of a House of Lords, and to that Hale, with the other judges, was summoned:[9] but parliament was again speedily dissolved; and Cromwell's death, which happened on the 3d Sept. 1658, put an end to every existing scheme.

Under the influence of growing experience, Hale again changed his course. He refused the mourning sent to him and his servants for the funeral; and the new commission, too, which Richard offered him. He was urged by the rest of the judges, as well as others, to alter his purpose, but every importunity was resisted, and he declared that he could no longer act under such authority.

Bishop Burnet is inaccurate when he says that Hale, until the parliament met which called home the king, (and to which he was returned as knight of the shire for the county of Gloucester,) lived as a private man. The fact is, that in the

[9] See the Parliam. Hist. vol. iii. p. 1519.

one summoned by the new protector, 1658, he represented the University of Oxford: [10] a distinction which must have been highly flattering to him, and one, had he needed such support, which was adapted to confirm him in the abandonment of his judicial functions.

A writer, who appears delighted with an opportunity of censuring Hale, has noticed, with some malignancy of emotion, his "serving in this parliament for Oxford University;" observing, that under Richard Lord Protector he could *make* laws, though he could not execute them; and adding, with no less insolence, "such was the correct judgment and consistent decision of this great lawyer and pre-eminent witch-finder." [11]

Public affairs soon became so very unsettled, as to terrify the young protector, and to indicate those changes, which ere long happened—the dissolution of the House, and the dethronement (it is Hume's word) of Richard.

The University now sought again to secure Hale's services. Various letters, which passed upon the occasion, are extant: some, of a mere private nature, between Dr. Edmund Staunton, of Corpus Christi College, and the parish minister of Alderley, "Mr. Francis Jacob;" the latter of which gentlemen says, in one of them, "Serjeant Hale will not stand to be chosen a

[10] The other member ............................ vol. iii. p. 1533.
[11] The ......

parliament man ; but if chosen he will stand, if new oaths or engagements be not laid in his way." [12]    Others were more directly official : all however, indicate the same indifference to the honours of office, and the same cautious vigilance, which on other occasions marked Hale's character.

Between the urgency of the University on the one hand, and the desires of nearer neighbours, for him once more to represent his native county, on the other, he was not a little perplexed. But the whole will be best explained by the two following letters :—

" *For the Honorable Justice Hale, at his house at Alderley, in Gloucestershire.    These.*

" S^r.

" There hath been, and still is, a great readiness in this place to choose you for one of their burgesses to sit in the next parliament. But a report (as we suppose without any just ground) hath been spread abroad here within these few days, that you will not accept of our choice. This hath somewhat discomposed and distracted the minds of some here who are, otherwise, cordially for you. Wherefore to settle men's thoughts, and to prevent the inconveniencies which may also befal us, tis humbly desired that you would be pleased positively to express your willingness, if chosen, to accept thereof. Herein you shall (as things are at present with us) greatly promote

[12] Orig. MS.

the interest of this place, and much quiet and oblige many here who honour you: and among them,

"Your most humble servant,

"JOHN CONANT, Vice Chan."

*"Oxford, April 2, 1660."* [13]

---

"Sir,

"I have received your letter: and, first of all, I must continue my acknowledgments of the great respects of the University to me, in thinking me worthy of such a trust as is communicated by your letter. Touching my resolution in general for serving in this ensuing parliament, this is all I can say, the expectation of the success of this parliament is great, and as I think and foresee that the businesses that are like to be transacted therein are like to be of great concernment to this nation, and therefore of great difficulty and intricacy ; and therefore I may well think any man (as I am) conscious of his own infirmity, may desire in his own particular to be excused ; yet, inasmuch as there seem to be no engagements to be prefixt to intangle the conscience, or to prevent the liberty of those that are chosen to act according to it, I shall not refuse, if I am freely chosen, to serve in it ; although, I must deal plainly with you, my own particular engagements do much persuade the

[13] Orig. MS.

contrary. But my difficulty at this present rests in this; I have not at all, till this time, heard any thing as from the University, touching their resolution. And upon that reason, the importunity of many in the county wherein I live, hath drawn from me this promise, that if I am chosen here I shall not decline it; and this is my great strait, that if I shall decline the service of the county in case they fix upon me, I fear I shall be unjust, much disappoint and discontent many; and if I shall decline the choice of the University, I shall seem ungrateful, especially when my last election seems to make me their debtor for ever [in the] present service: and I know not how to gratify both without a great discourtesy to one in my after relinquishment of either, and the expedient of deferring your choice till the success here were seen, would be too much below that weighty and honourable body of the University, and arrogance in me to expect it, and the choice here falls not before the 18th of this month, which may give too much advantage, it may be, to other's importunities, and leave you too little room after for your own choice. The sum is, if I am chosen here, I shall look upon myself as equally concerned for the good of the University as if chosen there. If I am chosen there, I shall serve, so it may be, without discontent to my native county. If chosen nowhere, I shall yet endeavour, in my private station, to serve both: consult the honour and service of the University: and follow that which is most conducible and suitable to it; and assure yourself, that whether I am chosen there, or here, or nowhere, I am,

> " Your's and the University's most faithful friend and servant.

" Perchance, if the election be not before Tuesday, I may, by conference with some, learn more of the sense and resolution of the country here, and send you notice of it."

" *To Oxford*."[14]

---

On the 25th of April, 1660, the famous " Convention" parliament (so called, because not summoned by the king's writ) met. Hale appeared among them as one of the members for Gloucestershire ;[15] and he bore a steady part in the attempt now triumphantly made, for restoring the legitimate and long-exiled sovereign. The design was *so* accomplished as actually to confound such as had attributed former successes[16] to an *approving* Providence, as an answer from heaven to the solemn appeals of the victorious. The restoration of the monarchical government was, undoubtedly, brought about with vastly *more* ease, more unanimity, and more dispatch[17] than its overthrow. To the occurrence just mentioned, the following memoranda, by Hale, were designed to refer.

---

[14] Orig. MS.  [15] See Note L.
[16] The fifth principle in Sancroft's Modern Policies. already referred to, was directed to this matter, and may at all times urnish a profitable topic for thought.  [17] See Note M.

" Where there are eminent dispensations con-
curring to ends unrighteous and unjust, the Divine
providence concurs permissively; and, for the
most part, the immediate consequence of such con-
currences obtaining their effect, is punishment and
judgment, though at a distance the issue may, by
the wisdom of God, be managed to a blessing.

" Where these eminent dispensations concur to
the effecting of righteous and just ends, the Divine
providence concurs positively and actively; and
the issue of such a dispensation is, commonly, a
blessing; though remotely, and at a distance, and
accidentally, by the unthankfulness of men, it
*may* produce a judgment.

" In the present transactions of things, there
hath been a most visible concurrence of Divine
providence and wisdom, which seems visibly distinct from the very instrumentality of the immediate actors:—1st. Infatuating those that were, for
their natural parts, not inferior to any that have
been, with less wisdom, more successful; so Fleet-
wood, Desborough, and other the officers of the
army, pulling down Richard, which was apparent
folly in them. 2d. Advancing the success of the
advices of men of no great eminency of judgment
in their counsels and advices, conducing to these
ends. 3d. Carrying the advices and activities of
men beyond their own design, to the producing of
that they intended not, as the sending up for
Monk, by a large party in the house, to counter-
work the designs of Lambert and Vane. 4th. In
permitting a spirit of jealousy and emulation to

D

arise between persons whose common interest lay in the same bottom, whereby they were divided and broken ; as between Haslerig and Vane in the house—between Lambert, and Desborough, and Packer, in the army. 5th. By mingling casual conjunctures in such order and method that they were each subservient one to another, and to the common cause of restoring the king ; the particulars are infinite and eminent, and such as could not fall under counsel or contrivance.

" All these tended to an end visibly righteous and just—the restoring of an oppressed, afflicted, forsaken prince, to that which the laws, both of God and the land, entitle him.

" Therefore, in all probability, an immediate blessing may be expected upon it, as a business agreeable to that method with which the Almighty is delighted, and whereby he doth govern mankind. And yet, accidentally, it may produce a judgment : not as a natural effect, but as a production of that corruption of the heart of man that commonly mingles itself with these occurrences. As, for instance, want of thankfulness to God, upon a sound conviction of his hand in it ; for I see people that would seem to be wiser than others, lay most, if not all, upon the prudent or imprudent conduct of the instruments. And likewise pride and vanity of mind swelling upon the issue of success, and too much looseness and profaneness, with, perhaps, vindictiveness, and insultation over others." [18]

[18] " Observations concerning the present Providences." Orig. MS.

# CHAPTER VI.

### A. D. 1660.

ALTHOUGH Hale was attached both to monarchy and his sovereign, he felt an objection to receive the king back without reasonable restrictions. He conceived the opportunity to be a favourable one for *limiting* the prerogative : a prerogative which, in his opinion, had given rise to those dire calamities under which the nation groaned so long. But Monk's policy defeated his " patriotic suggestion."[1] Indeed, the " hope," as Baxter expresses it, of being " delivered from the usurpation of the fanatics,"[2] led men, already beyond measure harassed, to dislike even the possibility of *delay :* besides which, those horrid commotions which followed the lately raging passion for liberty, had produced a spirit of obedience, miscalled loyalty, bordering upon servile subjection. Burnet remarks, with great seriousness, that, " To the king's coming in *without* conditions may be well imputed all the errors of his reign."[3]

[1] Hayley's Life of Milton, p. 150.    [2] Reliq. Baxter, p. 214.
[3] Own Time, vol. i. p. 152. 8vo. 1823.

On the 8th of May, 1660, his Majesty was proclaimed. The attendant circumstances were recorded by our author, and his manuscripts show how intently they occupied his mind; how the passing scene was beheld by him with the eye at once of a philosopher, a statesman, and a Christian. Scarcely in any case (if we except the Memoirs of Colonel Hutchinson, by his accomplished wife) have statements concerning the "unhappy distempers" been preserved, by one so competent to judge, and, because of his calm and impartial fidelity, so entirely to be relied upon.

While remarkable for a clear recognition of God's hand, and great foresight, they explain, in the amplest manner, the difficulties of the times. They satisfactorily evince the writer's sagacity; and they so explain the grounds of that steady moderation for which he is eminent, as to leave no doubt either of his honour or uprightness. But besides this, they strikingly disclose the evil and danger of civil animosities; they enforce that spirit of unambitious contentment which the gospel enjoins; they illustrate the necessity, on the part of rulers, of uniting justice with wisdom; and they present such an example of devout attention to passing events, as can neither be too much admired, nor too carefully imitated. On all these accounts the document, notwithstanding its length, establishes a powerful claim to the reader's notice. He will see, by its means, one of the most distinguished persons of the age retiring from the bustle of state affairs to the silence of his closet, for solemn meditation ; gazing, in the stillness of that exercise, upon all the pageantry with dignified indifference; loyally forming rules for the proper discharge of his public duty; and actually extracting from the troubles of his country, and their removal also, reasons for the better regulation of his heart and affections.

The paper thus referred to is dated 13th May, 1660, and entitled, "Considerations concerning the Present and Late Occurrences, for my own use and observation."

It is as follows :—

"The folly and corruption of our hearts is such, that it mingles itself with all concernments we meet with, and in a special manner, with the *great occurrences* of the present time ; as may appear in these ensuing evidences :

"1. It makes us so far set our minds and thoughts upon them, that it interrupts us in our very service and duty to God. When we should be praying, or hearing, or observing the duty of this day, or thinking upon our everlasting concernments, the thoughts of the occurrences past, or what will be next, or what is fit to be said or done in order to the present transactions, interpose, and steal away our hearts and intention of mind from that which is due to the present duty ; and leave little to God, but a bare shell or carcase of devotion, without a life or soul in it.

"2. It makes us set too high a rate upon these external concernments, and the glory, and splendour, and consequences of them; and stifles, and starves, and diverts those considerations which are of most absolute necessity for our christian walking. We have very seldom, or very flat, considerations of our latter end—of the vanity of the world—of the instability, and uncertainty, and emptiness, of the most splendid things the world can afford—of our own everlasting state after death —of the glory of the kingdom of heaven—the solemnity of the last judgment. The present noise and alarm of externals drive away and keep off those good, and serious, and necessary, entertainments of our souls; our ears, and our eyes, and our hearts, and our thoughts, are full of nothing but the presence, or expectation, or preapprehensions of a temporal kingdom—the state and magnificence of it—the provisions and preparations for it— triumphs, and acclamations, and coronations, and stately processions; counterplotting of oppositions, policies, and designs; suppressing and bringing down opponents; severity against injuries, public or private. And it is true, these have their use and season; but, in the mean time, such considerations as those seldom come athwart us; or, if they do, they stay but little with us. We are about restoring a temporal kingdom; but when we have done all, it is *but* a temporal kingdom—a kingdom that *may be shaken.* There *is* a kingdom of a higher constitution than this; a kingdom that 'cannot be shaken, eternal in the heavens.' While we take care of the former, let us be careful we neglect not our interest in the latter. We are about settling of our kingdom in glory, and power, and splendour; but, alas! the most glorious things in the world are but a 'shadow, that passeth away.' If we set our hearts upon it, it will either deceive, or not satisfy: death will come, and changes may come; and then 'whose shall all these things be?' We are providing to settle the nation in stability, and in peace, and in honour, and to prevent fears and dangers; and, when we have all done, unless God himself please to 'watch the city, the watchmen wake but in vain:' unless *he* add stability, our 'foundation is but rottenness' and sand. But, if he be pleased to lay the corner stone of our peace (it is but an outward and worldly peace), we may have a worldly peace: yet, if we have not peace with God, and with our own consciences, it is only a dry, and vanishing, disquieting peace.

"3. It is apt to make us look upon ourselves and instruments as the great contrivers and effecters of our desires. This man's folly, rashness, and cowardice, made way for the effecting of what we aim at; and it was such a contrivance, or direction, or advice, or speech, that contributed wonderfully to our settlement. And commonly, as we are wonderfully inclined to the admiration of the *means*, so we shift in somewhat of *ourselves*, or our own eloquence, or prudence, or conduct: and then, if we be commended we are admirably pleased; and rather than miss it, we will commend ourselves; and if we want *that* opportunity, we are apt secretly to admire ourselves. Thus, ostentation, and pride, and vain glory, and self-admiration, steal from God the glory that is due to him alone, when it is most evident to any man that shall but faithfully look into things, the whole honour of this great change is due only to *his* wisdom, and power, and goodness; to *his* timing of things, and mingling of circumstances, and managing of the hearts, and passions, and dispositions of men. Nay, if after all this that hath been hitherto brought, he should leave us without as signal an interposition as he hath hitherto shewn, the business would be lost, and disappointed, and broken; and when we think we are in the haven, we should either sink in it, or be suddenly driven out into a sea of storms, and tempests, and rocks, and shelves, much more dangerous than before. Certainly a wise and sober man, though never so active and successful in his part and share of this great transaction, upon a due and serious consideration, will easily find matter enough in it to attribute all the good that is past to God, and to depend singly upon him for what is to come; and with very much humility and despondency in himself, to look upon the past transaction, and the success that is to come.

"4. It is apt to put men upon greater expectation and hopes of temporal advantages and preferment, and to fill the mind with vain imaginations in order to it, when such thoughts as these have been apt to interpose:—' I have been greatly instrumental in promoting this event, and surely it is observed, or it is fit it should. I have been the man that

have contributed much in the satisfaction of others, and surely it cannot be forgotten, and there can be no preferment too great for me : and, besides, I have friends at court, those that represent my service, and my merits, and my works, and my popularity, and my interest ; and surely I may choose my own reward.' Thus, though we are but inconsiderable flies, that sit upon the chariot wheel, we attribute all the dust that is made to *our* weight and contribution ; and thereupon fancy up ourselves into an opinion of our merit, and of a most indisputable attendance of great honour, and place, and fame, and preferment attending it ; when, it may be, there is no such desert as is supposed ; or, if there be, yet not such observation of it by others ; or, if there be, yet the many rivals that attend such a change may disappoint me of it ; or if it do not, yet the preferment that befalls me is not such as I expected ; or if it be, yet it may be I am not suitable and fit for it ; or, if I am, yet I little consider the trouble, and dangers, and difficulty that attend it. Possibly it will make me obnoxious to much censure, as if all my former endeavours were basely ordered to my own ends and advantage ; or, it may be, it may subject me to the envy and emulation of others, which may, in time, undermine me ; or, if there be no such occasion of danger from that ground, yet the state of public affairs has various faces and occasions that may make it necessary to gratify other persons, or factions, or interests, with my removal ; or, if it do not, yet the engagement to a place of honour and profit, and the fear of the shame or loss in parting with it, may enslave me to those drudgeries, or at least engage me in them, that now I look upon as unworthy; or, if it do not, yet the very many and great difficulties that attend places of honour or profit, upon a change, may make my walk in them full of brakes and stones, that will perplex and scratch me, if not wholly bemire and entangle me; or, if none of all these things befall me, yet great places may rob me of serenity of mind, or withdraw my heart from God by the splendour of the world and multiplicity of secular concernments; or, at least, they most certainly will rob me of my quiet, rest, liberty, and the freedom of my opportunities to serve God with entireness and uninterruptedness.

" 5. It is very apt to carry men into insolence and insultation over the depressed party; or into such a kind of pity, as savours more of pride and scorn than compassion. And this men are apt to justify themselves in, as a just retribution of the like carriage formerly by that party that is now in disgrace; but let such men consider—

" That it is a carriage far unworthy of a christian profession, which teacheth us to return ' good for evil.'

" That it is the sign of a base and impotent spirit to make that use of a public calamity, even of an adverse party, to add to it by contumely and contempt.

" That it is an argument of infinite want of judgment, to return such a deportment by way of retribution, which, before, I looked upon in the adverse party as unseemly and unmanly when *they* were uppermost. Let me take my estimate of what is unfit for me to do *now* upon the change, by that judgment that I had of it before.

" It is a thing infinitely disadvantageous to that interest I profess to advance. It is most certain that my civil, moderate, and meek carriage, may make him that is an enemy to me and the king, a good friend or subject; but a sour, austere, insolent carriage, will make a disaffected or dissatisfied person worse in both relations.

" It is most certain that the world and the station of things are ever uncertain; and experience hath taught an ordinary capacity that lesson. We are yet but in a green and waterish condition; like a broken bone newly set, a small matter shatters it. Use the present hopes and dawnings of a settlement with moderation, for the ground we stand upon is unstable. Who knows whether that insolence that thou hast learned from the adverse party may be his by opportunity, and return upon thee with the same advantage?

" Let us all remember that the wise God observes our carriage in all conditions. It was *just* to punish the insolence of the adverse party toward thee with the like towards them : but that which is his justice may be thy sin; and, perchance, return upon thee as thy *punishment*. Remember the wise man's counsel — ' Rejoice not when thine enemy falleth, lest the Lord see it, and it displease him.'

" 6. It is apt to carry a man to an over-severe

animadversion of the supposed, or real, miscarriages of the adverse party. And men are apt to please themselves that *that* is an effort of their justice, which, for the most part, is but the issue of their passion and revenge. In these great convulsions, men are apt to make an estimate of things then done, as if they were done in a serene and settled condition of things upon their right basis; and, accordingly, they proportion their censures without giving things their due estimate and alloy, according to the variety of seasons and circumstances. That, perchance, may be a *crime* in one condition of affairs, which in another may be but a fault, or an infirmity; or, it may be, *neither* — the circumstances of times, and pressures and intentions considered. Nay, possibly, it may fall out that some things that were criminal in those times, yet upon a due and wise consideration of the present state of things, may be fit, either not to be touched at all, or with a very light hand. And let not men please themselves with a pretence that a zeal for justice must carry them to all severity; for *such* a kind of justice may be the greatest injustice and cruelty, when the issue of it must, in all probability, produce a public disturbance. The wise man tells us a man may be 'over just.' As equity may mitigate the severity of justice in particular cases, so may and must prudence some public and universal concernments; otherwise, it may become an act of frenzy, not of justice. I speak not of that unexampled villany against the king's life; wherein, nevertheless, though the punishment must be exemplary, perchance the present necessity may restrain the universality of the punishment, proportionable to the crime in reference to particulars.

" 7. Which is a yet farther and worse degree of immoderation, these and the like alterations carry men to vindictiveness of *private injury*, upon the opportunity given by such public mutations: wherein men must remember, that as all revenge is forbidden at all times, as a flower of that crown that God reserves to himself, who hath said, ' Vengeance is mine ;' so, most certainly, if at any time it is unseasonable, it is *then* most unseasonable, when the opportunity is given by a public change. A generous and manly mind will hold it unseemly to prostitute the opportunity of a public concernment, to right himself from a wrong, as much as might be, much less to revenge an injury. And, therefore, it is a shame to see how even clergymen most unhandsomely and indiscreetly catch at the present change to run into their benefices, and have not the patience to stay till things may have a little settlement. It is a sign of a mind too much set upon the *world*, and preferring men's own interest before the public settlement (which may chance to receive a brush by their hasty, inconsiderate, and tumultuous catching at the opportunity for themselves, without regarding the consequence): when, it may be, a little patience and moderation might, with more security to their private and the public interest, settle *both*.

" 8. It is apt to bring a prejudice into the minds

of men, and a contrariety of practice in some things. It is certain that in contrarieties of parties there may be, and for the most part is, somewhat that is good in the worst party, and somewhat that is bad in the best; and upon mutations people are apt, in their practice, if not in their judgment, to run quite counter to what was practised by the depressed party, whether the thing were good or not. *Sequitur fortunam semper et odit damnatos.* There was in many of the suppressed party much hypocrisy and dissimulation, much violence and oppression; but there was in them—sobriety in their conversation, pretence, and profession of strictness of life; prayers in their families; observation of the Sabbath. These were commendable in their use, though it may be they were in order to honour, and to disguise bad ends and actions. And I pray God it fall not out with us upon our change, that the detestation of their persons and foul actions may not transport us to a *contrary* practice of that, which was in *itself* commendable; lest we grow loose in religion and good duties, and in the observation of the Sabbath; and lest we despise strictness of life, because abused by *them* to base and hypocritical ends. Most certainly if we do, we shall gratify the devil in the greatest design that ever he yet practised; who, I doubt not, did with more industry prompt them to evil actions, that religion might be thereby disgraced, despised, and neglected, than to see disturbance of civil affairs; though either of them were a result well becoming a conclave of devils to produce. And I very much fear if this *be* the issue, our peace will not be lasting, nor our undertakings successful, nor restitution firm : for, certainly, irreligion will as soon rot *our* sinews, as hypocrisy and violence did *theirs.*

" 9. It is apt to carry men to expenses, and this to the great folly of mankind, in all their changes. We are like foolish passengers in a storm, that when the boat reels too much on one side, run all to the other ; which doth not cure, but increase, the danger. At the beginning of the troubles there was too much splendour and formality, and some superstition, mingled with, or creeping into, our worship : our cure of this was by running into the extreme. We must *take away* all decency, order, and uniformity. Our ecclesiastical government was too tyrannical and sharp :[4] and our cure was to have none at all. In the civil department our king and his council would govern without a parliament: our cure was—the parliament to govern without a king. And I pray God I be mistaken ; but I fear the detestation of the latter extreme under which we last smarted (and, therefore, the sense of it is most present with, and incumbent upon, us) will carry us over to the former extreme. A restitution of decency, order, uniformity of government in the church, is desired by all good and wise men ; but, methinks, I see those very extremities coming in apace upon us which we all generally disliked; which will, in a little while, give greater advantage to dissatisfied persons to shake all again, than ever before

[4] See Note N.

they had : for, by the long disusage of them, their return will be uncouth and unpleasing to many, and give an occasion of jealousy to more ; and besides, the numbers of persons of a contrary judgment is greatly increased, and they are twisted in with concernments that will make a third change grateful to many, and more easy to be effected : besides, our bones are but newly set, and easily put out again ; so that a relapse of it is more probable, and it will be most desperate and irrecoverable, both in civil and ecclesiastical concernments : and the discontents in both will make the commixtion in discontented persons more obvious and easy, and more formidable. Those, then, who wish well to the peace of Church and State, must use great *moderation* in the concernment of either, lest they undo both.

" 10. As it is apt to let out the activity of the passions and immoderation of men, so it is very apt to discover the imprudence and indiscretion of men ; and that, most of all, in those passages wherein they think their greatest wisdom and policy is eminent.

" To give instances in some particulars :—

" I have observed that many of these men that have been most obnoxious upon the change of times have been most forward, and foremost, and busy in the precipitating of it ; and most impatient of any delay in it ; most ambitious in discovering their desires of it. I have seen some that have been as great occasions of advancing our distractions as any have been under heaven, or at least never contributed to it till they saw it could not be hindered, yet the most importunate, violent, and hasty in the change when it needs them not; like the men of Israel that first entertained a defection from the house of David — upon the return of things, outrunning the fidelity of the men of Judah, that never forsook him utterly. But this violent conversion hath most ordinary one of these two interpretations upon which it withereth: either it is construed as a design to mischief, and endanger that return of things, things that they seem so hastily to advance (either by gaining themselves so much credit as to mingle with the counsels of the rising party according to the practice of Hushai with Absalom, thereby to disappoint them, or to bring discredit and precipitancy into the return of things which in every sober judgment must needs introduce the greatest danger that it is capable of), or it is construed an act constrained by necessity, or of adulation and flattery, or of self-seeking and interest, or of a pitiful and low-flying policy, to cover or obliterate the memory of former demerits, and to scrape a share of interest in the present returns; which, though it be made use of for the present advantage, yet it proves ineffectual for the end designed; and, commonly, such persons lose their interest and reputation on *both* sides; and, when turns are served, the memory of their former disservices returns with more acrimony; or, at least, they are laid aside as men that deserve no trust or confidence, by reason of their mutability or unfixedness. And the very party

which once they were of is sufficiently gratified
and pleased with it, and so they become the objects
of scorn and neglect to all parties.

" I have seen men that have been in some
degree obnoxious upon the change of times, who,
because they have not been *so* obnoxious as others,
fall foul, and fiercely, upon that party that have
been somewhat more obnoxious than themselves ;
not considering, that thereby they give a kind of
just occasion to others that are less obnoxious than
they, to use the same measure of severity towards
them, in a little while ; which either doth, or will
most certainly, happen ; and so that rod, whereby
they have whipped others, is most effectually and
indispensably delivered over from them that used
it, unto others, for *their own* correction, which they
intended not, till all that have had any concurrence or concomitancy in the change, have par-
taken in the same measure ; at least, till it stop in
the moderation of some persons: for it is most
certain and infallible, that unless there be a stop,
by moderation, in some middle parties, the animadversion against offenders, or such as are so reputed,
never ceaseth till it come to the most sublimated,
or, as they call it, refined interest. This was the
walk that things had in the late desolations, both
in ecclesiastical and civil matters. First, the animadversion began by the presbyterian interest,
upon the absolute royalist and episcopal man ; the
independent interest that ran along in that severity,
and thought the presbyterian not sufficiently contrary to the royal interest, is as severe upon the

presbyterian; the anabaptists, and other highflyers, think that went not high enough, but had a secret inclination to monarchy, and though in another line, fly upon the independent ; and when things were at the most refined and sublimest temper, they begin to return again, much by the same steps they went ; and every man, though subject to something that another will easily make a guilt, falls sharply upon another, which, it may be, hath exceeded : not considering that his turn may be next. Thus, he that hath sworn fealty to the late protector, falls sharply upon him that abjured ; he that took the Engagement, falls as sharply upon both the former ; he that took the Covenant only, is ready to fall upon the three former ; and he that never took any, is ready to inveigh as bitterly against the covenanter : he that acted regularly under the protector or commonwealth, falls generally upon the high court of justice men ; he that acted under the long parliament with the same severity, in-veighs against both the former ; and, perchance, invites thereby the spirits of those men that acted purely on the royal account, to fall as sharply upon all three; men, looking still, generally, upon that whereof they are innocent, and not consider-ing themselves in that whereof they are guilty, or so thought by others. This transition from one to another must needs be the issue of immoderate severity, upon these two accounts : 1st. The very reasons they use, and the severity they exercise upon others, gives the same weapon into the hands of others against *them:* puts them in mind of their sufferings; gives them hope and opportunity that the same measure may be used as successfully against others. 2d. The afflicted and upbraided party recriminates, and excites, and encourageth the more refined party to fall, with the same eagerness, upon the former; which either gives them a hope of security, or, at least, pleaseth them, to see their adversaries dealt with all in the same kind. This is, or will be, the issue of this gangrene, if not timely prevented by moderation; and would have been seasonably prevented, had the severity only rested in that which had the common odium of all men, and terminated in a few only; viz. those that actually condemned and executed the king.

"Hitherto, I have considered the miscarriages incident especially to the prevailing or rising party, upon such great mutations of state. I shall now consider the miscarriages incident to those persons that are of the declining party, or that were at all, in any sort, mingled with them.

"1. It is apt to breed a base despondency of mind, that a man scarce dares own that which was good, and well done, even in bad times. Doth thy conscience bear thee witness, that even in the worst of times thy *actions* have been *good*, and for the service of the unquestionable interest of the nation? Be not so vain as to seek thine own applause, lest thou be disappointed: but yet scorn to disown them, notwithstanding they are prejudicated, or misinterpreted. Content thyself with the serenity of thy own conscience, and the testimony it gives to thine integrity; and value not the descants of men. Good actions, happening in a time wherein there were many evil, may, in the tumult and hurry of a change, undergo the same, or very little better interpretation, than the worst actions. The indignation against the latter, or the times wherein they were acted, may cover the best actions and intentions with prejudice, and censure. But when things and persons grow a little calmer, they may be restored to their due estimate. Wait, therefore, with patience, upon the great Searcher and Judge of hearts, and actions, who, in his due time, will ' bring forth thy righteousness as the noon day ;' and, in the mean time, content thyself with the inward serenity of thy own conscience, in the midst of the mistakes, and prejudices of others.

" 2. It is apt to carry men to base and unworthy means to cover their former miscarriages, or avoid the shame, or danger of them : such as are falsities and untruths ; laying, sometimes, an undeserved blame upon the commands, counsels, and examples of others, which, for the most part, are detected, or, at least, suspected, to the greater disadvantage of the offender, than would ensue upon a manly and ingenuous confession.

" 3. It is apt to put men upon this ugly cover and diversion of the animadversion of their own guilt, either by a severe animadversion upon others, or an overhasty and unhandsome compliance with those things that, it may be, are unseemly, or unseasonable, if gratifying the rising party.    I have seen those men that have been most deeply obnoxious in their former occasioning of the late troubles, or opposing of the present change, or, at least, not contributing one grain to it before it came, to be the most severe censurers of those that were of their own party, and the most precipitate, and inconsiderate ; promoting of those things that seemed only to be grateful to those that are, or are like to be eminent, although, in truth, the things promoted have been most dangerous and destructive to them ; fearing to exercise any integrity, lest it might displease, and so bring their former sins to remembrance.

"4. It is apt to make men that either in truth, or in their own fears, are obnoxious, to be glad when others are drawn under the same calamity, or the danger of it ; and not only so, but to be secret promoters of it, which, though in some it seems only to be used as a base policy to secure themselves, yet, in most, it is a devilish mind that thinks their misery or misfortune is abated by the *multitude* of sharers in it ; thus I have seen some men who were out of hope of securing themselves from those miscarriages that they committed after the king's death, interest the actings and actors that preceded it in the time of the war in the same common guilt.

"5. It is apt to put men upon securing themselves by introducing a common calamity, or dissettlement, even upon the whole nation. I have reason to believe that there are some men that would be contented to see the nation in fire and blood, to see confusion spread over the face of the whole kingdom, though they could not but expect that the ruin of themselves and their posterity would, in probability, ensue, rather than to run the hazard of their own present shame or loss. Whereas a generous and noble, though a guilty, soul, would be glad to see the settlement of the nation, though with his own ruin and infamy.

" 6. It is apt to put men upon that cursed and tormenting distemper of envy, which looks upon all men that are like to be safer or greater than themselves, with indignation, and calumny: censuring their merit, blaming authority, whispering, backbiting, and slandering them. Men that cannot be contented to suffer, unless they draw others into the same calamity ; nor to be safe, unless they be also great.

" 7. It is apt to put discontented, discountenanced, and obnoxious men to secret machinations, making of parties, blowing up false reports, fomenting dissatisfactions and jealousies, thereby to occasion more divisions : and all this upon several base ends ; either to secure themselves from danger, or to satisfy their ambitious and restless spirits, which cannot be contented to enjoy peace, and their own rules, unless they may acquire power, and be masters of others : men that, having been accustomed to domination, had rather die than live without it. And I am very confident there be a sort of persons in the world, that do cunningly and artificially excite, and irritate some of good intentions, but of strong passions, prejudices, and severe principles, to immoderation, that thereby disunions, divisions, animosities, and discontents, may be raised; and the unanimity of the nation, especially, to the common interest, may be broken; the consequence whereof may engage the nation into parties, and new civil dissensions; or, at least, make them less cordial and unanimous in opposing a desperate party, if they should appear with specious pretences of more moderation, or indulgence: *quod Deus avertat.*

" And thus I have concluded my observations upon the present transactions, and various tempers of men under their different conditions; I shall now conclude with those counsels, or resolutions, which, though possibly they may be useful to others, yet are principally directed to myself.

" 1. Be not over-hasty in thy judgment concerning any person. First be certain of the truth of the fact. The prejudicate opinions of others, or common report, are but slight grounds for an accusation; but they are dangerous and unwarrantable grounds for a judgment; nay, though more particular evidence of the fact appear against a prejudiced person, yet they require an impartial discussion; partly, because men are apt to be too liberal in their endeavours against a prejudiced person; and naturally we are apt to take them in upon slight grounds, and with prepossessed minds, which are ready to make every mole-hill a mountain. Secondly, in cases of accusation of grea crimes, let there be great evidence; partly, because, where the crime is great, and consequently the punishment, the nature of both require the clearer evidence. Possibly the punishment may be such as the error therein may be fatal and irreparable; partly, because men are commonly too forward upon such censures, upon a vain fear, lest they should seem to countenance the crime : the odiousness of the fact many a time makes an imprudent judge too hasty and violent in the censure lest he should seem too remiss. Thirdly, in all cases weigh circumstances where the course of proceedings allows a latitude in the measure of the censure, for the very same fact may be so circumstantiated that it may put, at least, a different degree, if not a different denomination, in the thing objected; as on the one side malice, or deliberation, or base ends, may aggravate, so on the other side, fear, or inadvertence, or retractation, may extenuate the same fact.

" 2. In censuring of offences, beware of overmuch severity, especially in the station thou now standest in, and as the times are, upon these ensuing considerations.

" (1.) In respect of thy present station : thou art now purely in the case of a judge, who is bound up to the strict letter of a law. In case of a counsellor, and an adviser, that which thou art about is, not merely to measure the fact according to a law; but thou art in a parliament to fit a law in the particular case to the fact, wherein may be a latitude of prudential considerations. Again, thy king hath made thee a kind of chancellor, and hath much intrusted thee with some of his mercy :

E

as thou art not to be too lavish, so neither art thou to be too parsimonious of it ; for on either side there will be a breach of trust. In an ordinary course of criminal proceedings in other courts, the king intrusts thee only with justice, and reserves the dispensation of mercy to himself; and there thy rule of proceeding is according to the law. But here the king, as well by an implicit commission, as thou art a member of parliament, as by an express signification, hath committed the deliberation of his mercy to thee, wherein thou dost only advise ; the final decision is his.

" (2.) In respect of the present season : we are just now crept out of years of confusion, which involved a multitude in those actions that had they been done in sedate times, had been crimes of the highest nature ; which yet must come under another estimate (being done under the pressure, and upon the exigencies of former times) when the king is in a condition to protect his people. An oath of allegiance to another prince, serving in wars against him, raising monies against him, is a crime of the highest nature. But when force hath dispossessed him of his power, though that doth not absolve us from our duty, yet it takes off from the crime.

" (3.) In regard of the multitude of offenders : when *every* man is under a guilt, it gives a prudential dispensation both in the extent and severity of the punishment ; for, instead of justice, it would become a desolation. Almighty God that is Lord of the world may bring a deluge upon a sinful

world, and destroy them all; yet among men, when
the defection is almost universal, it is hard to press
an extent of punishment as large as the guilt;
especially since punishments, in all cases but of
blood, are, among men, by way of example, rather
than of retribution.

" (4.) In regard to the present state of things:
overmuch severity in point of justice, as the case
stands with England at this day, would, in common prudence, be the extremest injustice that
could be, when the issue of it, in all probability,
would be the production of new distempers, or, at
least, the seeds, or opportunities of them: and
then justice is ill placed or dispensed when the
consequence of it must introduce, not the good
and safety, but the danger and mischief, of a
nation.

" (5.) In regard to thy own self: the old gram-
mar rule is true, as well in point of judgment as
accusation, *Qui alterum accusat probri, liberum se
esse metueri oportet.* Thou art innocent of this or
that crime, or fact, and, therefore, thou art secure
against it; but art thou not guilty of something
else whereof another, it may be, is innocent? And
then thy severity teacheth him the like against
thee. Thou hast not taken the Oath of Abjuration,
and, therefore, thou art most severe, even to a
capital punishment, against him that hath: but hast
thou not taken the Engagement? or the Recognition, which, it may be, another hath? It may be
thy turn next to come under his rhetoric and
aggravations as now another is under thine. It was

a most wise answer of our Lord to the severe inquisition of Pharisees, ' He that is without sin, let him cast the first stone at her.' He did not acquit her from her fault, but he convinced them of partiality. Neither do I by this mean to countenance an impunity of offences at all times, nor of the great offence at this time, but to teach myself and others *moderation;* especially in such a time when the calamities of former times hath left so few clearly innocent.

" (6.) In respect of the nature of things : most certainly the safest error is to exceed in mercy rather than in severity, especially when both are, in a sort, in my power ; for it may be that person I now spare may upon that very account become a man of great service to the kingdom, that may with a redundant merit satisfy for his former demerit, which, by my severity, I may either make impossible, or very difficult. It is seldom seen that a man that hath undergone a public stigma, though he survive his punishment, ever grows eminent.

" 3. Again : suppose a guilty person escape, yet he is under the wrath of Divine justice, that can take him when he pleaseth, when the over severe punishment of one that seems guilty, but, it may be, is *not*, is oftentimes irreparable.

"God himself, whose justice is most pure, infallible, and absolute, is contented that *his* mercy should rejoice against his justice, and delights to be known by his mercy, rather than by the severity of his justice ; and this may be as well *our* example as his honour.

" Alas ! we are frail, weak men, that every moment stand in need of mercy from God. He forgives us our hundred talents, and yet we think much of pardoning our brother one hundred pence. The only objection that prevails and deludes many men in this case is this. But this is not vindictiveness in our own cause, but in the cause of the public ; and therein we are but their stewards, and trusted for them ; and therein if we show not severity, we perform not our trust. I answer—

" (1.) I fear that if men did impartially examine their own hearts, they would find that much of this severity ariseth from passion, animosity, and private revenge, which marcheth behind that painted cloth of the public interest. But,

" (2.) It is true that where a man is trusted purely with justice, and mercy is not committed to him, his rule must be to walk accordingly ; a judge of the common law must not walk by the rules of equity, nor a judge of criminal causes according to rules purely of mercy, because there is another tribunal reserved for them. But in the condition of a parliament, where my king and country trust me as a counsellor, or adviser, or under both considerations, certainly I do not discharge my trust if I think my rule must be severity, with an exclusion of moderation or mercy : and if I would blame that whole community whom I represent, if I should see them act according to *such* a method, I cannot acquit myself if I act so for them. God keep me from a corporation conscience, that think they are bound to use an extremity and severity because they act in a politic capacity."[5]

The king at a very early period proposed, in person, an act of indemnity, and Hale had the honour of being nominated one of the committee for forwarding the generous purpose. Wisely judging that the *sooner* it was carried the better, he exerted in its favour all the powers of his mind, and all the benevolence of his heart. He framed, carried on, and supported the bill;[6] and on the 11th of July, 1660, it passed the Commons.

[5] Orig. MS.      [6] Life by Runnington, p. 11.

# CHAPTER VII.

## FROM A. D. 1660 TO A. D. 1662.

WHATEVER opinion may be entertained of the Earl of Clarendon, Charles the Second's most confidential minister, in regard to his apparent bigotry and narrow mindedness respecting ecclesiastical matters, it seems generally agreed that in adjusting the affairs of the nation, and in the various appointments, especially to judicial offices, [1] he displayed the utmost penetration and wisdom.

The case before us is an instance of it. Mr. Hale's fame was too brilliant to allow of his being entirely overlooked; but amidst so much excitement, and even scrambling for preferment, it surely redounds to the premier's honour, as well as his own, that he should have been " sought out," [2] and at almost the earliest period of the restored government placed in a situation of first-rate dignity. He was included in the special

[1] This subject is noticed in connexion with Sir Matthew Hale in Mac Diarmid's Lives of British Statesmen, p. 538, 4to. 1807.

[2] Dr. Lingard attacks Lord Clarendon with more than insinuation as to this appointment.—History of England, vol. xii. p. 27, 8vo. 1829.

commission appointed for the trial of the regicides,[3] and he was elevated to a chief seat upon the bench. His reluctance to accept the appointment is no secret; but the following document, containing his reasons for that reluctance, is comparatively unknown. A relic so precious cannot be here omitted. While detailing the motives upon which he acted, it gives us a retrospective knowledge, curious, accurate, and unique, of his life. The answer furnished by it to invidious remarks will not escape observation.

*" Reasons why I desire to be spared from any place of public employment.*

" I. Because the smallness of my estate, the greatness of my charge, and some debts, make me unable to bear it with that decency which becomes it, unless I should ruin myself and family. My estate, not above 500*l.* per annum, six children unprovided for, and a debt of 1000*l.* lying upon me. And besides this, of all things it is most unseemly for a judge to be necessitous. Private condition makes that easier to be borne and less to be observed which a public employment makes poor and ridiculous. And besides this, it will necessarily lift up the minds of my children above their fortunes, which will be my grief and their ruin.

" II. I am not able so well to endure travel and pains as formerly. My present constitution of body requires now some ease and relaxation.

---

[3] See the State Trials, vol. ii. p. 304.

" III. I have formerly served in public employment under a new, odious interest, which by them
that understand not, or observe not, or will willingly, upon their own passions, or interest, mistake
my reasons for it, may be objected even in my
very practice of judicature, which is fit to be preserved without the least blemish, or disrepute in
the person that exerciseth it.

" IV. The present conjuncture and unsettlement
of affairs, especially relating to administration of
justice, is such ; the various interests, animosities,
and questions, so many ; the present rule so
uncertain ; and the difficulties so great; that a
man cannot, without loss of himself or reputation,
or great disobligations, exercise the employment
of a judge, whose carriage will be strictly observed,
easily misrepresented, and severely censured according to variety of interests. And I have still
observed that almost in all times, especially upon
changes, judges have been ever exposed to the
calumny and petulancy of every discontented or
busy spirit.

" V. I have, too, infirmities that make me unfit
for that employment. 1st. An aversation to the
pomp and grandeur necessarily incident to that
employment. 2d. Too much pity, clemency, and
tenderness, in cases of life, which may prove an
unserviceable temper for bustling *     *     *
    " VI. *     *     *     *     *     *     *     *
*     *     *     *     *     *     *     *     *     *

" VII. I shall lose the weight of my integrity
and honesty by accepting a place of honour or

profit, as if all my former counsels and appearances were but a design to raise myself.

"VIII. The very engagement in a public employment carries a prejudice to whatsoever shall be said or done to the advantage of that party that raised a man, as if it were the service due to his promotion. And so, though the thing be never so just, it shall carry no weight, but a suspicion of design or partiality.

"IX. I am sure in the condition of a private man declining preferment, my weight will be three to one over what it will be in a place of judicature.

"X. I am able in my present station to serve my king and country, my friend, myself, and family, by my advice and counsel.

"XI. I have, of late, declined the study of the law, and principally applied myself to other studies, now more easy, grateful, and seasonable for me.

"XII. I have had the perusal of most of the considerable titles and questions in law that are now on foot in England, or that are likely to grow into controversy within a short time : and it is not so fit for me, that am pre-engaged in opinion, to have these cases fall under my judgment as a judge, as I needs must either upon trials or judgment.

"If it be objected, that it will look as a sign of the displeasure of the king against me, or of a disserviceable mind in me towards the king, if I should either be past over, or decline a preferment in this kind, I answer that neither can reasonably be supposed——

" 1. In respect of my present condition as serving in the House of Commons, which excuseth the supposition of either.

" 2. His Majesty's good opinion of my fidelity may be easily manifested, and my fidelity and service to him will be sufficiently testified by my carriage and professions.

" But if, after all this, there must be a necessity of undertaking an employment, I desire——

" 1. It may be in such a court and way as may be most suitable to my course of studies and education.

" 2. That it may be the lowest place that may be, that I may avoid envy. One of his Majesty's counsel in ordinary, or at most, the place of a puisne judge in the Common Pleas would suit me best."

In the manuscript book from which what precedes is copied, it is here noted that "*desunt multa*, the paper being torn."[4]

On the 7th November, 1660, Hale was created Lord Chief Baron of England.

He received the commission from the hands of the Earl of Clarendon, then Lord Chancellor. The speech was more than mere ceremony; esteem was strongly expressed, and the new judge, among other things, was informed, in the complimentary style of Louis XIV., "that if the king could have found out an honester or fitter man for that

[4] Collection of Tracts relative to the Law of England, from MSS. now first edited by Francis Hargrave, Esq., Barrister at Law. 4to. 1787. Preface, pp. x—xii.

employment, he would not have advanced him to it: he had, therefore, preferred *him* because he knew none that deserved it so well."

"What but Christianity," asked the late Mr. Knox, with equal propriety and force, "could have given to Judge Hale that uniform ascendency over every thing selfish and secular, by means of which he so undeviatingly kept the path of pure heroic virtue, as to be alike looked up to and revered by parties and interests the most opposite to each other? Is there, in human history, any fact more extraordinary than that the advocate of Strafford and Laud, and of King Charles (had leave been given for pleading), should be raised to the bench by Cromwell? And again, that a judge of Cromwell's should be not only reinstated by Charles II., but compelled by him, against his own will, to accept of the very highest judicial trust? Such is the triumph of genuine *Christianity*; a triumph which is, in some degree, renewed, wherever the name of Hale is even professionally repeated : since the appeal is evidently made, not more to the authority of the judge, than to the integrity of the man."[5]

Like his great contemporary, Marshal Turenne, Lord Hale avoided the presence of his sovereign as well as the praise of men ; and thus, for a time, escaped the honour usually consequent upon his new office. This the Chancellor observed, and alluring him, at length, to his own house, at a

[5] Preface to the first Dublin Edition. p. xliv. Lives &c., by Burnet, ed. by Bishop Jebb, 8vo. 1833.

time when the king was there, presented the modest Chief Baron; and he was knighted.

With that precision and forecast which marked all his movements, Sir Matthew now framed those rules of conduct which even less admiration than they have enjoyed, would have entitled to a place in the present volume. Besides being worthy of attention as a manual of pious wisdom, they shed valuable light upon his history. They explain the unvarying homage he paid to his convictions: they show likewise why, with such undaunted intrepidity, he rebuked Cromwell; and by the prominence they give to personal infirmity, to that liableness to err which is human, and to determined watchfulness, resulting from the perception of it, they illustrate and commend principles the most sublime.

*" Things necessary to be continually had in remembrance.*

" I. That in the administration of justice, I am entrusted for God, the king, and country; and therefore,

" II. That it be done, 1st, uprightly: 2dly, deliberately: 3dly, resolutely.

" III. That I rest not upon my own understanding or strength, but implore and rest upon the direction and strength of God.

" IV. That in the execution of justice I carefully lay aside my own passions, and not give way to them, however provoked.

" V. That I be wholly intent upon the business

I am about, remitting all other cares and thoughts as unseasonable, and interruptions.

" VI. That I suffer not myself to be prepossessed with any judgment at all, till the whole business, and both parties be heard.

" VII. That I never engage myself in the beginning of any cause, but reserve myself unprejudiced till the whole be heard.

" VIII. That in business capital, though my nature prompt me to pity, yet to consider that there is also a pity due to the country.

" IX. That I be not too rigid in matters purely conscientious, where all the harm is diversity of judgment.

" X. That I be not biassed with compassion to the poor, or favour to the rich, in point of justice.

" XI. That popular or court applause, or distaste, have no influence into any thing I do in point of distribution of justice.

" XII. Not to be solicitous what men will say or think, so long as I keep myself exactly according to the rules of justice.

" XIII. If in criminals it be a measuring cast, to incline to mercy and acquittal.

" XIV. In criminals that consist merely in words when no more harm ensues, moderation is no injustice.

" XV. In criminals of blood, if the fact be evident, severity is justice.

" XVI. To abhor all private solicitations, of what kind soever and by whomsoever, in matters depending.

" XVII. To charge my servants : 1st, not to interpose in any business whatsoever : 2d, not to take more than their known fees : 3d, not to give any undue precedence to causes : 4th, not to recommend counsel.

"XVIII. To be short and sparing at meals, that I may be the fitter for business."[6]

Not only had Hale's prosperous course been hitherto, in a great degree, unchecked, but many of the common ills of life were scarcely known to him otherwise than by reading and observation. Whatever the trials he had endured, whether those of bereavement, or relative sorrows of any other description, innumerable providential favours, including good health, had reduced them in a sense to annihilation. It will be observed in the " Considerations" which follow, and which look back many years, only one exception to the statement just made is alluded to, and that of a trivial nature. It is, therefore, clear that his religious principles had hitherto been mainly tried by *prosperity ;* but through God's mercy, they had triumphed :[7] nor was the result different, when in infinite wisdom, they were subjected to another test : alarming disease—to the threatening of his life. His state and sentiments when so circumstanced are happily not left to conjecture. He wrote a memorial upon the occasion, which has been preserved ; and however it be viewed, whether as a narrative of facts, or as the thoughts of a spiritual mind, or as a

[6] Life by Burnet, pp. 35, 36.   See Note O.   [7] See Note P.

treasury of instruction, it imparts to this new era in his history special interest.

*" 1662. Considerations upon my late sickness, and what I learnt experimentally from it.*

" From this dispensation I find and learn that man is a very fragile, unstable, and weak creature. The chiefest occasion of my sickness I could visibly impute but to a little wet taken in my head in my journey to London. Thus a small cold; the obstruction of a little meat ill-digested; a small bruise or hurt; and a thousand such inconsiderable occurrences, may give opportunity to the humours and corruptions of the body, to distemper it into an ague, or fever, or palsy, or apoplexy, or any other disease that may destroy or endanger, or a long time discompose us.

" And truly though this seems to be a lesson that we may easily learn at an easier rate than experience from ourselves, by what we observe in others, and the weekly bills of mortality, and although every man hath the frailty and weakness and mortality of our condition at his tongue's end, yet it is a harder lesson *practically* to be learned than men in their firm state of health are aware of. And that it is so is most evident, because those very men that notionally know it, and can philosophise upon it excellently in their health, when sickness comes, are under as great a novelty and surprise and perturbation as if they had scarce supposed that possible before, which every day they saw and spake of: and their own experience in the time of sickness will make them know they have another kind of fear of it than they had before, viz. more deep, practical, and visible; and this was my condition as well as theirs.

" And the reason why the notion of our own frailty in the time of our health is so weak, waterish, and inoperative, is this—we are affected with what is present more strongly and intimately than with what is absent; and therefore we cannot, without much difficulty, have an affectionate apprehension or conviction of the latter: neither can we put ourselves by our imaginations or conception under a full and real impression of it, especially when that absent state or condition is, in its nature, grievous and displeasing. As we are under some kind of disability to have a deep and effectual apprehension of it because it *is* absent, so we are under an unwillingness to anticipate the notion of a change for the worse because it is *grievous*. And this difficulty, perchance, was much more upon me than upon others, because the Lord had been pleased to give me an uninterrupted state of health, without any considerable experience of sickness, or weakness, or pain, for above three and thirty years. But when this fever overtook me, and held me in continual burning for many hours together on successive days; when upon a sudden my sleep was troublesome and interrupted; when the offices of nature were in a great measure interrupted; when my spirits were exhausted and my sinews weakened, and my strength upon a sudden taken from me; *then* I found, experimentally, how soon I was brought low; how soon my strength was deranged; how easily I was brought even to the mouth of the grave. And though I could talk and think of this in my health, yet in my sickness I found my former apprehensions thereof were languid and formal. I now had another *kind* of sense and knowledge of it than I had before.

" And from this I learn, and hope ever to remember, after it hath pleased God to restore me in some measure to my health, never to put confidence in my own strength: but to look upon myself as a weak, fragile creature, crushed before the moth; ever in a tendency to death, and corruption, and dissolution; that even while I seem to be in a perfect state of health there may be growing in me a secret fermentation of corruption, or putrefaction, or the wasting humour that may bring me to the grave; a worm at the root of my life, as once there was at the root of Jonah's gourd, that, while it seems green and flourishing, may in a moment, an unexpected, unsuspected moment, wither it.

" I have found experimentally that it is of great necessity for men in their health and strength to walk with all piety and duty to God; with all watchfulness and sobriety, with all justice, honesty, and charity, and goodness to men; to work out their salvation with fear and trembling; to secure unto themselves that one thing necessary, the *magnum opus* of our lives—the pardon of sins and peace with God. Sometimes I have read over in the time of my health, that wise counsel of the wise man—"Remember thy Creator in the days of thy youth, before the evil days come, and the years draw nigh, when thou shalt say, I have no pleasure in them," (Eccl. xii.)—with a great sense of the necessity of it, and have accordingly applied myself unto it : many times I have read it without that due sense of the necessity of it, and as a counsel that did little at present concern me ; or, at least, the due weight of it did not sink into my soul, or so duly affect it as it should. But—my sickness made me understand, and sensibly feel the necessity and use of that counsel at another rate than formerly ; and these considerations and experiences laid the weight of it to my heart.

" 1. I experimentally found that as the past vanities and sins of my life were the greatest enemies I had, and the remembrance of them returned upon me with most trouble and perturbation, so I did feel that the care which in my health I took to make my peace with God, my frequent and humble addresses to him by prayer, and examination, and settling of my interest in Christ, his merits, righteousness, and intercession ; my endeavours to deny my lusts ; my endeavours, in an humble obedience, to observe the commands of God ; to sanctify his day ; to relieve the poor ; to be compassionate, and gentle, and charitable to those whom I found tender of the honour of God, and the duty they owed to him, though perchance dissenting in circumstantials ; the walking in the spirit of meekness, and tenderness, and compassion

to all, out of the sense of my own failings and
God's mercy; so now the secret witness of my
conscience that, though I had many failings, weaknesses, inadvertencies, passions, and lusts, yet I
had endeavoured to walk before God in truth, and
with a perfect heart, and to do that which was
good in his sight, and yet this very righteousness
I esteemed as nothing in the sight of God in its
own native worth, but rested only upon the Lord
our righteousness, the righteousness of God in
Christ, for my acceptation and justification in his
sight.   These, and the like transactions of my life
in the time of my health, and the returns of them
upon my memory, and the witness of my conscience
concerning the same, were more comfortable to
me than the best cordial : they brought me in much
comfort : and it eased my mind of very much care
and trouble, and gave it opportunity and leisure
to contest with the present infirmity of my body,
when I considered, that the greatest business and
concernment of my life was, in a great measure,
*well settled* in the time of my health, strength,
and integrity of body and mind.

" 2. I experimentally found that sickness is an
ill season to begin to compose and settle the great
concernment of our everlasting souls.   I have
many times known men that, out of inadvertence,
or perchance a foolish thought that the making of
their wills, or settling their temporal concernments,
might be a presage of death, have deferred the
same till sickness hath overtaken them ; and then
the man hath been so little himself, or so much

distracted with pain, or discomposed with weakness, or distemper, that, either he cannot do any thing at all; or if it be done, it is so broken and discomposed that the will speaks the distemper of the man; or it is, otherwise, the production of the discretion or design of those that are about him. And if it be so in case of matters of *worldly* concernment, and, therefore, even in that fit to be prevented by a timely disposition of temporals in time of health, much more care should be taken in the case of our *everlasting* concernments, because infinitely of greater moment. Believe it, it is business enough to be thoroughly sick; perchance the disease may preclude and bar up this intended enterprise of settling our peace with God; it may take thee with a frenzy, or apoplexy, or palsy, and cut off the use of thy understanding; or if it do not, yet it may be so acute, and violent, as may take thee away suddenly, in a day, or two, or three, (as the plague or pestilential fever, or it may be a misapplied, or unseasonable, or miscarrying, or mistaken medicine); or if it do *not*, yet it may be so full of pain, or high discomposure, that it gives thee not a moment of intermission, nor leaves thy thoughts free from the importunity of thy pains and distempers, till it carry thee to thy long home : or if thou hast some relaxation or intermission from the height of pain or distemper (as in dropsies, or agues, or consumptions), yet thou wilt most assuredly find the weakness of thy body, though without any great incumbent pain or distemper, will discompose the actings of thy soul, and have an influence upon it. Frowardness and peevishness will grow upon thee, and discompose thee. Faintness and lassitude will grow upon thee, and discompose thee. Ungrateful evaporations from putrefaction of humours will grow upon thee, and discompose thee. And hereupon thou wilt find, as well as I, by experience of this kind of sickness have found, that thy prayer will be as faint and as spiritless as thy body; and thou wilt not be able, either to hold up, or to hold out a prayer, or a contemplation, or meditation of what concerns thee most : thou wilt be scarce able to fix thy thoughts ; or if thou dost, they will soon flag and thou be weary of them.

"I do not deny but many a man may be converted to God in his sickness ; and I doubt not but the merciful God doth, and will, accept the weak, and faint, and languishing, and short prayers, and ejaculations, and repentings, and resolutions, of a sick, and dying, but sincere, heart : for he judgeth not as man judgeth, and his mercy is not confined to strong devotions. Neither do I deny but that it is the duty of the most confirmed soul under heaven, even in the time of his sickness, according to the measure of his strength and opportunity, to improve the assurance and the measure of his everlasting interest by renewed thanksgivings, intercessions, repentings, and other exercises of his faith and obedience : and without question those may be as acceptable to God as those that are done with the greatest mixture of the intention, and vigour of spirit : only this my experience tells me, and sickness will make thee know as well as I, that those exercises of piety are fuller of difficulty, and fuller of weakness, but not so full of comfort ordinarily, as when we take that opportunity of strength and health that God puts into our hands. And, therefore, they that burn out and lavish away the opportunity of health and strength in serving themselves, their lusts, their temporal interests, this world, and *procrastinate* their greatest concernment to the impotency of a sick bed—as it is a most ungrateful return to the Author of their health, so they venture they know not *how much :* possibly, they may meet with *prevention* in such a procrastination ; and if they do not, yet let them be assured they shall find greater difficulty and less comfort in it.

3. By the experience of this sickness I have found that the greatest perturbations of a sick bed are the sins of the past life ; therefore, let every man that means to have his sickness as easy and as comfortable as may be, be most careful to avoid all sin in his health, as much as possibly he can. It is most certain there is no man living without sin : and it is most certain that the more the sins are, the more the burden of sickness ; unless a man be under a stupidity. It is sure he that hath led a most strict life, and hath committed very few sins, at least of the greater magnitude, yet it is a thousand to one but the remembrance of those few sins, the sins of his youth, will visit him in his sickness, and trouble him so, and drive him to his great catholicon—the blood of Christ : and this may

come from several principles. It may be the merciful God doth a little awaken him, that he may take the *faster hold* upon his Saviour; and renew his repentings with more resolution; and his gratitude to the mercy of God with more cheerfulness. It may be, the evil one takes his advantage of a weaker and sick condition, of the impotency of the vital spirits, and the prevalence of the corruption of the body, and presents the memory, even of lesser faults, with greater aggravations, to the end to disturb and distract the mind, as well as the body; but God turns this also to a better end, even a faster clasping of the Redeemer of mankind. It may be the perturbation of the body, the putrefaction of humours, or the prevalence of them, may so fix and radicate a small or light remembrance of few and lesser sins in a good man's life, as that he cannot easily discharge himself of them. But certain it is, the less sin brings the less trouble: the more the goodness of a life past, the more comfort and overpowering and outweighing the trouble and discomfort of those fewer sins. Or, if the sins be many and great, yet a serious repentance takes away, through the blood of Christ, the venom and anguish of them. And they seldom gall the conscience in the time of sickness, because God is at peace with the soul, and witnesseth it in and to the conscience. But thou shalt find that a great stock of sins unrepented, will be the worst and most ungrateful and troublesome visitor in the world in the time of sickness. Let it, therefore, be thy care first to be watchful over thy life, and take heed of sin; for it will be most troublesome when thou art least able to bear it. Or if thou hast sinned, break off these sins by a timely and hearty repentance, before the evil day comes. By this means they will be put upon another's account—even the Lamb of God, that taketh away the sins of the world. And so *thou* shalt not be visited with these troublesome guests in thy sickness; or if thou *art*, thou hast wherewith to answer and dismiss them: ' Who is he that condemneth? It is Christ that died,' &c.

" 4. I experimentally learned that this world is a vain and empty thing; and that the generality of mankind are strangely and extremely deceived in their estimate and valuation of it, and miserably misled in their eager and violent prosecution of it. The Evangelist hath made a right testimony of it : ' All that is the *world*, is the lust of the flesh, the lust of the eyes, and the pride of life.' The great business of it is in subservience to the body, with pleasure, and profits, and honour : touch but the body with a disease, or with approaching death, there is no relish or taste in the best of these pursuits. It is true it is a popular theme that every man hath in his mouth from Solomon—*all is vanity ;* and yet those things that notionally and verbally we call so, we pursue as our greatest happiness ; as if those expressions of ours were not our meaning, but a design to discourage others from the prosecution of that which we would alone enjoy. And thus one man pursues honour and great place and authority, and prides himself much

F

in the acquest, and in the retinues, observances, distances, and addresses that wait upon such preferment. Another pursues after wealth, and makes it the whole business of his thoughts and life; and when he hath gotten it, blesseth himself with the rich man—' Soul, thou hast much goods laid up for many years ; eat, drink, and be merry. Others pursue the gratification of their senses and sensual appetite, rare pictures, and stately houses and gardens, luxurious diet, pleasant wines, choice meats and fruit, fine flowers, amorous and wanton company, and the fruition of unlawful lusts. And in these they place their *happiness*, and spend the flower and strength of their souls and bodies ; exhaust their supplies, and consume their time that will one day be wanted, but never recalled. And these for the most part are the business of the generality of mankind. But when the approaches of death come, nay, when a strong disease, a burning fever, or a violent ague, drinks up the blood, and consumes the spirits, and wastes the flesh, and contracts the sinews, and casts languishings and dimness upon the eye, nauseousness and loathing upon the stomach, pain and distemper upon the whole body—these conditions do undeceive the man, and render all those things that men make their business and their happiness, as nauseous and insipid as the most unacceptable thing in the world. The body is not only disabled to entertain the lusts of the flesh, of what kind soever, but the very thoughts and provisions of them are nauseous and odious. The eye rather

chooseth darkness to protect its weakness than the
most glorious sight in the world : an intermission
of pain for an hour; a relaxation of the burning
of an ague or fever for morning; an hour's quiet
composed sleep is then more valuable than the
greatest honours or treasures.   A man looks upon
all such as things out of date and of no use; as
vain and ineffectual helpers; and not only so, but
as vexing, and disquieting, and tormenting fruitions.
When a man shall be entertained with such
thoughts as these—' Lord, how have I spent my
time, my precious time, upon which my *eternity*
depends, for *bubbles* and *nothing;* things that give
a sick man no ease nor relish, and a dying man
no comfort.   I am never the *better* for the enjoyment, but much the *worse* for the precious hours
I spent to attain them (one whereof I cannot
redeem with all my acquests); for that excess
which I used in them, which increaseth my guilt
and doth not mitigate my disease, nor procrastinate
my approaching dissolution—when I must *leave*
them all, and all that is in them that carries in it
but the shadow of any comfort.   And I shall *take
along with me* into another world all the gall and
bitterness that I have extracted from them: the fear,
too, of that time I mispent about them that might
have been employed to my eternal advantage; the
guilt of that pride and vain glory, that oppression
and cruelty, that covetousness and uncharitableness,
that injustice and deceit, that worldly confidence
and forgetting of God, that intemperance and riot,
that luxury and wantonness, and those other

legions of sins that I committed either in the pursuit, or use, and enjoyment of them. And now I have but a little uncertain and unseasonable time in which I must gain my pardon, or carry those chains and shackles and furies about me to all *eternity*.' It concerns us, therefore, highly to have a right estimate of these externals : not to be over busy in the pursuit of them ; and to be very sober, vigilant, moderate, and cautious, in the enjoying of them ; to receive them, as from the hands of God, if he please to give them ; and to enjoy them, as in the presence of God, and according to the will of God, while we have them ; to set a value upon the goodness of God in dispensing them, but not to set *our hearts* upon them, as our rest or happiness ; not to spend too much time about them : to esteem them, in themselves, as temporal vanities, that in the end of our days they may not be our vexation. *This* is the lesson that sickness doth practically and experimentally teach ; and I pray God, if he please to restore me to my perfect health, I may never forget." [8]

[8] The orig. MS.

## CHAPTER VIII.

### FROM A.D. 1662 TO A.D. 1666.

How exactly the rules which Sir Matthew laid down for his governance as a judge were observed, is every where apparent. Because of his diligence, exactness, and impartiality, the practice of the Exchequer became vastly augmented; and, although some thought that he did not despatch matters quick enough, suitors found, to their great benefit, that while his anxiety to put a *final* end to causes made him somewhat slower in deciding them, those which he tried were seldom, if ever, tried again.

The following authentic anecdotes will remind the reader, not of the sage Antoninus and Aristides the Just only, but of those ancient judges whom an inspired writer expressively described as " fearers of God, men of truth, hating covetousness."

A nobleman called to explain a suit in which he was interested, and which was shortly to be tried, in order, as was alleged, to its being better understood when actually heard in court. The Chief Baron interrupted him, saying that he did not deal fairly to come to his chamber about such affairs, for he never received any information of causes but in open court, where both parties were to be heard alike. Nor would he suffer the noble duke to proceed. His grace retired dissatisfied, and complained of it to the king, as a rudeness not to be endured. But his majesty bid him content himself that he was no worse used; adding, that he verily believed he would have treated himself no better had he gone to solicit him in any of his own causes.

While on the circuit, a gentleman who had a trial, presented him with a buck. So soon as the trial commenced, Sir Matthew, remembering the name, asked whether "he was the same person who sent him the venison?" Finding that to be the case, he told him—" he could not suffer the trial to go on until he had paid him for it." The gentleman remarked " that he never sold his venison, and that he had done nothing to *him* which he did not do to every judge that had gone the circuit;" and his statement was immediately confirmed. But the Chief Baron remained firm, and the record was withdrawn.

On an occasion when the dean and chapter of Salisbury had a cause to try before him, he directed his servants to pay for the six sugar loaves which, according to custom, were presented to him on the circuit by that body.

In another case, the same principle is still further illustrated, and with some minuteness, and though occurring somewhat later than the period to which this chapter relates, may be inserted here.

The whole report[1] discovers Hale to the life; his sagacity, patience, kindness, and firm resolution, are all displayed : and, at the same time, such a degree of plainness of speech as (although, if estimated by modern times, bordering upon coarseness) was, it must be acknowledged, not uncommon with him.

The trial respected a charge by the preacher named in the note below, against Mr. Hawkins, for entering and robbing his dwelling-house ; but a full statement of particulars is rendered unnecessary by Hale's astounding address to the principal witness : *that* sufficiently discloses both the case and the testimony offered in its support. "Come, come, Larimore, thou art a very villain. Nay, I think thou art a devil." The prisoner was of course acquitted ; and the judge having expressed his opinion that Sir John Croke was concerned in the plot, the following singular dialogue commenced.

*Lord Chief Baron.*——(To the justices in court.) "Gentlemen, where is this Sir John Croke ?"

*Reply.*——" He is gone. "

---

[1] The Perjured Phanatick: or the malicious conspiracy of Sir John Croke of Chilton, Bart. Justice of Peace in Com. Bucks. Henry Larimore, Anabaptist Preacher, and other phanaticks, against the life of Robert Hawkins, M.A. now living, and late minister of Chilton, occasioned by his suit for tithes, discovered in a trial at Ailsbury before the Right Honorable Sir Matthew Hale, then Lord Chief Baron of the Exchequer, and afterwards Lord Chief Justice of England, published by his Lordship's command. Fol. 1710. The 2d edition.——See also the State Trials, vol. ii. p. 595, &c.

affairs, for he never received any information of causes but in open court, where both parties were to be heard alike. Nor would he suffer the noble duke to proceed. His grace retired dissatisfied, and complained of it to the king, as a rudeness not to be endured. But his majesty bid him content himself that he was no worse used; adding, that he verily believed he would have treated himself no better had he gone to solicit him in any of his own causes.

While on the circuit, a gentleman who had a trial presented him with a buck. So soon as the trial commenced Sir Matthew, remembering the name, asked whether "he was the same person who sent him the venison?" Finding that to be the case, he told him—" he could not suffer the trial to go on until he had paid him for it." The gentleman remarked "that he never sold his venison, and that he had done nothing to him which he did not do to every judge that had gone the circuit;" and his statement was immediately confirmed. But the Chief Baron remained firm, and the record was withdrawn.

. . . . . . . and chapter of . . . . . . . . . . . . before him, he di- . . . . . . . . . . . . for the six sugar loaves . . . . . . . . . . to custom, were presented to . . . on the circuit by that body.

In another case, the same principle is still fur- . . . . . . . . . . . . . . . and . . . . . . . . . . . . .

*Lord Chief Baron.*—"Is Sir John Croke gone? Gentlemen, I must not forget to acquaint you, for I thought that Sir John Croke had been here still, that this Sir John Croke sent me this morning two sugar loaves for a present, praying me to excuse his absence yesterday. I did not then know, so well as now, what he meant by them; but to save his credit I sent his sugar loaves back again. Mr. Harvey, did you not send Sir John his sugar loaves back again?"

*Clerk of the Assize.*—"Yes, my Lord: they were sent back again."

*Lord Chief Baron.*—"I cannot think that Sir John believes that the king's justices come into the country to take bribes. I rather think that some other person, having a design to put a trick upon him, sent them in his name." And so, taking the letter out of his bosom, shewing it to the justices, said,—"Gentlemen, do you know this hand?" To which some of them replied, they believed it might be Sir John Croke's own hand: which letter being compared with his mittimus, for he had no clerk, and some other of his writings there, it plainly appeared to be his own hand. So my Lord Chief Baron seeing that, putting up the letter again into his bosom, said,—he intended to carry that to London; and he added, farther, that he would relate the foulness of the business as he found occasions fit for it."[2]

Whatever sentiments may arise out of these examples of Hale's scrupulosity, it surely is impossible

[2] The Perjured Phanatick, p. 23.

to doubt, or not to respect, his motives. They were not only manifestly pure and disinterested, but they very obviously were associated with a conviction (notwithstanding the laxity given to the ancient oath against receiving from suitors " meat and drink"), that a gift, let it be managed as it may, *does*, according to Solomon's positive assertion, " pervert the ways of judgment." Besides which it is plain, that, even if, in either of the instances which have been adduced, Sir Matthew erred, the error was of such a nature as to inflict inconvenience only upon himself.

Happy for his own reputation, and the parties most interested, had this always been the case. But an occurrence *did* happen, in the early part of his career as Chief Baron, which was fearfully otherwise : and it having of late, as well as heretofore, been acrimoniously noticed, the reader will, it is hoped, bestow upon it his best attention.

At the assizes held March 10th, 1664, at Bury St. Edmund's, in Suffolk, two old women, named Rose Cullender and Amy Dumy, were indicted for bewitching seven persons.[3] One of the witnesses examined upon the trial was the celebrated Sir Thomas Browne, and he expressed his opinion that the parties named in the indictment *were* bewitched ; others present, though their reasons are not fully given, avowed a contrary belief. This was the case with Mr. Serjeant Keeling, who,

[3] Some remarks upon the trial may be seen in Dr. Hutchinson's Historical Essay concerning Witchcraft, pp. 139—157, 2d ed. 1720.

even admitting that the children in question were
in truth bewitched, doubted the sufficiency of the
evidence to convict the prisoners.   Sir Matthew,
evidently puzzled with the case, took especial
pains to arrive at the truth, and in his address to
the jury said he should not repeat the evidence,
lest by so doing he should wrong it on the one
side or the other.   Only this he acquainted them
with, that they had two things to inquire, 1st,
whether or not these children were bewitched;
and, 2d, whether the prisoners at the bar were
guilty of bewitching them ?   That there were such
creatures as witches he made no doubt at all, and
he appealed to the Scriptures, which had affirmed
so much, and also to the wisdom of all nations
which had provided laws against such persons ;[4]
and such hath been the judgment of this kingdom,
as appears by that act of parliament which hath
provided punishment proportionable to the quality
of the offence.   He desired them strictly to observe the evidence, and implored the great God of
heaven to direct their hearts in so weighty a matter ; for to condemn the innocent, and to let the
guilty go free, were both " an abomination to the
Lord."

Within the space of half an hour the jury found
the prisoners guilty upon the several indictments,
thirteen in number.   The judge, and all the
court, being fully satisfied with the verdict, judgment of death was given, and the penalty was
suffered.[5]

[4] See Note Q.                    [5] See Note R.

Such is a fair statement of this celebrated proceeding as reported in the scarce volume mentioned in the note; and in looking steadfastly upon it, and weighing, with impartial care, the phraseology of Scripture, to which our author conscientiously adhered; the time when the trial took place; the state of public opinion generally; that "popular cry" which made Lord Guildford himself, who seems to have had no religious scruples, "dread trying a witch;"[6] and the existing laws,[7] which the judges were sworn to administer; wonder will very much cease, and the conduct of Lord Hale, how erroneous soever it *now* appears, excite as little, as may be, of that astonishment which the reverend editor of his moral and religious works has bestowed upon it.[8]

The truth is—distressing, and humiliating, and even disgraceful as it may seem—that a belief in witchcraft has so prevailed in this country, not to mention others, as to hold in thraldom, as if spellbound, not merely the vulgar and credulous, but the wisest and best of men. Let the 72d canon made by the clerical convocation in 1603, and the laws enacted against " the crime" itself, and the contest respecting it carried on for many years by means of the press, from Scot's " Discovery" down to Glanville's " Sadducismus Triumphatus," and,

[6] Life of Lord Guildford, by the Honourable Roger North, vol. i. p. 266.

[7] This was honestly noticed by the Rev. Erasmus Middleton, Biog. Evan. vol. iii. p. 423.

[8] Vol. i. p. 147.

moreover, the authorized version of Holy Scripture, be but well considered, and it will be manifest that the superstition was actually a *national* one ; so much so, that the excellent Isaac Ambrose, in his Treatise on the New Birth, directs persons seeking salvation to inquire, while searching out their sins, whether they have not sometimes been guilty of—witchcraft.[9]

Nor is it immaterial to notice that the canon cited is *yet* in force ; that the laws which have been alluded to were not repealed till more than seventy years after the time in question ;[10] and that by such men as Bacon[11] and Addison,[12] notwithstanding the illuminations of reason and philosophy, the fact of witchcraft was admitted.   Dr. Johnson more than inclined to the same side of the question ;[13] and Sir William Blackstone[14] quite frowns upon opposers.   By the latter the " revealed word of God" was confidently alleged in support of his views ; and both of them regarded as conclusive the *universality* of a similar belief ; or, in the appropriate language of the eccentric James Howell, " the current and consentient opinion of all antiquity."[15]

[9] Prima, Media, and Ultima, p. 51, 4to. 1659.
[10] By statute 9 Geo. II. c. 5 : an act passed in Ireland in the 28 Eliz. is still in force.
[11] See his Natural History, Cent. X., works by Montague, vol. iv. pp. 512, 513 ; and his judicial charge upon the Commission for the Verge, ib. vol. vi. p. 91.
[12] Spectator, No. CXVII.
[13] Life by Boswell, vol. ii. p. 293, 7th ed. ; Tour to the Hebrides, pp. 33, 34, 3d ed.
[14] Com. vol. iv. p 60, 15th ed.          [15] See Note S.

Let it not be supposed that examples, like those here adverted to, are intended in justification of Lord Hale ; they are designed merely to shew the unfairness, to say the least, of so relating the circumstance which has elicited the foregoing remarks, as if *his* convictions respecting a superstition now appearing monstrous and degrading, had been singular ; as if only a small number had been weak enough to embrace it, instead of his opinions agreeing with those of the great bulk, not to say the most eminent, learned, and pious, of mankind.

How dishonourable to the writer, and how malignant, does the observation thus appear, that Hale's " piety and theological reading seemed only to have the effect of rendering him credulous, and unrelenting."[16]    On the contrary, how accordant with the love of truth, with good sense, and genuine charity, is that statement of Sir Michael Foster, when *he* adverted to the painful subject : " This great and good man," is his language, " was betrayed, notwithstanding the rectitude of his intentions, into a great mistake, under the strong bias of early prejudices."[17]

An able communicator to the Law Magazine has observed with equal candour and accuracy, that " it was during Sir John Holt's occupation of the bench the prosecutions for witchcraft, of which

[16] The General Biography, by Dr. Aikin, &c. vol. v. p. 11 ; and copied into the Retrospective Review, vol. v. part I. p. 118, 8vo. 1822.

[17] Report of Proceedings on the Trial of the Rebels in 1746, &c. Pref. p. vii. fol. 1762.

the piety and wisdom of Hale had not sufficiently enlightened him to discover the cruel and fanatical absurdity, began to fall into general discredit."[18]

With a curious memorandum, preserved by Sir John Keyling,[19] the chapter shall conclude. It illustrates the attention then, as now, commonly paid to etiquette; and that indifference to it on the part of Hale, for which, as we shall hereafter see, he never ceased to be distinguished.

"Upon Saturday the 28 of April 1666 An. 18 Car 2. all the Judges of England, viz. myself J. K. Lord Chief Justice of the King's Bench; Sir Orl. Bridgman, Lord Chief Justice of the Common Pleas; *Sir Matthew Hale*, Chief Baron of the Exchequer; my Brother Atkins, Brother Twisden, Brother Tyrell, Brother Turner, Brother Browne, Brother Windham, Brother Archer, Brother Raynsford, and Brother Morton, met together at Sergeant's Inn, in Fleet-street, to consider of such things as might in point of law fall out in the trial of Lord Morly, who was on Monday to be tried by his Peers for a murder, and we did all, *una voce*, resolve several things. First it was agreed that upon the letter of the Lord High Steward directed to us, we were to attend at the Trial in our Scarlet Robes, and the Chief Judges in their Collars of SS, which I did accordingly; but my Lord Bridgman was absent,

[18] Vol. xi. p. 47.

[19] In his Report of divers Cases in Pleas of the Crown in the reign of King Charles the Second, first published in 1708. fol. pp. 53, 54.

being suddenly taken with the gout; the Chief
Baron had not his collar of SS, *having left it
behind him in the country;* but we all were in
scarlet, but nobody then had a collar of SS but
myself, for the reasons aforesaid."

# CHAPTER IX.

### FROM A.D. 1666 TO A.D. 1671.

SIR MATTHEW was one of those who sat in Clifford's Inn[1] to settle the differences between landlord and tenant after the "dreadful fire." That calamitous event happened in the year 1665; and, eager at all times to do good, he was the first to offer his services for settling the numerous questions which arose out of it. Although ably assisted by Sir Orlando Bridgman, then Chief Justice of the Common Pleas, the rules laid down, and which prevented suits, perhaps not less chargeable than the destructive element, were of his contrivance. His skill, too, in architecture, and readiness in arithmetic, proved of singular advantage; and to *him* has been ascribed the chief instrumentality in accomplishing the re-edification of the city with such astonishing speed and quiet. The citizens, as a testimony of their gratitude and respect, caused his portrait and the portraits of his coadjutors to be placed in Guildhall. They presented him, likewise, with a handsome silver watch, now in Mr. Hale's possession at Cottles.

[1] See Herbert's Antiquities of the Inns of Court, p. 275.

In the year 1667, Lord Hale, having removed to Acton, then the residence of Baxter, an acquaintance commenced between them, which, owing to more than common similarity of taste and pursuit, ripened into friendship;[2] and as no inconsiderable portion of the particulars which can be depended upon respecting the Judge is known to us *only* through the medium of that fellowship, the following narrative of its commencement can scarcely be deemed out of place.

" We sat," says Baxter, " next seats together at church many weeks; but neither did he ever speak to me, nor I to him. At last my extraordinary friend (to whom I was more beholden than I must here express), Serjeant Fountain, asked me why I did not visit the Lord Chief Baron? I told him, because I had no reason for it, being a stranger to him, and had some against it, viz. that a judge, whose reputation was necessary to the ends of his office, should not be brought under court suspicion or disgrace, by his familiarity with a person whom the interest and diligence of some prelates had rendered so odious (as I knew myself to be with such), I durst not be so injurious to him. The Serjeant answered, It is not meet for him to come first to you; I know why I speak it; let me entreat you to go first to him. In obedience to which request I did it; and so we entered into neighbourly familiarity. I lived then in a small house, but it had a pleasant garden and backside,

[2] See Note T.

which the honest landlord had a desire to sell.
The Judge had a mind to the house; but he
would not meddle with it till he got a stranger to
me to come, and inquire of me, whether I was
willing to leave it? I told him I was not only
willing, but desirous, not for my own ends, but for
my landlord's sake, who must need sell it; and so
he bought it, and lived in that poor house[3] till his
mortal sickness sent him to the place of his inter-
ment."[4]

It is delightful to mark the courtesy of these
eminent persons: the kindly feeling, sense of
honour, and contentment of the Judge: and the
delicacy, respect, and desire to please, of the Non-
conformist. In spite of his natural reserve, Hale
made, it will be noted, the first advances: but the
circumstance, notwithstanding disparity of station,
need occasion no surprise, for Baxter was then
well known, and likely, on many accounts, to
attract a person of Hale's discernment. A celebrated prelate,[5] indeed, affirmed of him, that had
he lived in the primitive times he would have been
one of the Fathers of the Church.[6]

The gratification afforded by the intimacy was
mutual, and there can be little doubt that its
influence extended far beyond the limits of private
friendship. It may not unreasonably be supposed
to have had a propitious bearing upon the proposal

[3] See Note U.
[4] Hale's Works, vol. i. p. 95.
[5] Bishop Wilkins.
[6] Dr. Bate's Funeral Sermon for Baxter, p. 106. 12mo. 1692.

made by the Lord Keeper Bridgman the following year, 1667-8, for a " Comprehension :" an advance, by the way, towards peace and liberty at that time of astonishing boldness, and so captivating to Hale as instantly to rivet his attention. But Bishop Burnet having furnished an account of the matter, and a correct representation of the views and feelings Sir Matthew indulged, his statements shall be given at length : only premising that Baxter was one of the Presbyterian divines referred to, and Dr. Manton the other.

" Besides great charities to the Nonconformists, who were then, as he thought, too hardly used, he (Lord Hale) took great care to cover them all he could from the severities some designed against them ; and discouraged those who were inclined to stretch the laws too much against them. He lamented the differences that were raised in this church very much, and, according to the impartiality of his justice, he blamed some things on both sides, which I shall set down with the same freedom that he spake them. He thought many of the Nonconformists had merited highly in the business of the *king's restoration*, and, at least, deserved that the terms of conformity should not have been made stricter than they were before the war. There was not then that dreadful prospect of popery that has appeared since. But that which afflicted him most, was, that he saw the heats and contentions which followed upon those different parties and interests did take people off from the indispensable things of religion, and slackened the zeal of (otherwise) good men for the substance of it, so much being spent about external and indifferent things. It also gave advantage to atheists to treat the most sacred points of our holy faith as ridiculous, when they saw the professors of it contend so fiercely, and with such bitterness, about lesser matters. He was much offended at all those books that were written to expose the contrary sect to the scorn and contempt of the age in a wanton and petulant style; he thought such writers wounded the christian religion through the sides of those who differed from them; while a sort of lewd people, who having assumed to themselves the title of the wits (though but a very few of them have a right to it) took up from both hands what they had said to make another shew ridiculous, and from thence persuaded the world to laugh at both, and at all religion, for their sakes: and, therefore, he often wished there might be some law to make all scurrility, or bitterness in disputes about religion, punishable. But as he lamented the too rigorously proceeding against the Nonconformists, so he declared himself always on the side of the Church of England, and said those of the separation were good men, but they had narrow souls, who would break the peace of the church about such inconsiderable matters as the points in difference were.

" He scarce ever meddled in state intrigues; yet upon a proposition that was set on foot by the Lord Keeper Bridgman, for a comprehension of the more moderate dissenters, and a limited indulgence towards such as could not be brought within the comprehension, he dispensed with his maxim, of avoiding to engage in matters of state. There were several meetings upon that occasion. The divine of the Church of England that appeared most considerably for it, was Dr. Wilkins, afterwards promoted to the bishopric of Chester, a man of as great a mind, and as true a judgment, as eminent virtues, and of as good a soul as any I ever knew. He being determined as well by his excellent temper as by his foresight and prudence, by which he early perceived the great prejudices that religion received, and the vast dangers the Reformation was like to fall under by those divisions, set about that project with the magnanimity that was, indeed, peculiar to himself; for though he was much censured by many of his own side, and seconded by very few, yet he pushed it as far as he could. After several conferences with two of the eminentest of the Presbyterian divines, heads were agreed on, some abatements were to be made, and explanations were to be accepted of. The particulars of that project being thus concerted, they were brought to the Lord Chief Baron, who put them in form of a bill,[7] to be presented to the next session of parliament.

"But two parties appeared vigorously against this design; the one was of some zealous clergymen,[8] who thought it below the dignity of the Church to alter laws, and change settlements, for the sake of some whom they esteemed schismatics. They also believed it was better to keep them out of the church than bring them into it, since a faction upon that would arise in the church which they thought might be more dangerous than the schism itself was. Besides, they said, if some things were now to be changed in compliance with the humour of a party, as soon as that was done another party might demand other concessions, and there might be as good reasons invented for these as for those ; many such concessions might also shake those of our own communion, and tempt them to forsake us, and go over to the Church of Rome, pretending that we changed so often that they were thereby inclined to be of a church that was constant and true to herself. These were the reasons brought and chiefly insisted on against all comprehension, and they wrought upon the greater part of the house of commons, so that they passed a vote against the receiving of any bill for that effect.

" There were others that opposed it upon very different ends. They designed to shelter the Papists from the execution of the law, and saw clearly that nothing could bring in popery so well as toleration ; but to tolerate popery barefaced would have startled the nation too much, so that it was necessary to hinder all the propositions for union, since the keeping up the differences was the best colour they could find for getting the toleration to pass, only as a slackening the laws against dissenters, whose numbers and wealth made it advisable to have some regard to them; and under this pretence popery might have crept in more covered, and less regarded. So these councils being more acceptable to some concealed Papists, then in great power, as has since appeared but too evidently, the whole project for comprehension was let fall, and those who had set it on foot came to be looked on with an ill eye as secret favourers of the dissenters, underminers of the church, and every thing else that jealousy and distaste could cast on them." [9]

That inaccuracies are discoverable in the foregoing citations, will scarcely be questioned; but, notwithstanding such is the case, the merest notice of the impolicy [10] as well as iniquity of *imposing*, as of the highest importance, " matters" thus admitted to be " inconsiderable," might have sufficed, had it not been for the observations made upon them by Mr. Knox, [11] and not long ago reprinted by the late lamented Bishop of Limerick.

The observations alluded to arose *professedly* from fear lest the narrative just given " might, at first view, be thought to bear a favourable testimony to the cause of nonconformity;" and the apprehension, no doubt, was distressing to the writer of them; but it is quite obvious that their main design, instead of being to " throw useful light" upon the subject proposed, was to eulogize the national hierarchy, to justify those arbitrary

[9] Life by Burnet, pp. 39—44. 12mo. 1682.   [10] See Note Z.
[11] In his Preface to the *second* Dublin edition of the Life of Hale by Burnet.

measures which disgraced the Stuarts; and, by thus feeding animosities, to uphold, with a better grace, a system of civil ignominy and exclusion,[12] because of religious opinions. Had Mr. Knox done this elsewhere no one can question his perfect liberty on the subject, but to do it at Hale's expense is matter of just reprehension.

Mr. Knox contends, without other evidence than his active fancy could detect in the statements of Burnet and Baxter, and without the slightest benefit, that the wish " for lowering the terms of conformity" which Hale encouraged, is to be accounted for upon *other* grounds than those of "unbiassed reason and penetrating sagacity;" as if the attachment Hale himself avowed, and discovered for the Church of England, was necessarily defective because unconnected with ignorance, bigotry, or pride.

But, allowing ever so much force to his Lordship's intercourse with Baxter: to the tutorship of Sedgwick: and, if the reader pleases, to Mr. Kingscot, and the "scandalous vicar" of Wotton[13] also; as well in producing those marks of " puritanic prepossession" which, while Mr. Knox impugns them, he acknowledges added to Hale's " moral respectability," still that gentleman's love of philosophising became excessive, when he imputes, *therefore*, to a man so distinguished for the opposites,—" partiality" and error.

Modesty should have taught Mr. Knox better: especially since, although entitled to the praise of

[12] See Note AA.      [13] See ante, p. 2.

talent, and taste, and piety, his feelings (which were strangely Quixotic) rather than his judgment, too often governed him : so much so, and it was the case with Origen, whom he strikingly resembled, as to make any effort on *his* part to detract from the honest impartiality and profound sagaciousness of " the great Hale"[14] presumptuous. Nothing could have been less adapted to measure the vast scope of Hale's intellect than a heated imagination ; and few persons were more unfit for the attempt than Mr. Knox. They were entirely different in the constitution of their minds. Besides which, so completely was Mr. Knox captivated by his own prepossessions, as to be indisposed even to *consider* the cases of not a few " sincere, true-hearted Christians." [15] He neither sympathized with their doubts, nor their distresses. The numerous matters of ecclesiastical jurisdiction which affected *them* presented no difficulties to *him*. Hale, on the contrary, perceived the difficulties alluded to, and was grieved, and afflicted by them. This is demonstrated in his manuscripts, as well as elsewhere. Those invaluable relics consist of diffuse and interesting tracts upon " the Church," and " Church Government," " and things indifferent," all shewing the most searching examination of the subjects in question. There is one entire folio upon " Policy, and the use thereof in matters of religion." [16]

[14] Lord Erskine's Speeches, vol. iii. p. 337.

[15] Hale, Orig. MS.

[16] These MSS. were bequeathed by the judge to his widow. See the Will, *post.* They are carefully preserved at Cottles.

G

The truth is, that in the case of Mr. Knox, love
to the established hierarchy was passion : in Hale
it was intelligent, conscientious regard.    Knox
viewed objections, if not objectors, with the stern
indifference of high-minded disdain ; Hale, under
a deep consciousness of human imperfection, with
the most considerate and accommodating kindness :
Knox was naturally pugnacious, and seems to have
been swayed by civil distinctions, by worldly respectability, by the principles of intellectual refinement : upon each and all of those things Hale
placed a subordinate value only : and none at all
in comparison with the higher interests of truth,
forbearance, and charity.

Had Mr. Knox contented himself with his *first*
preface, and left the matter as Burnet fairly put it,
his judgment and impartiality, so far as the present
affair is concerned, would have stood firm : but as
it is, they are both impeached ; for, in the warmth
of his zeal to maintain high-church notions, by
charging so eminent a man with undue leaning and
want of penetration, he overlooked the numerous
celebrated persons, ecclesiastics and laymen, not
subjected to any suspicion of improper influence,
who thought *with* Hale on that occasion, and on a
subsequent occasion also of the same kind.[17]    He
lost sight, likewise, of the possibility, that even if
Hale's piety *were*, in some degree, " tinged with
the prejudices of nonconformity," it was quite as
likely that *his own* might take its hues from other
prejudices no less baneful.    Nor does he seem to

[17] See Note BB.

have been otherwise than stark blind to the fact, that there is no part of his advocacy that the Church of Rome might not press in commendation of most, if not all, those very claims which led to "the bright and blissful Reformation," and which still detach her from the bulk of Christendom.

This will be a proper place to notice Lord Hale's aversion to the Roman Catholic religion: not, however, because of unacquaintedness or prejudice, but from deep conviction, the effect of a diligent and impartial scrutiny. A pretty large manuscript is mainly devoted to the consideration of the subject. The history of the Church of Rome is therein traced; its rise and progress marked; its unsound doctrines and antiscriptural practices described; its arrogant pretensions exposed: in short, the entire scheme, nature, and quality of the papal monarchy; the extent of its jurisdiction; its subordinate officers, ministers, and dignities; its corruptions, revenues, and supplies; and its collateral contributions and contrivances, both for establishment and advance; pass under full and scrutinizing review. He so exemplifies the operations of that evil policy,—"the wisdom of the serpent *without* the innocence of the dove,"—which he wished to expose, upon the whole framework, upon its inventions and appointments, as to make it evident that all are "subservient" to domination and wealth, and repugnant, therefore, as well as injurious, to religion.

"Religion,"—they are his own remarks,—"is a thing of a pure and excellent nature; a delicate and tender matter; and receives rather detriment and dishonour when politic tricks, and devices, and shufflings, are used in it, or for it, or by it. But of all religions in the world, the christian religion is most profaned when it is prostituted to secular ends, or made to dissemble with God or men *for* secular ends. It is religion that teacheth simplicity, integrity, sincerity, truth, innocence, plain dealing; that teacheth self-denial, contempt of the world, humility; that teacheth to carry up all our thoughts, endeavours, and hopes, for a life after this; a religion that hath persecution rather than splendour, and external equipage—the badge of it; a religion that, with the greatest indignation, disparageth and condemneth lying, dissimulation, hypocrisy, carnal ends, and covetousness, ambition, love of the world, or of the gains thereof. This the Author of this religion taught by the constant tenor of his example: this he left behind him as the tenor of his last will and testament,—the rule of his order. And, therefore, on the one hand, to pretend to propagate such a religion as this by frauds, or tricks; or, on the other, to make this excellent religion to be a cloak and convoy to secular ends; is the highest injury that can be done to religion—to christian religion; to Christ Jesus the founder of it." [18]

In another part of the same manuscript some observations occur which it will be scarcely possible to read without admiring the acumen of the judge: they are unusually ironical: and the impression

[18] Hale, Orig. MS.

conveyed by them is almost irresistible—that, how applicable soever they may be to the abettors of the papacy, they touch the core of not a few ecclesiastical questions among such as professedly hold the tenets of the unreformed in abhorrence.

" I do not so much attribute those errors of the Roman Church wherein we differ from them, either to want of learning or judgment; for it is plain they have great advantages in both, being, many of them, men of profound learning, knowledge, and judgment. But I do really attribute them, or the most part of them, to politique design and contrivance to support the dignity, power, wealth, splendour, and magnificence of their ecclesiastical state, or church, as they call it.

" And, therefore, I have not, without some compassion upon our protestant divines, looked upon the great pains they have taken to confute them out of the Scriptures, Fathers, church histories, and reason; and the great indignation the protestant divines have had at their pertinacity, blindness, ignorance, and impenetrableness, as if they were stupid, dull, or ignorant; when all the while our Protestants consider not the *reason* of this pertinacity of the Romanists : perchance they understand the truth as well as some of ours, and understand the edge and weight of the reasons given against them. But can we reasonably expect that a society, or body of men, that have set their hearts upon wealth and greatness, that know there is no way to support it but by upholding and maintaining these tenets that maintain *them;* can we think that they that have proclaimed themselves over all the world *infallible*, and that have gained a competent persuasion among the ignorant sort, that they are so; and that by that very tenet have maintained much of their power and wealth; can we imagine, I say, that these men should be content to deliver up all this upon any reasons, or declare themselves to have been the deluders of the world, and thereby to dissolve their state, to lose their grandeur, to cut off those pipes, and stop those channels, that with so great ease and affluence pour the greatest part of the wealth of Christendom into their lap?    A man might as soon, by syllogisms, persuade the king of Spain that he hath no title to the Indies, or make the Grand Seignior deliver up Constantinople.    In things of speculation and notion, sometimes, we may have a man brought over with reasons; but it is rarely seen in matters of *interest*, especially of so great moment, and when the possessors are numerous, and impatient of the dishonour of retractation." [19]

To return to the narrative.    Although Lord Hale and his fellow-labourers were defeated in their attempt at a comprehension, one happy consequence, at all events, resulted from their laudable efforts, and one that, to the disappointed Chief Baron, was a source of lasting pleasure; namely, a steady friendship with Bishop Wilkins; [20] and so entire did it become, that notwithstanding his esteem for Dr. Ward, the Bishop of Salisbury; Dr. Barlow,

[19] The Orig. MS.
[20] See *ante*, p. 117.

the Bishop of Lincoln ; Dr. Barrow, Master of Trinity College ; Dr. Tillotson, afterwards Archbishop of Canterbury ; and Dr. Stillingfleet, subsequently Bishop of Worcester ; the apostolical Primate Usher ; and the illustrious Richard Baxter, there was about his converse with Wilkins a peculiar freedom ; and, the better to enjoy his conversation, he sometimes (which was remarkable) dined with him.

About this time Sir Matthew published, anonymously, his address to the " Young Students of the Common Law." It was prefixed to Rolle's " Abridgment."[21] That curious collection, since used by Viner, and praised by Hargrave,[22] elicited in its commendation his solid and masculine powers to the utmost.

The whole Preface may be regarded as a record of his own doings and experience ; and it partakes, throughout, of the sedate wisdom and other excellencies which render his compositions valuable. Many confirmative extracts might be given ; but regard to brevity will not admit of more, in this place, than the graphic sketch it embodies of Lord Rolle himself. As the result of intimate knowledge, on the part of the writer, that sketch is invaluable ; and while singularly adapted to enkindle in the professional aspirant laudable emulation, it can hardly fail to please and instruct the general reader.

[21] See Note C C.
[22] See Co. Litt. 9 a. (3), note 49.

" Lord Rolle was a man of very great natural abilities ; of a ready and clear understanding, strong memory, sound, deliberate, and steady judgment ; of a fixed attention of mind to all business that came before him ; of great freedom from passions and perturbations ; of great temperance and moderation ; of a strong and healthy constitution of body, which rendered him fit for study and business, and indefatigable in it.

" He spent his time under the bar, and for some years after, in diligent study of the common law, neglecting no opportunity to improve his knowledge therein ; and he had this happiness in relation thereunto, that, from his first admission to the Society of the Inner Temple, which was 1st February, 6 Jac., and till his call to be a serjeant, he had contemporaries of the same society of great parts, learning, and eminence ; as, namely, Sir Edward Littleton, afterwards Chief Justice of the Common Pleas, and lord keeper of the great seal of England ; Sir Edward Herbert, afterwards attorney general ; Sir Thomas Gardyner, afterwards recorder of London ; and that treasury of all kind of learning, Mr. John Selden : with these he kept a long, constant, and familiar converse and acquaintance, and thereby greatly improved both his own learning and theirs, especially in the common law, which he principally intended ; for it was the constant and almost daily course for many years together of these great traders in learning, to bring in their several acquests therein, as it were, into a common stock, by mutual communication, whereby each of them became, in a great measure, the participant and common possessor of the other's learning and knowledge.

"He did not undertake the practice of the law till he was sufficiently fitted for it, and then he fixed himself unto one court, namely, the King's Bench, where was the greatest variety of business; by this means he grew master of the experience of that court, whereby his clients were never disappointed for want of his experience or attendance. He argued frequently and pertinently; his arguments were fitted to prove and evince, not for ostentation; plain, yet learned; short (if the nature of business permitted), yet perspicuous; his words few, but significant and weighty; his skill, judgment, and advice, in points of law and pleading, was sound and excellent.

"Although, when he was at the bar, he exceeded most others, yet when he came to the exercise of judicature, his parts, learning, prudence, dexterity, and judgment, were more conspicuous. He was a patient, attentive, and observing hearer, and was content to bear with some impertinences rather than lose any thing that might discover the truth or justice of any cause. He was a strict searcher and examiner of businesses, and a wise discerner of the weight and stress of them, wherein it lay, and what was material to it. He ever carried on as well his search and examination as his directions and decisions with admirable steadiness, evenness, and clearness; great experience rendered business easy and familiar unto him, so that he gave convenient dispatch, yet without precipitancy or surprise. In short, he was a person of great learning and experience in the common law, profound judgment, singular prudence, great moderation, justice, and integrity."[23]

In concluding the present chapter, an occurrence shall be noticed which, though collateral in its subject to Lord Hale, is closely connected with his history; it is introduced the rather because every part of it does honour to him; to the sincerity of his friendship, the moderation of his principles, and the tenderness of his disposition.

" When I went," says Baxter, " out of the house[24] in which he succeeded me, I went into a greater, over against the church-door. The town having great need of help for their souls, I preached between the public sermons in my house, taking the people with me to the church (to common-prayer and sermon) morning and evening. The judge told me that he thought my course did the church much service, and would carry it so respectfully to me at my door, that all the people might perceive his approbation. But Dr. Reeves could not bear it, but complained against me; and the Bishop of London caused one Mr. Rosse, of Brainford, and Mr. Philips, two justices of the peace, to send their warrants to apprehend me.

[23] Abridgment, Preface, pp. i. ii. and Collect. Jurid. vol. i. pp. 264, 265.   See Note D D.

[24] In 1670.   See Dr. Calamy's Abr. of Baxter's Life and Times, vol. i. p. 324. 8vo. 1713.

I told the judge of the warrant, but asked him no counsel, nor he gave me none, but with tears showed his sorrow (the only time that ever I saw him weep). So I was sent to the common gaol for six months by these two justices, by the procurement of the said Dr. Reeves (his Majesty's Chaplain, dean of Windsor, dean of Wolverhampton, parson of Horseley, parson of Acton).[25] When I came to move for my release upon a habeas corpus (by the counsel of my great friend Serjeant Fountain) I found that the character which Judge Hale had given of me stood me in some stead ; and every one of the four judges of the Common Pleas did not only acquit me, but said more for me than my counsel (viz. Judge Wild, Judge Archer, Judge Tyrrel, and the Lord Chief Justice Vaughan), and made me sensible how great a part of the honour of his Majesty's government, and the peace of the kingdom, consisted in the justice of the judges ; and, indeed, Judge Hale would tell me that Bishop Usher was much prejudiced against lawyers, because the worst causes find their advocates ; but that he and Mr. Selden had convinced him of the reasons of it to his satisfaction : and that he did, by acquaintance with them, believe that there were as many honest men among lawyers, proportionably, as among any profession of men in England (not excepting bishops or divines).

[25] Bishop Jebb remarks, that "these are ostentatiously expanded, as though they were separate and independent benefices, when, in fact, several of them were comprehended in one, and were merely titular or nominal."—Lives, *ut sup.* p. 152.

" And I must needs say, that the improvement of reason; the diverting men from sensuality and idleness; the maintaining of propriety and justice; and, consequently, the peace and welfare of the kingdom, is very much to be ascribed to the judges, and lawyers.

" But this imprisonment brought me the great loss of converse with Judge Hale: for the parliament in the next act against conventicles, put into it divers clauses suited to my case; by which I was obliged to go dwell in another county, and to forsake both London and my former habitation; and yet the justices of another county were partly enabled to pursue me.

" Before I went, the judge had put into my hand four volumes (in folio) which he had written, to prove the Being and Providence of God, the immortality of the soul, and life to come, the truth of Christianity, and of every book of the Scripture by itself, besides the common proofs of the whole. Three of the four volumes I had read over, and was sent to the gaol before I read the fourth. I turned down a few leaves for some small animadversions, but had no time to give them him. I could not then persuade him to review them for the press. The only fault I found with them of any moment, was that great copiousness, the effect of his fulness and patience, which will be called tediousness by impatient readers.

" When we were separated, he (that would receive no letters from any man about any matters which he was to judge) was desirous of letter-

converse [26] about our philosophical, and spiritual
subjects. I having then begun a Latin Methodus
Theologiæ, sent him one of the schemes (before-
mentioned),[27] containing the generals of the philosophical part, with some notes upon it ; which he
so over-valued that he urged me to proceed in the
same way. I objected against putting so much
philosophy (though mostly but *de homine*) in a
method of theology : but he rejected my objections, and resolved me to go on." [28]

[26] See Note EE.
[27] See *post*, ch. xii.
[28] Hale's Works, vol. i. pp. 105—107.

# CHAPTER X.

## FROM A.D. 1671 TO A.D. 1676.

EARLY in May, 1671, Sir John Keyling, Lord Chief Justice of the King's Bench, died. On the 18th of the same month Hale succeeded him : and still pursued the same exemplary, and intrepid course. Against oppression his opposition even increased : he so lifted up his voice as to confound and overwhelm aggressors. An instance occurred, in a case reported by Ventris,[1] where a Captain C——, and one of his serjeants, thinking fit to carry military tactics into civil affairs, had rescued, by means of twenty or thirty soldiers, an individual arrested for debt after enlisting. His lordship there, indeed, furnished an illustration of what he meant by " personated *anger*."[2] " Whatever you military men think," was his address in open court, " you shall find that you are under the civil juris-diction ; and you but gnaw a file ; you will break your teeth ere you shall prevail against it." He committed both the culprits to Newgate ; and on

[1] Reports, p. 250, part i.
[2] Sometimes a personated anger, managed with judgment, is of singular use, especially in persons in authority ; but such an anger is but a painted fire, and without perturbation. Works, vol. ii. p. 390.—" Of Moderation of Anger."

their subsequent appearance before him, he asked
" why an information was not exhibited ? " telling
the city counsel, " that if the sheriffs did not prosecute, the court would, for it was a matter of great
example, and ought not to be smothered."

Laudably anxious to satisfy the public, and
suitors especially, that what he did was *right*, he
not only gave the *reasons* of his judgments in
intricate cases, but by eliciting observations, and
his own remarks, constantly took pains to make
whatever passed intelligible, and instructive. " I
have known," says Roger North, " the Court of
King's Bench sitting every day from eight to
twelve, and the Lord Chief Justice Hale managing
matters of law to all imaginable advantage to the
*students*, and in which he took a pleasure, or
rather pride. He encouraged inquiry when it
was to the purpose, and used to debate with the
counsel, so as the court might have been taken for
an academy of sciences, as well as the seat of
justice." [3]

Nor was he content with this service, valuable
as it was, and novel also, and interesting. He
assisted in *private* such as applied to him ; he
advised them to use their books diligently, and
directed their studies. [4] When he saw any thing
amiss, particularly if he observed a love of finery,
he did not withhold admonition. It was done,
however, in a smiling, pleasant way ; usually by

[3] Roger North on the Study of the Laws, 8vo. p. 32, first published in 1824. See Note F F.

[4] See Note G G.

observing that *that* did not become their profession. The sight of students in long periwigs, or attorneys with swords, was known to be so offensive to him, as to induce those who loved such things to avoid them when they waited upon him, in order to escape reproof.

In 1673 his lordship printed an Essay touching the gravitation, and non-gravitation of fluid bodies, and the reasons thereof. This, two years afterwards, was followed by another treatise, entitled, " Difficiles Nugæ ; or, Observations touching the Torricellian experiment, and the various solutions of the same, especially touching the weight and elasticity of the air." But of these more hereafter.

His incessant labours began now to tell visibly upon his constitution. The firm and vigorous health he had hitherto enjoyed, and to which his great temperance and equanimity had conduced, suddenly gave way. In two days inflammation brought him low ; asthma ensued ; and that was followed by dropsy.[5] " He had death," says Baxter, " in his lapsed countenance, flesh, and strength, with shortness of breath." [6] *So* enfeebled was he, all at once, as to be scarce able, though supported by his servants, to walk through Westminster Hall.

Perceiving that his days were nearly numbered, he resolved upon retirement from office : a resolve, however, not unattended, in his apprehension,

[5] See Note H H.
[6] Works, by Thirlwall, vol. i. p. 107.

with difficulties. They are expressed in the following memoranda :—

" First, If I consider the business of my profession, whether as an advocate or as a judge, it is true I do acknowledge, by the institution of Almighty God, and the dispensation of his providence, I am bound to industry and fidelity in it. And as it is an act of obedience unto his will, it carries with it some things of religious duty, and I may and do take comfort in it, and expect a reward of my obedience to Him, and the good that I do to mankind therein, from the bounty and beneficence, and promise of Almighty God ; and it is true also, that without such employments civil societies cannot be supported, and great good redounds to mankind from them ; and in these respects, the conscience of my own industry, fidelity, and integrity in them, is a great comfort and satisfaction to me. But yet, this I must say concerning these employments, considered simply in themselves, that they are very full of cares, anxieties, and perturbations.

" Secondly, That though they are beneficial to others, yet they are of the least benefit to him that is employed in them.

" Thirdly, They do necessarily involve the party whose office it is, in great dangers, difficulties, and calumnies.

" Fourthly, That they only serve for the meridian of this life, which is short and uncertain.

" Fifthly, That though it be my duty faithfully to serve in them while I am called to them, and till I am duly called from them, yet they are great consumers of that little time we have here; which, as it seems to me, might be better spent in a pious, contemplative life, and a due provision for eternity. I do not know a better temporal employment than Martha had, in testifying her love and duty to our Saviour, by making provision for him; yet our Lord tells her, That though she was troubled about many things, there was only one thing necessary, and Mary had chosen the better part." [7]

As soon as his determination was known, he was beset by the importunities of friends, and an almost universal clamour, that the event, which seems to have been regarded as a national calamity, might, if possible, be averted. He, however, " resolvedly petitioned" for his writ of ease. His Majesty, unwilling to comply, proposed that he should retain the office, doing what business he could in his chamber; but he said, that being unable longer to discharge the attendant duties, he could not with a good conscience consent.

The king felt that the request could not be denied, but still deferred granting it; nor could the Chancellor, although often urged to it by the Chief Justice, be prevailed upon to move his Majesty to dispatch.

At length, upon the 20th February, 1675-6, weary of waiting, and stimulated by increasing infirmities, he surrendered, in person, at Secretary

[7] Works, vol. i. pp. 42, 43.

Coventry's lodgings,[8] his high office to the king. Charles treated him with the affability for which he was remarkable; wished him the return of his health; and assured him, that he would still look upon him as one of his judges; that he should have recourse to his advice when his health would permit; and, likewise, continue his pension so long as he lived.

The day following, February 21st, Sir Matthew attended a Master in Chancery with a deed of resignation,[9] drawn and written upon parchment by himself; and, having executed and acknowledged it for enrolment, proceeded with it to the Chancellor.

He informed his lordship the reasons of his conduct. He wished, he said, to show the world his own free concurrence in his removal : and also to obviate an objection, that a chief justice, being placed by writ, was not removable at pleasure, as judges by patent were; *that* opinion was once held, he remarked, by his predecessor;[10] and, although his own was different, he thought it reasonable to prevent the scruple.

His Majesty's bounty, with respect to the continuance of his pension, made upon him, always grateful and susceptible, a deep impression. At that time a judge's salary was not ascertained and established, nor his commission, as it is now, placed beyond the power of the crown. The good man, therefore, thinking the favour intended him would

---

[8] See Keble's Reports, vol. iii. p. 622. fol. 1685.
[9] See Note II.  [10] Lord C. J. Keyling.

be an ill precedent, actually wrote to the Lord Treasurer, and desired that the pension might be continued only during pleasure. But the king, greatly to his credit, was firm, and ordered it to be paid quarterly.

When the first payment was made, Sir Matthew consigned a great part of it to charitable uses, and avowed his design so to employ it in future.

The same liberality was shewn by him on the dismissal of his servants—that is, all who were not domestics. To some he gave considerable presents; to each a friendly token.

No sooner was he fully discharged, and all his arrangements completed, than he returned home with as much cheerfulness as the want of health would allow. He felt emancipated from a state of thraldom, as one delivered from a heavy burden. This gave him a temporary elasticity, and he perpetuated his emotions in a paraphrase upon the much admired lines in Seneca's Thyestes,—Act II. If the paraphrase be less poetical than the " Imitation" of them by Andrew Marvell, and Cowley, the verses themselves are perfectly characteristic both of his lordship's taste, and virtues.

> " Stet, quicunque volet, potens,
> Aulæ culmine lubrico :
> Me dulcis saturet quies.
> Obscuro positus loco,
> Leni perfruar otio :
> Nullis nota Quiritibus
> Ætas per tacitum fluat.
> Sic cum transierint mei
> Nullo cum strepitu dies,

Plebeius moriar senex.
Illi mors gravis incubat,
Qui, notus nimis omnibus,
Ignotus moritur sibi."

" Let him that *will*, ascend the tottering seat
Of courtly grandeur, and become as great
As are his mounting wishes : as for me,
Let sweet *repose* and *rest* my *portion* be.
Give *me* some mean, obscure recess ; a sphere
Out of the road of business, or the fear
Of falling lower ; where I sweetly may
Myself, and dear retirement, still enjoy.
Let not my life, or name, be known unto
The grandees of the time, toss'd to and fro
By censures or applause ; but let my age
Slide gently by ; not overthwart, the stage
Of public action, unheard, unseen,
And unconcern'd, as if I ne'er had been.
And thus, while I shall pass my silent days
In shady privacy, free from the noise
And bustles of the mad world, then shall I,
A good old innocent plebeian, die.
Death is a mere surprise, a very snare
To him that makes it his *life's greatest care*,
*To be a public pageant ; known to all,*
*But unacquainted with himself* doth fall." [11]

Sir Richard Rainsford[12] succeeded Lord Hale :
and when the commission was delivered to him, he
was thus addressed by Sir Heneage Finch, then
Lord Chancellor :—

[11] Works, by Thirlwall, vol. ii. p. 179. " The modesty and reasonableness of Jacob's desire."

[12] " The Lord Chief Justice Rainsford," says Baxter, " falling
into some melancholy, came and sent to me for some advice. He
did it, as he said, because Judge Hale desired him so to do. He
expressed great respect for his judgment and writings." Additional Notes ; Hale's Works, vol. i. p. 91.

" The vacancy of the seat of the Chief Justice
of this court, and that by a way and means so unusual as the resignation of him that lately held it ;
and this, too, proceeding from so deplorable a
cause, as the infirmity of that body which began to
forsake the ablest mind that ever presided here ;
hath filled the kingdom with lamentations, and
given the king many and pensive thoughts how to
supply that vacancy again." And a little after
speaking to his successor, he said: " The very
labours of the place, and that weight and fatigue
of business which attends it, are no small discou-
ragements ; for what shoulders may not justly fear
that burthen, which made *him* stoop that went
before you? Yet, I confess, you have a greater
discouragement than the mere burthen of your
place, and that is, the inimitable example of your
last predecessor: *Onerosum est succedere bono prin-
cipi,* [13] was the saying of him in the panegyric : [14]
and you will find it so too, that are to succeed
such a chief justice of so indefatigable an industry, so invincible a patience, so exemplary an integrity, and so magnanimous a contempt of worldly
things, without which no man can be truly great :
and to all this, a man that was so absolutely a
master of the science of the law, and even of the
most abstruse and hidden parts of it, that one may
truly say of his knowledge in the law, what St.
Austin said of St. Hierome's knowledge in divinity—*Quod Hieronimus nescivit, nullus mortalium*

[13] It is a troublesome task to succeed a virtuous prince.
[14] C. Plinii Secundi. Paneg. xliv. 4.

*unquam scivit.* [15]   And, therefore, the king would
not suffer himself to part with so great a man, till
he had placed upon him all the marks of bounty
and esteem which his retired and weak condition
was capable of." [16]

To this high character, in which the expressions, as they well became the eloquence of him
that pronounced them, so they agree exactly with
the subject without the abatements that are often
to be made for rhetoric, " I shall add," says
Burnet, " that part of the Lord Chief Justice's
answer, in which he speaks of his predecessor."

" A person in whom his eminent virtues and
deep learning have long managed a contest for the
superiority, which is not decided to this day,
nor will it ever be determined, I suppose, which
shall get the upper hand ; a person that has sat
in this court these many years, of whose actions
there, I have been an eye and an ear witness ; that
by the greatness of his learning always charmed
his auditors to reverence, and attention : a person
to whom, I think, I may boldly say, that as former
times cannot shew any superior to him, so am I
confident succeeding and future times will never
shew any equal.   These considerations, heightened
by what I have heard from your lordship concerning him, made me anxious and doubtful, and put

---

[15] " What Jerome was ignorant of, no man ever knew."—In
the recent edition of Burnet's Lives, by Bishop Jebb, a note is
appended to this citation, shewing that the passage does not occur in the *genuine* works of St. Augustine.

[16] Works, vol. i. pp. 82, 83.

me to a stand how I should succeed so able, so
good, and so great, a man. It doth very much
trouble me, that I, who in comparison of him, am
but like a candle lighted in the sunshine, or like a
glow-worm at mid-day, should succeed so great a
person, that is, and will be, so eminently famous to
all posterity: and I must ever wear this motto in
my breast to comfort me, and in my actions to
excuse me, — *Sequitur, quamvis non passibus
Æquis.*"[17]

[17] " He follows his steps, though at a distance."

# CHAPTER XI.

SIR MATTHEW now left Acton, and retired to his seat at Alderley,[1] in Gloucestershire, " in likelihood," observed Baxter, " to die there. Nor is it," continued that great man, " the least of my pleasure that I have lived some years in his more than ordinary love and friendship, and that we are now waiting which shall be *first* in heaven, whither, he saith, *he* is going with full content and acquiescence in the will of a gracious God, and doubts not but we shall shortly live together. Oh what a blessed world were this were the generality of magistrates such as he!"[2]

The change, though to his native air, was unavailing. He retained, however, his delight in devotion and study. The "sanctuary" continued to be loved. His closet was still his element; and such was his relish for its pleasures, that when unable to walk, he was carried, into it.

---

[1] A drawing of the house, &c. may be seen in " Atkyn's Gloucestershire," p. 208.

[2] Reliq. Baxter, part 3, p. 176.

In connexion with these habits Lord Hale appears to advantage; and he cannot be too closely observed. To *them*, indeed, particularly on "the first day of the week," must be attributed not only his maturity for heaven, but some of his most valued works.

How exemplary and instructive was his observation of the Lord's day!

Instead of counting the Sabbath[3] a "weariness," or employing it, as many do, in idle or frivolous occupations, he attended, with pious constancy, upon public worship. There, in the exquisite language of the Litany, he "meekly" heard the Word of God; "he received it with pure affection, and brought forth the fruits of the Spirit." Afterwards, he watered the good seed, by repeating before his family, often with judicious additions, an outline of the truths taught in the pulpit; and then, between the evening service and supper time, secluding himself entirely from others, he indulged in meditation, employing his pen merely to aid the fixing of his thoughts, and to preserve[4] them the better for future reference, and domestic instruction.

The *publication* of those sacred lucubrations formed, it should be observed, no part of his design. That was the act of Mr. Stephens; who, having obtained a perusal of them, instead of

[3] See *post*, Chap. XII. and Note K K.

[4] Mr. Stephens's Preface to the Contemplations, 12mo. 1721, pp. 1 and 2; also the Discourse on the Knowledge of God and Ourselves. 8vo. 1688. Preface.

contenting himself with a transcript, published them.[5]  One portion of the papers was submitted to Baxter's[6] judgment; he thought them worthy of the public eye; and in ignorance of the writer, for the name had been concealed from him, freely altered such phraseology in the piece entitled the " Right Knowledge of Christ Crucified," as seemed liable to be mistaken.

In the preface before quoted, Mr. Stephens makes out, with a view to his own justification, as good a case, perhaps, as the circumstances would admit: but the necessary consent, although importunately sought, having been withheld, he had, obviously, some difficulty in silencing the misgivings of his conscience.  The honesty of the intention, Sir Matthew's candour and goodness,[7] and the omission of his name (some passages being purposely left out which would too plainly have made him known[8]) were severally brought forward in apology: a distinction was attempted, also, between the reasons which induced the author not to consent, and such as would be of no force against a publication *without* his privity, or knowledge.  But no ingenuity can make a thing straight which is so essentially crooked, nor atone

[5] Pref. to the Contemplations. 8vo. 1679.  Reliq. Baxter, part 3, p. 181.

[6] Reliq. Baxter, part 3, p. 176.

[7] In Mr. Stephens's Preface to the second part of the Contemplations, he notices having craved and obtained Lord Hale's pardon for publishing the first part.—Contempl. parts 1 and 2. 1679. Part 2, Pref. 2.

[8] Pref. to the Contempl. 1679.

for that want of delicacy, to say the least, towards his " very good friend," which Mr. Stephens ought to have shewn. When Baxter was similarly treated, as to one of *his* sermons, he unceremoniously pronounced the act an injury.[9]

In spite of every precaution, it transpired who wrote " the books," and they were presently bought up."[10]

Nor will the reader wonder at the discovery, when he peruses the commencement of the " Contemplation" on Hebrews xiii. 14,—" *For here we have no continuing city, but we seek one to come.*" It is as follows:

" I have, in my course of life, had as many stations, and places of habitation, as most men. I have been in almost continual motion; and although of all earthly things I have most desired rest, retiredness, and a fixed private station, yet the various changes that I have seen and found, the public employments that, without my seeking, and against my inclination, have been put upon me, and many other interventions, as well private as public, have made the former part of this text true in me in the letter,—that I have had no continuing city, or place of habitation. When I had designed unto myself a settled mansion in one place, and had fitted it to my convenience and repose, I have been presently constrained by my necessary employments to leave it, and repair to

---

[9] See the Preface to his Directions for Weak and Distempered Christians. Works, vol. viii. p. 258.

[10] Reliq. Baxter, part 3, p. 176.

another; and when again I had thoughts to find repose there, and had again fitted it to my convenience, yet some other necessary occurrences have diverted me from it; and thus, by several vicissitudes, my dwellings have been like so many inns to a traveller, though of some longer continuance, yet of almost equal instability and vicissitude. This unsettledness of station, though troublesome, yet hath given me a good and practical moral; namely, that I must not expect my *rest* in this lower world, but must make it as the place of my journey and pilgrimage, not of my repose and rest, but must look further for that happiness: and, truly, when I consider that it hath been the wisdom of God Almighty to exercise those worthies which he left as patterns to the rest of mankind, with this kind of discipline in this world, I have reason not to complain of it as a difficulty or an inconvenience, but to be thankful to him for it, as an instruction and document, to put me in remembrance of a better home, and to incite me to make a due provision for it, even that everlasting rest which he hath provided for them that love him; and by pouring me thus from vessel to vessel, to keep me from fixing myself too much upon this world below." [11]

Sir Matthew about this time committed to the press his Treatise on the Primitive Origination of Mankind, a section only of a direct and systematic

[11] Works, vol. ii. pp. 379, 380.

attack upon atheism, which he had then completed, and which yet remains in manuscript. The first part was intended to prove the creation of the world, and the truth of the Mosaic history, "shewing," says Dr. Birch, a " great force of reasoning, and an equal compass of knowledge." [12] The second part was of the nature of the soul, and of a future state. Part the third concerned the attributes of God, both from the abstract ideas of him, and the light of nature, the evidence of Providence, and the notions of morality, and the voice of conscience : and the fourth part was concerning the truth and authority of the Scriptures, with answers to objections.

Upon these volumes, the first of which only has appeared, the judge was occupied seven years, writing them in vacant hours upon the circuits ; [13] but with so much consideration, as that one who perused the original in his own hand, which was the first draft, told Bishop Burnet he did not remember any considerable alteration, perhaps not twenty words in the whole.

When this important undertaking was finished, Sir Matthew sent it by a stranger to Bishop Wilkins, for the benefit of his judgment, with no other account of the author than that he was not a clergyman. It is almost necessary, however, to conjecture from the sequel, that a transcript, and not the original manuscript, was communicated ; else the hand-writing, which in general was rather

[12] Life of Tillotson, p. 47.
[13] Reliq. Baxter, part 3, p. 47.

difficult to read,[14] must have been detected, which
was not the case. The bishop, and his friend
Dr. Tillotson, read long in utter ignorance of the
writer, and were much puzzled that one who
appeared to be so great a " master" should be
unknown to them. At last, Dr. Tillotson guessing
Lord Hale, they immediately went to him. The
bishop at once thanked him for the entertainment
his work had afforded. The judge blushed extremely; and apprehending that he had been betrayed by his messenger, was somewhat displeased.
The bishop soon removed the impression; and
assured him that he had discovered *himself* by the
various learning of the book; it was such as none
but he could have written. With his usual freedom, but, at the same time, with great plainness
and prudence, the excellent prelate added, that
nothing could surpass the arguments, if only the
bulk could be *reduced*; and that if Sir Matthew's
leisure would not permit of that, he thought it
much better the whole should be published,
though a little too large, than that the world
should be deprived of the treasure. A time for
revisal not arriving, the first part only, under the
title of the Primitive Origination of Mankind,[15]
considered and examined according to the light of
nature, was ever sent to the press; but its author

[14] Mr. Hargrave's Preface to the volume on the Jurisdiction
of the Lord's House, p. ccxviii.

[15] Notice was taken of it in the Philosophical Transactions,
No. 136, p. 917. See the Philosophical Transactions Abridged,
vol. ii. p. 411.

died, as we shall presently see, before the day of publication.

The following accurate summary of its contents is from the pen of Bishop Burnet:—

"In the beginning of it he" (Sir Matthew) "gives an Essay of his excellent way of methodizing things; in which he was so great a master, that whatever he undertook, he would presently cast into so perfect a scheme, that he could never afterwards correct it. He runs out copiously upon the argument of the Impossibility of an eternal Succession of Time, to show that time and eternity are inconsistent with one another; and that, therefore, all duration that was past, and defined by time, could not be from eternity; and he shows the difference between successive eternity already passed, and one to come; so that though the latter is possible, the former is not so; for all the parts of the former have actually been, and, therefore, being defined by time, cannot be eternal; whereas the other are still future to all eternity: so that this reasoning cannot be turned to prove the possibility of eternal successions that have been, as well as eternal successions that shall be. This he follows with a strength I never met with in any that managed it before him.

"He brings, next, all those moral arguments to prove that the world had a beginning; agreeing to the account Moses gives of it, as that no history rises higher than near the time of the Deluge; and that the first foundation of kingdoms, the invention of arts, the beginnings of all religions,

the gradual plantation of the world, and increase
of mankind, and the consent of nations to agree
with it.   In managing these, as he shows profound
skill both in historical and philosophical learning,
so he gives a noble discovery of his great candour
and probity, that he would not impose on the
reader with a false show of reasoning, by arguments that he knew had flaws in them ; and, therefore, upon every one of these, he adds such alloys,
as in a great measure lessened and took off their
force, with as much exactness of judgment, and
strictness of censure, as if he had been set to plead
for the other side : and, indeed, sums up the whole
evidence for religion as impartially as ever he did
in a trial for life or death to the jury : which, how
equally and judiciously he always did, the whole
nation well knows.

  " After that, he examines the ancient opinions
of the philosophers ; and enlarges, with a great
variety of curious reflections, in answering that only
argument that has any appearance of strength for the
casual production of man, from the origination of
insects out of putrified matter, as is commonly supposed ; and he concluded the book, showing how
rational and philosophical the account which Moses
gives of it is.   There is in it all a sagacity, and
quickness of thought, mixed with great and curious
learning, that I confess I never met together in any
other book on that subject.   Among other conjectures, one he gives concerning the Deluge is : ' That
he did not think the face of earth, and the waters,
were altogether the same before the universal

deluge and after; but, possibly, the face of the earth was more even than now it is; the seas, possibly, more dilated and extended, and not so deep as now.' And a little after: ' Possibly the seas have undermined much of the appearing continent of earth.' This I the rather take notice of, because it hath been, since his death, made out in a most ingenious and elegantly writ book, by Mr. Burnet of Christ's College, in Cambridge, who has given such an essay towards the proving the possibility of an universal deluge; and from thence has collected with great sagacity what Paradise was before it, as has not been offered by any philosopher before him." [16]

Such was the last effort made by this " most learned and religious person" [17] for the service of his generation.

The subject, it may be well supposed, had very especially interested him, so great a portion as seven years of his busy and industrious life having been devoted to its completion. And that is not the only evidence of the ardour of his mind in counteraction of error; his writings abound with brief descriptions of the " strange spirit of atheism;" and in his Letter of Advice to his Grandchildren, when he was " grown to a great age," and all his anxieties for them were in the liveliest exercise, he says, emphatically—" Read often the first chapter of Solomon's Proverbs, and the first chapter of the Wisdom of Solomon; though the

[16] Life, pp. 52—54. 12mo. 1682. See Note LL.
[17] Wood's Ath. Oxon. vol. iii. p. 1095.

latter be not any part of the canonical Scripture, yet it excellently describes the folly and miserable end of atheists." [18]

The termination of his lordship's earthly pilgrimage now rapidly approached; and, like one wearied with a long and sorrowful day, he wished for night. He looked *through* " the mists of mortality," and associated with dying, as do the Scriptures, images full of loveliness and peace.

When in health he thus wrote; and it shows how familiar he had made the subject of death; with what becoming and serious thoughts he had contemplated it.

" I will learn, and often return upon the consideration of my own mortality; and look upon my life here as but a shadow, and a pilgrimage; as a journey to my home, and not as an abiding place. I will learn not to make this life, or this world, the subject of my chiefest care; but make my everlasting home—eternity—the one thing necessary: the presence of God, to be that which I will mainly provide for; to pass the time of my sójourning here in fear; to wait all my appointed time till my *change* come; to work out my 'salvation with fear and trembling; to make my calling and election sure; and to spend my time, and employ my parts, and to use my wealth, and to improve my opportunities, that I may with comfort give an account of my stewardship, that I may be *ready* for death, and *welcome* it as the *passage* unto my *Master's* joy." [19]

[18] Page 39. 12mo. 1823. second edition. [19] Hale, Orig. MS.

His sufferings, oftentimes, were distressingly great. For more than a year before they ceased, he had been obliged, by a constant asthma, to sit, rather than lie, in his bed. Amidst all, however, patience had her "perfect work;" and such was his submission to the will of God, and such his unruffled calmness, as forcibly to recommend Christianity to observers.

During his illness, his parish minister, the Rev. Evan Griffith, M. A. assiduously attended upon him; and it was noticed that, in spite of bodily anguish, whenever that gentleman offered up prayer, not only was every complaint and groan suppressed, but with uplifted hands and eyes he proclaimed the fixedness, and piety of his mind. On being informed by the same worthy divine, not long before his departure, that the communion was to be observed at church on the approaching Sunday, and that as it was not likely *he* could be present, it should be administered at his own house, the dying saint replied, with the reverence and humility which were habitual to him,—"No; my heavenly Father has prepared a feast for me, and I will go to my Father's house to partake of it." Accordingly he was carried thither: "and received the sacrament," says Bishop Burnet, "on his knees, with great devotion; which it may be supposed," he adds, "was the greater, because he apprehended it was to be the *last*, and so took it as his viaticum and provision for his journey."

Like Henry the Great, [20] Lord Hale had some

[20] See Note MM.

secret unaccountable presages of his death; and said,—"that if he did not die on such a day, the 25th of November, he believed he should live a month longer;" and that accordingly happened.

To the latest moment, the use of his reason, a blessing for which he had often and earnestly prayed, was mercifully continued to him; and when his voice became too feeble for articulation, he gave almost constant signs, that his heart, as well as his treasure, was in heaven. Thither he was translated, without a struggle, in the afternoon of December 25, 1676-7, between two and three o'clock.

For many years Christmas-day had been employed by Lord Hale as a season of extraordinary devotion; and he had accustomed himself, after attending public worship and receiving the sacrament, to give utterance to his feelings in verses sacred to the Redeemer. This circumstance rendered the event which now had happened the more observable; a source, too, of innocent pleasure, no doubt, to his friends, that the chaunts, in which he had so often indulged, were *on that day* [21] exchanged for angelic songs and the Saviour's presence. Seventeen of the effusions referred to were printed with the "Contemplations." One other, and probably the last he wrote, shall here be introduced, not because of poetical merit, but for the sake of the thoughts, and the testimony it affords

[21] His death happening upon the quarter day, might have occasioned a dispute as to his pension; but that matter the king decided by ordering it paid to his executors.

to the holy satisfying nature of that "peace" which, "being justified by faith," he consciously possessed.

> " Bless'd Creator! who before the birth
> Of time, or e'er the pillars of the earth
> Were fix'd, or form'd, didst lay that great design
> Of man's redemption ; and didst define
> In thine eternal counsels, all the scene
> Of that stupendous business, and when
> It should appear ; and, though the very day
> Of its Epiphany concealed lay,
> Within thy mind, yet thou wert pleas'd to show
> Some glimpses of it, unto men below,
> In visions, types, and prophecies ; as we
> Things at a distance in perspective see.
> But thou wert pleas'd to let thy servant know,
> That *that* blest hour, that seem'd to move so slow
> Through former ages, should at last attain
> Its time, e'er my few sands that yet remain
> Are spent ; and that these aged eyes
> Should see the day when Jacob's star should rise.
> And now thou hast fulfill'd it, blessed Lord,
> Dismiss me now, according to thy word ;
> And let my aged body now return
> To rest, and dust, and drop into an urn ;
> For I have liv'd enough ; mine eyes have seen
> Thy much-desir'd Salvation, that hath been
> So long, so dearly wish'd ; the joy, the hope
> Of all the ancient Patriarchs ; the scope
> Of all the prophecies, and mysteries,
> Of all the types unveil'd ; the histories
> Of Jewish Church unriddled ; and the bright
> And orient sun arisen, to give light
> To Gentiles, and the joy of Israel,
> The world's Redeemer, bless'd *Emmanuel.*
> Let this sight close mine eyes ; ' tis loss to see,
> After this vision, any sight but thee."[22]

---

[22] Life, pp. 68, 69.   Works, vol. i. pp. 48, 49.

` Sir Matthew often said that churches were for the living, and church-yards for the dead ; and accordingly, a few days before his own exit, he went into that at Alderley, and fixed upon a spot for interment ; where, on the 4th of January, his remains were safely laid up [23] until the morning of the resurrection.

The same day, Mr. Griffith improved the sad occasion, in a sermon on Isaiah lvii. 1, which afterwards was published.[24]

A plain and decent monument was erected to his memory ; the stone of black, and the sides of black and white marble. The inscription he had himself provided ; and Mr. Mason has remarked, that although there is the utmost simplicity in the words, there appears a certain air of dignity, owing to the feet that compose them being all of the most generous quality.[25]

HIC INHUMATUR CORPUS
MATTHÆI HALE, MILITIS ;
ROBERTI HALE, ET JOANNÆ
UXORIS EJUS, FILII UNICI.
NATI IN HAC PAROCHIA DE ALDERLEY,
PRIMO DIE NOVEMBRIS,
A.D. 1609.
DENATI VERO IBIDEM
VICESSIMO QUINTO DIE DECEMBRIS,
A.D. 1676.
ÆTATIS SUÆ LXVII.

[23] Reliq. Baxter, part 3, p. 181.
[24] A Sermon preached at Alderley, in the county of Gloucester, 4th January, 1676, at the funeral of Sir Matthew Hale, Knight, late Lord Chief Justice of his Majesty's Court of King's Bench. 4to. 1677.
[25] Life by Runnington, p xxix.

Here is buried the body of Matthew Hale, Knight, the only son of Robert Hale, and Joanna his wife ; born in this parish of Alderley on the 1st day of November, in the year of our Lord 1609, and died in the same place on the 25th day of December, in the year of our Lord 1676 ; in the 67th year of his age.[26]

Of Sir Matthew's person, a correct idea may be formed from some, at least, of the numerous portraits which have appeared. Most of them, not to mention the one prefixed to the present volume, justify and illustrate the picture Burnet himself sketched.

" The last year of his (Lord Hale's) being in London, he came always on Sundays (when he could go abroad) to the chapel of the Rolls, where I then preached. In my life I never saw so much gravity, tempered with that sweetness, and set off with so much vivacity, as appeared in his looks, and behaviour, which disposed me to a veneration for him, which I never had for any with whom I was not acquainted."[27]

Sir Matthew was twice married. His first wife was Anne, daughter of Sir Henry Moore, of Faly, in Berkshire, and grandchild to Sir Francis Moore, serjeant-at-law ; by her he had ten children ; the four first died young, the other six lived to be married. He outlived them all, except his eldest daughter, and his youngest son, who at the time Bishop Burnet wrote the Memoir, were alive.

[26] The Works, vol. i. p. 60.
[27] Life. The Preface. The Works, vol. i. p. 5.

His eldest son, Robert, married Frances, the daughter of Sir Francis Shock, of Avington, in Berkshire. They both died early, leaving five children, two sons, Matthew and Gabriel, and three daughters, Ann, Mary, and Frances.[28] Having, by the judge's advice, made him their executor, he took his grandchildren under his own care, and left them his estate.

His second son, Matthew, married Anne, the daughter of Mr. Matthew Simmonds, of Hilsley, in Gloucestershire, and shortly afterwards died, leaving one child, named Matthew.

His third son, Thomas, married Rebecca, the daughter of Christian le Brune, a Dutch merchant, and died without issue.

His fourth son, Edward, married Mary, the daughter of Edmund Goodyere, Esq. of Heythorp, in Oxfordshire. He had two sons and three daughters.

His eldest daughter, Mary, was married to Edward Alderley, son of Edward Alderley, of Innishannon, in the county of Cork, in Ireland. She was left a widow with two sons and three daughters, but afterwards married Edward, son of Edward Stephens, Esq. of Cherrington, in Gloucestershire.

His youngest daughter, Elizabeth, was married to Edward Webb, Esq., barrister-at-law. She had two children, a son and a daughter.

[28] The fourth chapter of the Letter of Advice to his Grandchildren, contains a very curious description of their " constitutions and complexions."—Pp. 29—33.

The judge's second wife was Anne, the daughter of Mr. Joseph Bishop, of Faly, in Berkshire, by whom he had no issue; she resided in the house at Alderley with his family, but not, as North has ill-naturedly alleged, in the situation of a servant.[29]

" Some," says Baxter, " made it a scandal, but his wisdom chose it for his convenience, that, in his age, he married a woman of no estate, suitable to his disposition, to be to him as a nurse."[30] " The good man," says the same writer elsewhere, " more regarded his own daily comfort than man's thoughts and talk."[31] Indeed the union seems to have been a source of unmingled satisfaction and comfort to both parties. In the Letter of Advice to his Grandchildren, which will be noticed hereafter, and which he wrote in the year 1673, he bears the highest testimony to her varied excellencies.[32] In his will,[33] too, she is much distinguished; eulogized as a most dutiful, faithful, and loving wife, and appointed one of the executors. To her care the judge committed his grandchildren. Baxter, much to his credit, notices her as " the Lady Hale."[34] She was buried at Alderley in the year 1694; and it deserves mention, that her good management increased the property of the family.[35]

[29] Information from R. H. Blagden Hale, Esq.
[30] Reliq. Baxter, part 3, p. 176.
[31] Additional Notes. Hale's Works, vol. i. p. 89.
[32] At p. 21.      [33] See the Appendix.
[34] Hale's Discourse on Religion. 4to. 1684. Preface.
[35] Information from Mr. Hale.

The male line of Lord Hale's family became extinct in 1784, by the death of his great grandson, Matthew Hale, Esq., barrister-at-law.[36]

[36] Chalmers's General Biog. Dict. vol. xvii. p. 28.

# CHAPTER XII.

## HIS HABITS AND CHARACTER.

HAVING traced the life of this truly illustrious man to its close, it remains, by collecting together those fragments of information which lie scattered abroad, to endeavour yet further to delineate his character and habits. Besides other advantages incident to the attempt, will be an exemplification of the connexion established by Divine wisdom between humility and honour; between industry and success; between "well-doing," and the fairest, richest rewards. "The most wise God," they are the judge's words, "though he reserve his predeterminations and councils in his own hand, yet hath given mankind an ordinary track to walk by; and hath ordinarily placed *good* events in ways of virtue, human prudence, counsel, and the like; and hath placed *evil* events, ordinarily, in ways of folly, imprudence, and vice; and by this economy keeps the world in right order and discipline."[1]

In *private* there was every thing to render Lord Hale beloved, and revered. The whole of his

[1] Orig. MS.

carriage indicated a constant remembrance of the "great and glorious King of heaven and earth."[2]

His temper was admirably equal; he was cheerful rather than merry; and lived with both his wives in the happiest intercourse. His habits were strictly domestic; fashionable and formal visiting was shunned, that in the enjoyment of his beloved privacy he might cultivate the endearments of home; and, while pursuing his studies, surrender himself to the interests of his offspring.[3]

After noticing the death of his youngest child— a little girl about four months old—and the lessons the event was adapted and intended to teach, he adds, "I learn my duty of *christian education* when my children come to any measure of understanding; viz. that they may understand their natural condition; the use of their baptism; the merits and righteousness of Christ; that they may renew their covenant with God, and grow up in it, and in his presence; to keep them from the vanities, and levities, and follies, and excesses, and pollutions, of the times and places wherein they live."[4]

In the same manuscript he enjoined upon himself "to be more solemn and faithful in the performance of the great duty of baptism:" he, likewise, acknowledges his "own sin, and the sin of divers others, in using that ordinance as a piece of state, or formality, or custom, without a deep

[2] Works, vol. ii. p. 485. Medit. on the Lord's Prayer.
[3] Ib. vol. i. pp. 89, 205.
[4] Hale, Orig. MS.

and serious consideration of its greatness, use, and consequence."[5]

His paternal vigilance is manifest from the extracts just adduced, and from the "letters" of counsel and advice especially, which have long since been included in his works. Nor is it less evident that he felt an increasing concern that his example might serve as a "visible direction"[6] to others.

The following transcript from an unpublished relic, furnishes a pleasing specimen of the familiarity he cultivated as a parent; and it so confirms existing representations of his thoughtfulness in that capacity, and so discloses the grounds upon which it proceeded, as that it will not fail to be read with interest.

"ROBIN,                                    "*November* 30, 1659.

        "YOU are now about sixteen years old; you have passed the more innocent part of your life, and are come to that age wherein the vanity of youth, and the necessity of an education more distant from your father's eye, do expose you to more dangers and temptations than formerly.

"You are like a small pinnace beginning to put out to sea, wherein are many rocks and quicksands, which, besides accidental storms and tempests, may endanger you in your voyage. And many times youths do contract those ill customs, about your age, that either ruin them betimes, or, like *mali*

[5] Hale, Orig. MS.
[6] Works, vol. i. p. 194. Letter I. touching the Lord's Day.

*genii*, follow them to their graves, or at best, are not without much difficulty, and loss of time broken. My business at this time is to give you some counsels in writing that may abide with you, and may be frequently considered by you, for the avoiding those rocks and dangers that are incident to your age, complexion, and future condition. And it will be your wisdom, reputation, and advantage, often to consider them; constantly to observe them, and in them to look upon me as present, advising you, observing you, and reprehending your neglect, or commending your observance. And, indeed, you have a stricter eye upon you than mine can be; which is upon your ways, though mine always cannot be. The advice that is given you comes from a father, and, therefore, carries in it love, and authority: and it comes from one that hath, by God's assistance, passed through your age, and the dangers incident to it; and hath had a strict observation, and long experience, and, therefore, carries in it more weight, and safety."[7]

In his family, the judge maintained the daily worship of God; and, unless a clergyman was present, officiated himself. From an expression in one of his letters,[8] it is evident that he attended, likewise, to the "ancient and venerable usage" of catechising; nor will it escape remark that his "Contemplations" contain at least one allusion to the "Church Catechism;"[9] as also to the

---

[7] Hale, Orig. MS.
[8] The second, concerning Religion. Works, vol. i. p. 209.
[9] Works, vol. i. p. 291. Discourse of Religion.

shorter formulary of the "Westminster Assembly."[10]

Towards his servants his gentleness was habitual; if offended with them he allowed no interview until his displeasure had abated; when the merited reproof was administered, he made it appear that he was more concerned for the fault committed as before God, than for the offence given to himself. In cases of immorality and ungovernableness, he proceeded to a dismissal; observing sometimes, that as he was bound officially to punish delinquents, he could not suffer *such* offenders, when they happened in his own house, to escape.

In the *promotion* of his dependants, he observed order, regulating the movement by the time of service: he thus avoided those causes of envy which so commonly attend changes of that nature. They all received from him the treatment of a friend rather than a master, and the best instruction and advice, also, in his power. From those who filled the more lucrative places, he required contribution to the receivers of fixed wages only. Each of them enjoyed a legacy at his death; and one of the number, Robert Gibbon, of the Middle Temple, Esq. was placed among his executors. At the desire of that gentleman it was that Bishop Burnet wrote the judge's life: and through him most of the materials were obtained.[11]

Lord Hale's *diligence* was remarkable. Upon

[10] Works, vol. ii. pp. 310, 319. Of the chief end of Man.
[11] Ib. vol. i. p. 66.

"time" he placed the highest possible value, and he redeemed it with great care. He allowed only a short season for taking his food; he rarely discoursed concerning news; he entered into no correspondence, except about necessary business, or matters of learning; he studiously avoided all unnecessary familiarity with great persons;[12] he shunned the diversions and vanities of the world;[13] he abstained from public feasts; and, confining his own entertainments almost exclusively, as we shall see presently, to the poor, much time, usually wasted, was *so* redeemed.

Besides his tract on the *redemption*[14] of the fleeting treasure; and, besides the evidence afforded by his doings, there are various and very touching passages in his printed works, relating to the same matter. One of them, by the allusion it makes, though in few words, to his early days; "to long feastings, seeing of interludes, and impertinent studies;" and to the impressions produced upon him by "concernments of everlasting importance,"[15]—presents in strong colours those mingled emotions which haunt, not unfrequently, the awakened mind—regret for past negligence, and anxiety for future improvement.

An attentive reader will notice that the first letter "to his children" was penned "while he lay at an inn;"[16] and that in others of his writings

---

[12] Reliq. Baxter, part 3. p. 47.    [13] Ib. p. 176.
[14] Works, vol. ii. pp. 239—252.
[15] Ib. vol. ii. pp. 268—271.—The Good Steward.
[16] Ib. vol. i. p. 204.

I

hints occur of a similar description; all shewing the hate he bore to idleness, and how incessant his efforts were to employ his hours,[17] especially his " Horæ Sacræ," *well*.[18] Many of his "Contemplations" were written during journeys, which, by reason of company, were ill adapted for the exercise.[19]

To such *constancy* of occupation, combined with abstemiousness, systematic arrangements, and early rising,[20] must be ascribed those results which, otherwise, would have been impossible.

He delighted in rural walks; and these, while promoting his bodily health, acted beneficially upon his mind; expanding it, and imparting to it a vigorous freshness, favourable to studious, and successful application. With what edifying attention he was accustomed to observe visible objects, the " Good Steward" informs us; and the example he left of a due regard to exercise will not, it is hoped, be slighted. It is, no doubt, owing to the *neglect* of such attention, including diet, and not to hard reading, that the health of many has been impaired, and the lives of not a few sacrificed. That wonderful man, and intense pursuer of knowledge, Mr. Baxter, was of opinion that diligence in study tends to long life; and in his " Address" prefixed to the Memoir[21] of the Rev. John Janeway, Fellow of King's College, Cambridge, he seems, unanswerably, to have supported it.

[17] See Note NN.
[18] The Contemplations, Oct. 1679. Part 2. Pref. p. 4.
[19] Ib. p. 3.     [20] See Note OO.     [21] 12mo. 1672.

The *modesty* of Lord Hale was as conspicuous as his attainments, and industry. Like Erasmus, he took more care to avoid the legitimate honours and preferments of his profession, than others do to secure them; and when *constrained* to accept them, which was literally the case, he has shewn, by his general demeanour, as well as in his "Works," how wisely, and devoutly they were used.

To others, his conduct was fair, kind, and obliging. Instead, in the progress of a cause, of taking triumphant advantages where the arguments of a junior, on the opposite side, betrayed either inexperience, or imbecility, he would often give strength to weakness, supply what was defective, and, in noticing the objections themselves, *commend*, if possible, the gentleman who had pressed them; and few things operated so favourably upon a young practitioner as his good word.

While at the bar, his practice, owing to his freedom from the love of money, was far less lucrative than it might have been. But the luxuries of benevolence, as he passed along, more than compensated him. In ordinary cases requiring little time, or study, when those who asked his counsel gave him a "piece," being satisfied with ten shillings, he used to give back the half.

He deemed it the honour of English gentlemen to employ their time in husbandry; in planting; in raising stocks of sheep, cattle, and horses:[22] and it is obvious, that it was no abstract sentiment:

[22] Letter of Advice, pp. 97, 112.

besides other evidence, his will shews that what he could conveniently spare was laid out in the purchase of land, and its improvement.

As a landlord, he discovered the remoteness of his disposition from every thing grasping, and covetous : times, and circumstances were duly regarded; and he was ready, upon any reasonable cause, to make abatements. In short, opportunities to do *good*, of whatever kind, were eagerly embraced by him; nor did he ever suffer his zeal to languish, either under the influence of expense, or trouble. On a widow in London, who possessed a small estate near his house in the country, making known to him her distress, because of the ill payment of her rents, and the expensive mode of obtaining them, he directed his steward to transact the necessary business without charge ; and when a reduction became inevitable, to allow what was necessary to the tenant; but he forbad the slightest deduction from the income of the receiver.

Counterfeit coin once paid, he never suffered to be circulated. He thought the imposition practised upon himself afforded no pretext for a repetition of the evil. In time, a considerable heap of that sort of money had accumulated; and it is probable he intended to have destroyed it. Some thieves, however, saved him the trouble, by breaking into, and stealing it from, his chamber ; a circumstance which he sometimes amused himself by narrating, and by imagining their feelings when the nature of the prize was ascertained.

The truths Lord Hale deduced from "Jacob's vow,"[23] (and which show the strongest possible conviction of the danger, as well as vanity, and transitoriness of grandeur, power, and wealth,) were, in fact, the constant guide of his desires, and conduct. Mr. Baxter, noticing the smallness of his estate,[24] notwithstanding the opportunities he had enjoyed for its increase, accurately remarked, that, " as he had little, and desired little, so he was *content* with little, and suited his dwelling, table, and retinue, thereto. His housekeeping was according to the rest, like his state of mind, but not like his place, and honour. His great advantage for innocency was, that he was no lover of riches, or grandeur."[25]

This indifference to appearances extended itself to his furniture, which was exceedingly plain. Economy reigned over every part of his establishment, without hurtful parsimony. " Be frugal in my family," was his direction, " but let there be no want : provide conveniently for the poor."[26]

In accordance with such a system, his temperance was strict. He even lived so philosophically as to rise from table with an appetite. In that affecting narrative, which may be regarded as the commencement of his religious history, we have seen the reason of this extraordinary care ; and it is observable in his works, when he adverts to the

---

[23] Works, vol. ii. p. 169.
[24] See *post*, ch. xiii.
[25] Works, vol. i. p. 89, and Reliq. Baxter, part 3, p. 47.
[26] Third Letter to his Children ; Works, vol. i. p. 222. See also his account of the Good Steward ; Works, vol. ii. p. 286.

subject, how invariably the vigilance, and caution then inspired are discovered.[27]

Being of a " cold constitution," he took " much tobacco," not as an " incitement to drinking" (for he never drank with it), but as physic; and he considered it a great preservative of his health.[28] He, at the same time, warned others against the practice, unless they were of the same " complexion, government, and prudent ordering,"[29] as himself.

Of excess in drinking, he cherished, ever after the time he was startled into thoughtfulness,[30] the utmost dread : and his testimony was thus solemnly recorded.

" The places of judicature which I have long held in this kingdom, have given me opportunity to observe the original cause of most of the enormities that have been committed for the space of near twenty years; and by a due observation, I have found, that four out of five of them have been the issues, and product of excessive drinking at taverns, or alehouse meetings."[31]

To his attire, Lord Hale appears to have been blamably inattentive; and although the love he once discovered for finery makes it apparent that even his negligence resulted from *principle*, yet it would, surely, have been commendable had the

[27] See particularly his Fourth Letter, Works, vol. i. p. 239, and vol. ii. p. 555. Meditations on the Lord's Prayer.
[28] Letter of Advice, p. 154.
[29] Ib. p. 126; and see p. 155.
[30] See *ante*, pp. 6, 7.
[31] Letter of Advice, p. 126.

lesson taught him by slovenliness,[32] induced a greater regard to the etiquette of his station. " His habit," says Baxter, " was *so* coarse, and plain, that I, who am thought guilty of a culpable neglect therein, have been bold to desire him to lay aside some things which seemed too homely. The house which I surrendered to him, and wherein he lived at Acton, was well situated, but very small, and so far below the ordinary dwellings of men of his rank, as that divers farmers thereabouts had better; but it pleased him."[33]

He tells his grandchildren that he never changed the fashion of his clothes after he was thirty years old; and that *they* would have no cause to repent, if they followed his example.[34]

The noble Pieresc was a judge, as well as a man of letters, and " supported his rank, more by his character than either by luxury, or parade;" but Gassendi's captivating memoir shows how well this was done, *without* a departure from ordinary fashions, so entire as that alluded to.

While it is, and must be, a matter of just regret that Hale had not, like Pieresc, a biographer to whom he was " familiarly known;" one who could have given an account of his feelings, and perpetuated the numerous influences which acted upon him, and portrayed their effects in the modification of his mind, and described him in social life with an approach, at least, to Boswell-like minuteness, it is pleasant, so far as Baxter's intercourse

[31] See *ante*, p. 6.    [33] Hale's Works, vol. i. p. 89.
[34] Letter of Advice, p. 160.

with him extended, that the regret is capable of diminution. Some extracts, therefore, from a letter that celebrated man addressed to Mr. Stephens, subsequently to the bishop's publication, shall now be introduced, and they will be found to be of the deepest interest.

" I will truly tell you the matter and manner of our converse. We were oft together; and almost all our discourse was philosophical, and especially about the nature of spirits, and superior regions; and the nature, operations, and immortality of man's soul. And our disposition and course of thoughts were in such things so like, that I did not much cross the bent of his conference. He studied physics, and got all new or old books of philosophy that he could meet with, as eagerly as if he had been a boy at the University. Mousnerius and Honoratus Faber he deservedly much esteemed; but yet took not the latter to be without some mistakes. Mathematics he studied more than I did, it being a knowledge which he much more esteemed than I did, who valued all knowledge by the greatness of the benefit, and necessity of the use; and my unskilfulness in them I acknowledge my great defect, in which he much excelled. But we were both much addicted to know, and read all the pretenders to more than ordinary in physics: the Platonists, the Peripatetics, the Epicureans (and especially their Gassendurs), Teleius, Campanella, Patricius, Lullius, White, and every sect that made us any encouraging promise. We neither of us approved of all in Aristotle, but he valued him more than I did. We both greatly disliked the principles of Cartesius and Gassendus (much more of the Bruitists, Hobbs, and Spinosa), especially their doctrine *de motu*, and their obscuring or denying nature itself, even the *principia motus*, the *virtutes formales*, which are the causes of operations.

" Whenever we were together, he was the spring of our discourse (as choosing the subject), and most of it still was of the nature of spirits, and the immortality, state, and operations of separated souls. We both were conscious of human darkness, and how much of our understandings, quiet in such matters, must be fetched from our implicit trust in the goodness and promises of God, rather than from a clear, and satisfying conception of the mode of separated souls' operations ; and how great use we have herein of our faith in Jesus Christ, as he is the undertaker, mediator, the Lord, and lover of souls, and the actual possessor of that glory. But yet we thought that it greatly concerned us to search, as far as God allowed us, into a matter of so great moment ; and that even little, and obscure prospects into the heavenly state are more excellent than much, and applauded knowledge of transitory things.

" He was much in urging difficulties and objections ;[35] but you could not tell by them what was his own judgment ; for, when he was able to

---

[35] His very questions, and objections did help me to more light than other men's solutions. Reliq. Baxter, part 3, p. 47.

answer them himself, he would draw out another's answer.

" He was but of a slow speech ; and, sometimes, so hesitating, that a stranger would have thought him a man of low parts, that knew not readily what to say, though ready at other times. But I never saw Cicero's doctrine, *de Oratore*, more verified in any man, that, furnishing the mind with all sorts of knowledge, is the chief thing to make an excellent orator ; for when there is abundance, and clearness of knowledge in the mind, it will ever furnish a slow tongue to speak that which, by its congruence and verity, shall prevail. Such an one never wants moving matter, nor an answer to vain objectors.

" The manner of our converse was as suitable to my inclination as the matter ; for, whereas many bred in universities, and called scholars, have not the wit, manners, or patience, to hear those that they discourse with speak to the end; but, through list and impotency cannot hold, but cut off a man's speech when they hear any thing that urgeth them, before the latter part make the former intelligible or strong (when oft the proof and use is reserved to the end), liker scolds than scholars ; as if they commanded silence at the end of each sentence to him that speaketh, or else would have two talk at once. I do not remember that ever he and I did interrupt each other in any discourse. His wisdom, and accustomed patience, caused him still to stay for the end. And though my disposition have too much forwardness to speak, I had not so little wit or manners, as to interrupt *him;* whereby we far better understood each other, than we could have done in chopping and maimed discourse.

" He was much for coming to philosophical knowledge by the help of experiments; but he thought that our new philosophers, as some called the Cartesians, had taken up many fallacies as experiments, and had made as unhappy a use of their trials, as many empirics and mountebanks do in medicine; and that Aristotle was a man of far greater experience, as well as study, than they. He was wont to say, that lads at the Universities had found it a way to be thought wiser than others, to join with boasters that cried down the ancients, before they understood them; for he thought that few of these contemners of Aristotle had ever so far studied him to know his doctrine, but spoke against they knew not what; even as some secular theologues take it to be the way to be thought wise men, and orthodox, to cant against some party or sect, which they have advantage to contemn. It must cost a man many years' study to know what Aristotle held. But to read over Magirus (and, perhaps, the Conimbricenses, or Zabarell), and then prate against Aristotle, requireth but a little time, and labour. He could well bear it, when one that had thoroughly studied Aristotle dissented from him in any particular upon reason; but he loathed it in ignorant men, that were carried to it by shameful vanity of mind.

" His many hard questions, doubts, and objections to me, occasioned me to draw up a small tract, Of the Nature and Immortality of Man's Soul, as proved by Natural Light alone, by way of questions and answers. In which, I had not baulked the hardest objections and difficulties that I could think of; conceiving that Atheists and Sadducees are so unhappily witty, and Satan such a tutor, that they are as like to think of them as I. But the good man, when I sent it to him, was wiser than I, and sent me word, in his return, that he would not have me publish it in English, nor without some alterations of the method; because, though he thought I had sufficiently answered all the objections, yet ordinary readers would take deeper into their minds, such hard objections as they never heard before, than the answer, how full soever, would be able to overcome; whereupon, not having leisure to translate and alter it, I cast it by.

" He seemed to reverence and believe the opinion of Dr. Willis, and such others, *de animis brutorum*, as being not spiritual substances. But when I sent him a confutation of them, he seemed to acquiesce, and, as far I could judge, did change his mind, and had higher thoughts of sensitive natures than they that take them to be some evanid qualities, proceeding from contexture, attemperation, and motion.

" Yet he and I did think that the notion of immateriality had little satisfactory to acq with the nature of a spirit, not telling

what it is, but what it is *not;* and we thought that the old Greek and Latin doctors (cited by Faustus Rhegiculus, whom Mamertus answereth) did mean by a body or matter, of which they said spirits did consist, the same thing as we now mean by the substance of spirits, distinguishing them from mere accidents; and we thought it a matter of some moment, and no small difficulty, to tell what men mean here by the word *substance,* if it be but a relative notion, because it doth *substare accidentibus et subsistere per se;* [36] relation is not proper substance. It is substance that doth so subsist; it is somewhat, and not nothing, nor an accident; therefore, if more than relation must be meant, it will prove hard to distinguish substance from substance by the notion of immateriality. Souls have no shadows; they are not palpable and gross, but they are SUBSTANTIAL LIFE, as VIRTUES; and it is hard to conceive how a created *vis vel virtus* should be the adequate *conceptus* of a spirit, and not rather an inadequate, supposing the *conceptus* of *substantia fundamentalis* (as Doctor Glisson calls it *de vita naturæ*), seeing *omnis virtus est rei alien virtus.* [37]

" Yet he yielded to me, that *virtus seu vis vitalis,* is not *animæ accidens,* but the *conceptus formalis spiritus,* supposing *substantia* to be the *conceptus fundamentalis;* and both together express the essence of a spirit.

" Every created being is passive; for *recipit in*

[36] It subsists to accidents, and subsists of itself.
[37] Every virtue is the virtue of a thing foreign to it.

*se fluxum causæ primæ.*[38] God transcendeth our defining skill; but where there is receptivity, many ancients thought there was some pure sort of materiality, and we say, there is receptive substantiality; and who can describe the difference (laying aside the formal virtues that difference things) between the highest material substance, and the lowest substance, called immaterial?

"We were neither of us satisfied with the notions of penetrability and indivisibility, as sufficient differences; but the *virtutes specificæ* plainly difference.

"What latter thoughts, a year before he died, he had of these things, I know not; but some say that a treatise of this subject, the soul's immortality, was his last finished work (promised in the end of his treatise of Man's Origination); and if we have the sight of that, it will fuller tell us his judgment.

"One thing I must notify to you, and to those that have his manuscripts, that when I sent him a scheme with some elucidations, he wrote me on that, and my treatise of the soul, almost a quire of paper of animadversions, by which you must not conclude at all of his own judgment, for he professed to me that he wrote them to me not as his judgment, but (as his way was) as the hardest objections which he would have satisfaction in; and when I had written him a full answer to all, and have been oft since with him, he seemed satisfied. You will wrong him, therefore, if you should print that written to me as his judgment.

[38] It receives a supply from the first cause.

" As to his judgment about religion, our discourse was very sparing about controversies; he thought not fit to begin with me about them, nor I with him; and as it was in me, so it seemed to be in him, from a conceit that we were not fit, to pretend to add much to one another.

" About matters of conformity, I could gladly have known his mind more fully; but I thought it unmeet to put such questions to a judge who must not speak against the laws; and he never offered his judgment to me : and I knew that as I was to reverence him in his own profession, so in matters of my profession and concernment, he expected not that I should think as he, beyond the reasons which he gave.

" I must say, that he was of opinion that the wealth and honour of the bishops was convenient, to enable them the better to relieve the poor, and rescue the inferior clergy from oppression, and to keep up the honour of religion in the world. But, all this on supposition, that it would be in the hands of wise and good men, or else it would do as much harm. But when I asked him, whether great wealth and honour would not be most earnestly desired and sought by the worst of men, while good men would not seek them ? and whether he that was the only fervent seeker was not likeliest to obtain, except under some rare, extraordinary prince ? And so, whether it was not like to entail the office on the worst, and to arm Christ's enemies against him to the end of the world, which a provision that had neither alluring, nor much discouraging temptation might prevent, he gave me no answer. I have heard some say, if the pope were a good man, what a deal of good might he do? But have popes, therefore, blessed the world?

" I can truly say, that he greatly lamented the negligence, and ill lives, and violence of some of the clergy;[39] and would oft say, What have they their calling, honour, and maintenance for, but to seek the instructing and saving of men's souls?

" He much lamented that so many worthy ministers were silenced, the Church weakened, papists strengthened, the cause of love and piety greatly wronged and hindered, by the present differences about conformity; and he hath told me his judgment, that the only means to heal us was a new Act of Uniformity, which should neither leave all at liberty, nor impose any thing unnecessary.

" I had once[40] a full opportunity to try his judgment far in this. It pleased the Lord Keeper Bridgman to invite Dr. Manton and myself (to whom Dr. Bates, at our desire, was added) to treat with Dr. Wilkins and Dr. Burton, about the terms of our reconciliation, and restoration to our ministerial liberty. After some days' conference, we came to agreement in all things, as to the necessary terms; and because Dr. Wilkins and I had special intimacy with Judge Hale, we desired him to draw it up in the form of an act, which he willingly did, and we agreed to every word. But it pleased the

[39] See Reliq. Baxter, part 3, p. 47.
[40] See *ante*, p. 115.

House of Commons, hearing of it, to begin their next session with a vote that no such bill should be brought in ; and so it died.

" *Query* 1. Whether, after this and other such agreement, it be ingenuity, or somewhat else, that hath ever since said, we know not what they would have ? and that at once call out to us, and yet strictly forbid us to tell them what it is we take for sin, and what we desire ?

" 2. Whether it be likely that such men as Bishop Wilkins, and Dr. Burton, and Judge Hale, would consent to such terms of our concord as should be worse than our present condition of division and compulsion is ? and whether the maintainers of our dividing impositions be all wiser and better men, than this judge and that bishop were ?

" 3. And whether it be any distance of opinion, or difficulty of bringing us to agreement, that keepeth England in its sad divisions, or rather some men's opinion, that our unity itself is not desirable, lest it strengthen us ? The case is plain.

" His behaviour in the church was conformable, but prudent. He constantly heard a curate too low for such an auditor. In common prayer he behaved himself as others, saving that to avoid the differencing of the gospels from the epistles, and the bowing at the name of Jesus, from the names Christ, Saviour, God, &c., he would use some equality in his gestures, and stand up at the reading of all God's word alike.

" I had but one fear or suspicion concerning him, which since, I am assured, was groundless. I was afraid lest he had been too little for the practical part of religion, as to the working of the soul towards God, in prayer, meditation, &c., because he seldom spake to me of such subjects, nor of practical books, or sermons; but was still speaking of philosophy, or of spirits, souls, the future state, and the nature of God. But at last I understood that his averseness to hypocrisy made him purposely conceal the most of such of his practical thoughts and works, as the world now findeth by his Contemplations, and other writings.

" He told me, once, how God brought him to a fixed honour and observation of the Lord's day: that when he was young, being in the west, the sickness, or death, of some relation at London, made some matter of estate to become his concernment; which required his hastening to London from the west: and he was commanded to travel on the Lord's day; but I cannot well remember how many cross accidents befel him in his journey; one horse fell lame, another died, and much more; which struck him with such a sense of Divine rebuke as he never forgot.[41]

" When he had striven awhile under disease, he gave up his place, not so much from the apprehension of the nearness of his death (for he could have died comfortably in his public work) but from the sense of his disability to discharge his

[41] See the Note K K, *ante*, p. 146.

part; but he ceased not his studies, and that upon points which I could have wished him to let go; being confident, that he was not far from his end.

"I sent him a book, which I had newly published, for reconciling the controversies about predestination, redemption, grace, free-will; but desired him not to bestow too much of his precious time upon it; but, before he left his place, I found him at it so oft, that I took the boldness to tell him, that I thought more practical writings were more suitable to his case, who was going from this contentious world.[42] He gave me but little answer; but, I after found, that he plied practicals and contemplatives in their season; which he never thought meet to give me any account of. Only, in general, he oft told me, that the reason and season of his writings (against atheism, &c. aforesaid) were, both in his circuit and at home, to set apart some time for meditation, especially after the evening public worship every Lord's day; and that he could not so profitably keep his thoughts in connexion and method, otherwise, as by writing them down; and withal, that if there were any thing in them useful, it was the way to keep it for after use; and, therefore, for the better management, for the accountableness and the after use, he had long accustomed to pen his meditations; which gave us all of that nature that he hath left us.

"Notwithstanding his own great furniture of

---

[42] See Reliq. Baxter, part 3, p. 181.

knowledge, (and he was accounted, by some, somewhat tenacious of his conceptions; for men that know much cannot easily yield to the expectations of less knowing men), yet, I must say, that I remember not that ever I conversed with a man, that was readier to receive and learn. He would hear so patiently, and recollect all so distinctly, and then try it so judiciously (not disdaining to learn of an inferior in some things, who, in more, had need to learn of him), that he would presently take, what some stand wrangling against many years. I never more perceived in any man, how much great knowledge and wisdom facilitate additions, and the reception of any thing not before known. Such a one presently perceiveth that evidence, which another is incapable of.

" For instance, the last time but one that I saw him, in his weakness at Acton, he engaged me to explicate the doctrine of divine government and decree, as consistent with the sin of man. And when I had distinctly told him, 1st, what God did as the author of nature, physically; 2d, what he did as legislator, morally; and, 3d, what he did as benefactor, and by special grace; 4th, and where permission came in, and where actual operation; 5th, and so, how certainly God might cause the effects, and not cause the volitions, as determinate to evil, (though the volition and effect being called by one name, as theft, murder, adultery, lying, &c. oft deceive men), he took up all that I had said, in order, and, distinctly, twice over, repeated each part in its proper place, and with its reason; and when he had done, said that I had given him satisfaction.

" Before I knew what he did himself in contemplations, I took it not well that he more than once told me, ' Mr. Baxter, I am more beholden to you than you are aware of; and I thank you for all, but especially for your scheme, and your Catholic theology.' For I was sorry, that a man that I thought so near death, should spend much of his time on such controversies, though tending to end them. But he continued after, near a year, and had leisure for contemplations which I knew not of.

" When I parted with him, I doubted which of us would be first at heaven; but he is gone before, and I am at the door, and somewhat the willinger to go, when I think such souls as his are there.

" When he was gone to Gloucestershire, and his Contemplations were published by you, I sent him the confession of my censures of him; how I had feared, that he had allowed too great a share of his time and thoughts to speculation, and too little to practicals, but rejoiced to see the conviction of my error; and he returned me a very kind letter, which was the last.

" Some censured him for living under such a curate at Acton, thinking it was in his power to have got Dr. Reeves, the parson, to provide a better, of which I can say that I once took the liberty to tell him that I feared too much tepidity in him, by reason of that thing; not that he needed himself a better teacher, who knew more, and could overlook scandals; but for the sake of the poor ignorant people, who greatly needed better help. He answered me, that if money would do it, he would willingly have done it; but the doctor was a man not to be dealt with; which was the hardest word that I remember I ever heard him use of any: for I never knew any man more free from speaking evil of others, behind their backs.[43] Whenever the discourse came up to the faultiness of any *individuals*, he would be silent; but the *sorts* of faulty persons he would blame with cautelous freedom; especially idle, proud, scandalous, contentious, and factious clergymen. We agreed in nothing more than that, which he oft repeateth in the papers which you gave me; and which he oft expressed, viz. that true religion consisteth in great, plain, necessary things; the life of faith and hope, the love of God and man, an humble self-denying mind, with mortification of worldly affection, carnal lust, &c. And that the calamity of the Church, and withering of religion, hath come from proud and busy men's additions; that cannot give peace to themselves and others, by living, in love and quietness, on this christian simplicity of faith and practice, but vex and turmoil the Church with these needless and hurtful superfluities; some, by their decisions of words, or unnecessary controversies; and some, by their restless reaching after their own worldly interest, and corrupting the Church, on pretence of raising and defending it; some, by their needless ceremonies; and some, by their superstitious and causeless

[43] See Note P P.

scruples. But he was especially angry at them, that would so manage their differences about such things, as to show that they had a greater zeal for their own additions, than for the common saving truths and duties, which we were all agreed in; and that did so manage their several little and selfish causes, as wounded or injured the common cause of the christian, and reformed churches. He had a great distaste of the books called ' A Friendly Debate,' &c. and ' Ecclesiastical Polity;' as, from an evil spirit, injuring Scripture phrase, and tempting the Atheists to contemn all religion, so they might but vent their spleen, and be thought to have the better of their adversaries; and would say, how easy is it to requite such men, and for all parties to expose each other to contempt! Indeed, how many parishes in England afford too plenteous matter of reply, to one that took that for his part; and of tears, to serious observers!

" His main desire was, that as men should not be peevishly quarrelsome against any lawful circumstances, forms, or orders, in religion, much less think themselves godly men, because they can fly from other men's circumstances, or settled lawful orders, as sin; so especially, that no human additions of opinion, order, modes, ceremonies, professions, or promises, should ever be managed, to the hindering of christian love and peace, nor of the preaching of the gospel, nor the wrong of our common cause, or the strengthening of atheism, infidelity, profaneness, or popery; but that christian verity and piety, the love of God and

man, and a good life, and our common peace in
these, might be first resolved on and secured, and
all our additions might be used, but in due subor-
dination to these, and not to any injury of any of
them ; nor sects, parties, or narrow interests be
set up against the common duty, and the public
interest and peace.

" As Mr. Selden was one of those called Eras-
tians (as his book, *de Synedriis*, and others, show),
yet he owned the office properly ministerial; so, most
lawyers that ever I was acquainted with, (taking
the word 'jurisdiction' to signify something more,
than the mere doctoral, priestly power, and power
over their own sacramental communion, in the
Church which they guide,) do use to say, that it is
primarily in the magistrate; as, no doubt, all power
of corporal coercion, by mulcts and penalties, is.
And as to the accidentals to the proper power of
priesthood, or the keys, they truly say, with Dr.
Stillingfleet, that God hath settled no one form.

" Indeed, the Lord Chief Justice thought, that
the power of the word and sacraments, in the
ministerial office, was of God's institution ; and
that they were the proper judges, appointed by
Christ, to whom they themselves should apply
sacraments, and to whom they should deny them.
But, that the power of chancellors' courts, and
many modal additions, which are not of the essence
of the priestly office, floweth from the king, and
may be fitted to the state of the kingdom. Which
is true, if it be limited by God's laws, and exercised in things only allowed them to deal in, and

contradict not the orders and powers, settled on by Christ and his apostles.

" On this account, he thought well of the form of government in the Church of England; lamenting the miscarriages of many persons, and the want of parochial reformation; but he was greatly for uniting in love and peace, upon so much as is necessary to salvation, with all good, sober, peaceable men.

" And he was much against corrupting the Christian religion (whose simplicity and purity he justly took to be much of its excellency), by men's busy additions; by wit, policy, ambition; or any thing else, which sophisticateth it, and maketh it another thing, and causeth the lamentable contentions of the world."[43]

Whatever opinion may prevail as to the indulgence of metaphysical propensities, after the manner of Hale and Baxter, or whatever surprise may be excited by *some* parts of the foregoing narrative, it is not easy to peruse it as a whole, without admiring each of the distinguished persons to whom it refers. The attention must be confined, however, to Hale, and his title to it is vastly increased by the circumstance, that, with what we have thus seen and heard in *private*, every thing that was *public* corresponded;—the same conscientiousness; the same spirit of cautious vigilance; the same balancing of opinions; the same freedom from intermeddling with others;

[43] Hale's Works, vol. i. pp. 95, &c.

K

and the same absence of every species of slander.[44]

Fond as Hale was of retirement; and free, as he also was, from the vices of conversation, he had a true relish for social enjoyments. He *loved*, particularly for an hour or two at night, to be visited by some of his friends. His deportment was marked by the loveliest simplicity, and the entire absence of what was rude, or harsh. None were uneasy in his presence, and if he chanced to be impertinently addressed in matters of justice, the intrusion was only repelled by a slight elevation of his voice. Private discourse of public affairs he avoided, and, although when at the Bar, he was free in solving the doubts of young and inquiring lawyers, he grew, in that respect, after his elevation to the Bench, more reserved. It was not possible to obtain his opinion until he was obliged to declare it in open court, and *there* it was delivered with caution. We have before seen how the feeling was inspired by a sense of liability to mistake; and how his vigilance against error, consequent upon that perception, was exercised; both have been illustrated in his rules for judicial conduct; and as an instance of the full exemplification, whether of scrupulosity, or a nicely adjusted love of rectitude, the legal reader may be referred to the case of Goff *v.* Lloyd. Lord Hale there, upon a question, whether a smith's forge was within the Acts relating to

[44] See Note QQ.

hearth-money, observed, that it was a matter of fact into which he had not inquired; and that he should be loath to deliver an opinion without much inquiry.[45]

In cases of importance, such was his studied silence, in court, as to render it impossible to guess at the inclination of his mind; he acted so, because he thought it the duty of every individual with whom he was associated, to pronounce judgment strictly according to his own conscience, and convictions. Sometimes, and it shows the deference paid to his opinion, the other judges, after expressing their sentiments with entire unanimity, felt so strongly the reasons he assigned in favour of a different decision, as, actually, to retract what had been said, and concur with him.

The *prudence* he thus practised was discernible (and it was the case with Pomponius Atticus, [46] whom he so much admired,) in every thing he did; a feature in his character well evinced by a letter yet in existence,[47] addressed to him by " the Lord Herbert."

Observing that mankind, notwithstanding prudence is the " grand point of philosophy," generally fail in it; he remarked, that if they would but pause in actions or speeches of moment, so long as might serve to repeat the Creed, or Lord's

[45] Ventris's Reports, p. 192, part 1.

[46] See Hale's Translation of the Life of Atticus; Works, vol. i. p. 417.

[47] Orig. MS. at Cottles.

Prayer, many follies and mischiefs would be avoided.[48]

How he extended the principle to another class of duties, may be advantageously collected from the observations with which he concluded the tract on "Contentation:" observations which deserve, especially by new converts to Christianity, frequent perusal; as do those on the same subject,[49] in the twelfth division of the account of "the Good Steward."

The passages referred to may be safely regarded as a register of his Lordship's own doings; and they include, at least, *one* preventive of evil,—the making of a will—which, because connected with the relinquishment of "things temporal," is often shrunk from; postponed, frequently, to a season of extreme hurry, and perturbation. He not only arranged his earthly concerns before he was frightened to do so, but he took pains to expose the "vain foolish conceit" of those, who treat such a consideration of their "latter end" as "ominous," and a "presage of death."[50]

In his apprehension, the work just mentioned was part of that righteousness which, at all events, pertains to a husband, and a father.

There was about his whole conduct a marked, visible, and comprehensive *fidelity;* a respect to the confidence reposed in him, whether specific

[48] Works, vol. ii. p. 27, "On Wisdom and the Fear of God."
[49] See Note RR.
[50] Works, vol. ii. p. 5. "Of the Consideration of our Latter End."

or implied, which amounted to an identifying of the interests of others with his own.　A spirit of litigation, therefore, he opposed; recommending, when a case appeared doubtful or weak, an amicable adjustment rather than a suit.　To such an extent did his virtuous integrity in such cases go, as that, for a time, if the matter so much as *seemed* unjust,[51] he declined further interference. Ultimately, he became less scrupulous about appearances; for he found, in unison with the experience of all lawyers, how much depends upon *ex parte* statements, and how easily, and not uncommonly, the truth suffers from the narrator's perverseness, ignorance, or stupidity.

Of him, as of his patron, the attorney-general Noy, it may be said, that he never pleaded a cause in which his tongue was *opposed* to the dictates of his conscience;[52] he associated dishonour with saying or doing for hire, otherwise than as he thought;[53] and ascribed a contrary habit to that "love of money," which is condemned alike by Scripture, and reason.　But the reader will do well to refer to his own remarks in the "Good Steward," upon the "gift of elocution:" his practice, and the considerations which influenced it, are there fully described.

In pleading, Sir Matthew, as a matter of course, disliked, and consequently avoided, the mis-reciting

[51] See Note SS.
[52] The Life of Sir W. Noy, prefixed to his " Grounds and Maxims of the Laws of England," by W. M. Bythewood, Esq. 1821, p. ix.
[53] See Note TT.

of evidence, the making of false quotations, and such confident assertions as were calculated to mislead. Nor was he more favourable to inordinate sallies of wit and eloquence, than to some other forensic artifices;[54] he contended, that if the judge or jury had a right understanding it signified nothing; it was a waste of time, and a loss of words; and that, if the parties addressed were easily wrought upon, the course pursued, by bribing the fancy and biassing the affections, was only a more decent way of corrupting them. He marvelled, and attributed it to affectation, that the French lawyers, who enjoyed the privileges of a monarchy, should, in their pleadings, imitate the Roman orators, whose style was occasioned by the popular nature of their government; by the consequent factions of the city; and a special training in the schools of the Rhetors, adapted to such a state of affairs. That the orations of Cicero were contaminated by the corrupt fountain alluded to, can hardly be questioned; and the attempt to make them acceptable to the auditory, rather than satisfactory to himself, has rendered them less cogent, and less beautiful than his other writings. They are more to be regarded as essays of wit and sophistry, than as *pleadings*, at all calculated to succeed with such a judge as Hale.

In avoidance of what was thus looked upon by him as an evil, he argued direct to the point, in a calm, dispassionate, and, probably, low tone of

[54] A remarkable, and very disgraceful manœuvre, may be seen in Lord North's Life, vol. i. p. 89.

voice; which led an old, and valuable reporter occasionally to complain, that " he could not hear Hales[55] well."[56]  This latter habit was, obviously, a defect; nor will it escape notice, that had that, and some other parts of his practice been imitated; or had all his views as to the duties of an advocate, been universally cherished, our country had lost those superlative specimens of oratory which have made the English bar renowned.

It ought to be mentioned, that if Sir Matthew undervalued the rhetoric of the Romans, he much liked their custom of having, as jurisconsults, men of the highest quality, trained to a fitness for the chief employments of the state: the persons so elected were, in truth, the masters of the law; they gave their opinions, when consulted, freely, judging it below them to accept even a gratuity; and their resolutions were of such weight as to make one classis of those materials, out of which the Digests were compiled.  The Orators, or Causidici, who pleaded causes, were well nigh unacquainted with the law, and, accordingly, they aimed principally, if not exclusively, at the affections, either of the prætors, the people, or the senate.  The ignorance of Sulpicius, notwithstanding his great eminence, and the effect upon him of a well administered rebuke, have been made familiar by the elegant narrative of the Honourable Mr.

[55] See Note UU.
[56] Styles.  More v. Earl Rivers, p. 222; and Wats v. Dix, p. 204.

Justice Blackstone, in his Commentaries.[57] Suffice it, therefore, to add, that Lord Hale thought it might become the greatness of an English prince to encourage a class, similar to that which has been described; and had it devolved upon him to select one individual as a specimen of the nearest approach to the jurisconsults of ancient Rome, the choice would, in all probability, have fallen upon his friend, Selden.

Before his elevation it happened to Lord Hale, as to most upright and industrious lawyers, that differences were referred to his judgment: when this was the case, his services were freely rendered: he would not accept a reward, even when offered it by both parties. In those particular instances he considered himself a judge, and a judge, he maintained, ought not to take money. The loss of his time being urged as a reason why he should act differently, he asked — Whether he could employ his time better than in making people friends? Must no time be allowed me, said he, in which to do good?

Towards the needy, like his excellent contemporary, Sir Thomas Crew,[58] he was most pitiful and compassionate.

Esteeming the practice of God's ancient people

[57] Vol. i. Introduction, s. 1.

[58] See the Bride's longing for her Bridegroom's coming; a Sermon preached at the funeral of the right worshipful Sir Thomas Crew, Knight, Serjeant at Law to his Majesty, by Richard Sibbs, p. 124. 24mo. 1638.

not merely a sufficient warrant, but instruction also,[59] (an opinion held by many other Christians) he appropriated to the poor, the tenth part of his increase.[60] He took pains to be informed of proper objects for his bounty, but when they were ascertained, or when he discharged necessitous prisoners, (to which object many of his perquisites of office were applied,) he concealed from them their benefactor. On his promotion to the Chief Justiceship of the King's Bench, he stipulated for the marshal's accustomed new year's gift to be presented in money instead of plate, that *it* might be so disposed of : and he would not have accepted the donation at all, had not the other judges urged it as a thing pertaining to his appointment, and his refusal as a prejudice to his successors.

He invited his poorest neighbours to dinner, making them, as did Bishop Bedell,[61] sit at his own table; and to those whom sickness prevented attending, he sent a supply. Nor was this kindness restricted to his own parish ; it embraced, as occasion required, the surrounding districts. The poor, as such, were *considered;* and, ever remembering that they were of the same nature with himself, and reduced to no other necessities than those to which he was exposed, they were treated with the utmost familiarity, and tenderness. Such common beggars as could work, he paid liberally to gather stones, and then used his own carts to

[59] Works, vol. ii. p. 272. " The Good Steward."
[60] See Note XX.
[61] Life of Bedell by Burnet, p. 224. 8vo. 1685.

carry them for reparation of the highways. His " Discourse touching provision for the poor," is well known. It unfolds his many excellent qualities, and represents "populousness" as a blessing.

Some complained of his alms to street beggars, alleging that he thereby encouraged idleness, and that most of those he so assisted were cheats. He admitted it might be so; nay, that he believed most of them *were* such; but he contended, that some among them were great objects of charity; and said, that he had rather give relief to twenty who might, perhaps, be rogues,[62] than that one of the other sort should perish, for want of the small assistance he bestowed.

He was fond of architecture, and his love to it was increased by the employment it created for the poor. His judgment in it as a science was good; in the indulgence of his taste, however, he avoided vanity and pomp, and connected utility with every contrivance, and every change.

When the Duke of Beaufort was improving his mansion at Badminton, Lord Hale, at that time his neighbour, paid him a visit; and noticing his Grace's plans, craved leave to suggest one which he thought would be serviceable:—to have no more than one door to the house, and the window of the study most open upon that.[63] How impracticable soever such advice may appear, it was founded

[62] See Note YY. "It is better to relieve twenty drones than let one bee perish."—*Sir Matthew Hale*, Quarterly Review, vol. xix. p. 11 [63] Life of Lord Guilford, vol. i. p. 276.

upon a conviction that a regard to economical arrangements, instead of being incompatible with an exalted station, is necessary to the security and permanence, of even splendid fortunes.

The *pity* of this good man reached to his beasts. When his horses became aged and infirm, instead of selling them, they were, in the spirit of Virgil's advice, turned loose upon his grounds; seldom used, and then at easy work, such as going to market, and the like. His dogs, also, were treated with similar care. Information having reached him that his shepherd was about to kill, or lose a dog of his own, because blind, he sent for the animal, and, while life lasted, had it fed. Never was his anger seen to glow so hot, as towards one of his servants, who had negligently starved a bird to death, for want of food.

Although he could not say that hunting was, in itself, an unlawful exercise, yet he observed, that he could never approve of "pursuing the harmless hare for no other end than sport;"[64] and, that after he reached years of discretion, he never joined in it.

The same temper marked the whole of his *judicial* character, and it was regulated by the wisest discretion; the strictest impartiality; the most intrepid firmness;[65] by an unceasing regard to

[64] Letter of Advice, pp. 137, 138.
[65] Baxter says, that when blamed for doing that which he supposed was justice, he often offered to the Lord Chancellor to resign his place. Reliq. Baxter, part 3, p. 47.

God, the Supreme Judge. He has, approvingly, noticed that recognition of the " all-seeing eye," which some of the heathen intended, by fixing, in the place of judicature, an empty chair.[66]

North bore a noble testimony, without, perhaps, intending it, when, alluding to a cause heard in the King's Bench, he says,—" It was tried, I think, twice, but I am sure once, before the Lord Chief Justice Hales, who was most propitious to a poor man's cause; and before him, *if any leaning were*, it was of his favour to that side that most seemed to be oppressed."[67]

But it is truly lamentable, that when it suited his purpose to revile, the same writer should have so represented this propensity to kindness, as seriously to affect his Lordship's integrity. He affirms, with an air of unhallowed exultation, that Hale *had* a bias for *and* against characters, and denominations; and how he was once caught. " A courtier," is the statement, " who had a cause to be tried before him, got one to go to him as from the king, to speak for favour to his adversary, and so carried his point; for the Chief Justice could not think any person to be in the right, that came so unduly recommended."[68]

The foregoing passage would have been omitted as too slanderous for introduction, had not Sir Walter Scott used it, without comment, as a note to Dryden's Essay on Satire, where Charles II. is

[66] Works, vol. ii. pp. 22, 23. "Of Wisdom, and the Fear of God."
[67] Examen. p. 530. Life of Guilford, vol. i. p. 139.
[68] Life of Guilford, vol. i. pp. 119, 120.

made to reflect upon Hale, though "doubtless an uncorrupt and upright man," as a favourer of the cause of a poor person—*right, or wrong.*[69]

How far the encomium and illustration agree, the reader will decide.

Lord Hale rendered his high office strictly subservient to the interests of virtue; and, disregarding alike station or consequences, publicly bore his testimony against evil, and evil doers. He checked a horse-race wager, by threatening to allow the defendant, the loser, to put off the cause from time to time—by perpetual imparlances.[70]

The immoralities of Sir William Scroggs, afterwards Chief Justice of the King's Bench, excited in him the strongest detestation;[71] and when arrested for debt, by a King's Bench warrant, he refused him the privilege he claimed as a serjeant: a circumstance which is said to have made a great talk at the time.[72] Nor was Sir Matthew less observant of, or less severe upon, the intemperance and odious conduct of another subsequent Chief Justice—the eccentric and witty, but notoriously vulgar, Sir Edmund Saunders.[73]

Those who argued before him he confined to the point at issue; by which course much time was saved, and the main difficulties of a case were better

---

[69] Dryden's Works, by Scott, vol. xiii. p. 67.
[70] See the case of Sir Brazill Firebrass *v.* Brett. 1 Vern. p. 489, and 2 Vern. p. 70.
[71] Life of Guilford, vol. i. p. 314.
[72] Woolrych's Memoirs of Judge Jeffreys, p. 52.
[73] Life of Guilford, vol. ii. p. 43.

cleared, and stated. The inequality in the ability and learning of the advocates he supplied : and he would not permit the use of apparently legitimate argument to prevail beyond proper limits. On its being insisted by the counsel employed for a Quaker, who was sued for debts contracted by his wife, *dum sold*, that the marriage, not having been solemnized according to the rites of the Church of England, was *no* marriage, Hale at once started. He saw the consequences to be the bastardizing of the children of all Quakers; and regarding marriage, and succession, as a right of nature, from which none, how mistaken soever in points of revealed religion, ought to be barred—he prevented so much as the partial determination of the question, by directing a special verdict. Roger North, in the plenitude of his ill-will, selected the case in proof of Hale's "fondness and partiality."[74] But in spite of that " unjust reporter,"[75] not only was his Lordship obviously governed by conscientiousness and impartiality,[76] but, likewise, by the law of Christ ;[77] and, *therefore*, because he would have thought it a hardship, not without cruelty, if, among Papists, marriages were annulled, which had not been made with all the ceremonies of the Roman ritual ; so applying this to the case of sectaries, he thought marriages solemnized according

[74] Life by North, vol. i. pp. 126—134.
[75] Hale on the Jurisdiction of the Lords. Pref. by Hargrave, p. lxxx. *post.*
[76] See Note ZZ.
[77] Matt. vii. 12.

to their several persuasions ought to have effect in law.[78]

Nor is it unworthy of observation, little as it would have suited Roger North to have noticed it, that Hale's conduct upon the occasion just instanced, appears the more creditable, in proportion as his disapproval of the " affected superadditions," and " unwarrantable singularities"[79] of the Quakers, is taken into account.

When trying prisoners his *vigilance* was taxed to the utmost, in order that no circumstance might be neglected which could, in any way, elucidate the facts. His whole conduct displayed a disinterested regard to truth, and was marked by the most instructive gravity, and compassion ; not, however, that *false* compassion (as the Honourable Daines Barrington has accurately noticed) which some judges have thought it right to manifest ; he never discovered an anxiety to find out such niceties as would enable criminals improperly to escape:[80] a temptation, and source of perplexity, too, in a great measure now, happily, removed by law.

His whole demeanour towards witnesses was that of patience, and gentleness. They were borne with, though tedious ; and protected against those rude buffetings which, commonly, instead of . eliciting truth, suspend the memory, produce confusion, and pervert justice. He " summed up " with

---

[78] See Note A A A.
[79] Works, vol. i. p. 301. " A Discourse of Religion."
[80] Observations on the more Ancient Statutes, p. 248, 4to. 1775. 4th ed.

studied fairness; and when it devolved upon him to pass sentence of death, such was his attention to decency, both of speech and manner; such his entire freedom from affectation; and such the instructions he imparted, as to occasion many to declare, they heard few such sermons. Roger North admits, that he " became the cushion exceedingly well: his manner of hearing was patient, his directions pertinent, his discourses copious, and although he hesitated often, fluent. His stop, for a word, by the produce, always paid for the delay; and on some occasions, he would utter sentences heroic."[81]

Deeply as he was impressed with the solemn responsibility attached to that part of his office which has been just alluded to, he was proof against tenderness, when the gratification of that feeling would amount to " merciful injustice. " It was, as we have seen, one of the things he determined to have continually in remembrance, that in business " capital," although his nature prompted him to pity, he should consider, also, that there is a pity due to the country.[82]

Being once pressed for a recommendation to the royal favour, he answered—that he could not think *they* deserved a pardon, whom he had adjudged to die ; and all he could be prevailed upon to do, was to make a statement of the circumstances, leaving the result entirely with the king.

[81] Life of Lord Guilford, vol. i. p. 120.
[82] Ante, p. 86 ; and see Note B B B.

Stern as is the appearance of such immovable decision ; and much as, at first sight, there may seem in it of the *want* of humility ; that excellent virtue will well consist with it ; there may even be "tender yearnings," all the while, towards the guilty. In one of his tracts he has carefully distinguished upon this matter ; and disclosed so fully the maxims upon which he acted,[83] as to justify, both Dr. Parr's description of him, as " wise, *humane*, and pious," and the christian-like assumption of the same distinguished scholar, that he must often have had occasion to exclaim, as Boerhaave was said to do, when a criminal was condemned, " May not this man be better than I ? If otherwise, the praise is due not to me, but the grace of God."[84]

Another instance of his Lordship's firmness, and self-control, may be noticed in the case of one whom he had displaced for ill behaviour. The individual urged him to sign a certificate for his restoration, or else to provide him with another place ; he was told that his fault was such that it could not be done. The other pressed the matter vehemently, and, on his knees, entreated him with tears ; perceiving *this* effort unavailing, he said he should be utterly ruined if it were denied, and that he should curse him for it every day. When this threat was found ineffectual, under the full excitement of passion and despair, he poured forth words of reproach. The judge continued unmoved,

[83] Works, vol. ii. pp. 132, 133. "Of Humility."
[84] Dr. Parr's Works, vol. iv. pp. 161, 171.

and merely replied, that he could very well bear all that, but he could not set his hand to the certificate. He, however, bestowed upon him something considerable because of his poverty, and sent him away.

We have before seen the care Lord Hale, knowing its blinding and perverting influence, took not to receive a gift; but that was not all: after he had a seat upon the bench, his anxiety to prevent even *suspicion* attaching to his conduct was so great, that he insisted upon paying *more* for every purchase than the price required, or than the article bought was worth. On his attention being drawn to the subject, and his ill bargains noticed, he maintained that it became judges to act *so,* as that none with whom they dealt might imagine themselves, because of such transactions, entitled to favour; so as that the world might *see,* that none were too well used on some secret account.

Mr. H. Roscoe,[85] noticing this particularity, has discovered a strong disposition to sneer; but how closely soever such conscientiousness may border in some men's judgment, either upon fastidious scrupulosity, or mistake, the display of it is not without a charm; especially when it is borne in mind, for how long a period prior to the example thus set, the very grossest venality had, occasionally, disgraced the coif; a circumstance which should lead us, instead of attributing the habit in question to any thing fantastical, to

[85] Lives of Eminent British Lawyers, pp. 75, 76.

admire the elevated virtue manifested by it, and to ascribe it to those sacred motives by which Sir Matthew was actuated. Such, indeed, *was* the effect upon the public mind; he seems to have won the love and reverence of all; and from almost every quarter[86] praise was awarded to him. Nor has his laurel withered; a circumstance delightfully opposed to the strange sentiment, that " strict rectitude of conduct is generally an impediment to lasting fame,"—a sentiment, nevertheless, with which, in spite of the common opinion of mankind to the contrary, to say nothing of the most distinguished moralists, and holy Scripture also, the writer of Sir Julius Cæsar's Life commences that deeply interesting, and instructive record.[87]

Lord Hale sat as a judge in all the courts of law, and in two of them as chief. Wherever he presided, most business of consequence followed him, and few persons were content with any judgment which he had not given, or at least participated in. His opinion being once known, it rarely happened that an attempt was made to controvert it; indeed, when it was otherwise, the party being looked upon as contentious, encountered great disadvantage.

Men did not reverence his judgment in the courts of law only; his authority was equally great in those of *equity;* and oftentimes was he called upon to assist, and advise the Great Seal.[88] Viewing equity

[86] See Note C C C.
[87] Life of Sir Julius Cæsar, 4to. 1827, p. 10.
[88] See Note D D D.

as part of the common law, and one of its grounds,
he endeavoured to reduce it to fixed rules and
principles ; not merely to aid the study of it as a
science, but to prevent the surmise that in its administration it involved any thing arbitrary, or
uncertain.     He felt that it concerned *him*, as
he notices it did Henry IV., " to be just to the
people ;"[89] which led Sir James Mackintosh to observe, that while the opinions of Hale were often
those of a tory philosopher, his knowledge made
him frequently a whig lawyer.[90]     Mr. Hallam
has noticed,[91] that Hale was Chief Baron of the
Exchequer at the time the practice of fining
jurors for giving a verdict contrary to the direction
of the court, was effectually opposed : and Dr.
Parr, enumerating the distinguished persons from
whom his own politics were chiefly drawn, mentions *Hale* as well as Sidney, Selden, and Locke.[92]

But nothing was more admirable than his
*patience*.     Though in disposition quick, and sensitive, yet he had so subdued the propensity, as
never, in matters of importance, to arrive at a
sudden conclusion.     *Festina lente*,[93] was his beloved motto, and he engraved it upon the head of
his staff.     He observed, sometimes, that many men
of talent and discernment, commit great errors, for

[89] Collection of Tracts by Hargrave, p. 184.     Hale on the Customs, chap. xi.
[90] History of England, vol. i. p. 352.
[91] Constitutional History of England, vol. ii. pp. 348, 849, 4to
1827.
[92] Works, vol. iii. p. 476.
[93] See Note E E E.

want of taking time to *think*; indulging a heated imagination, they suffer themselves to be governed by mere impulses; whereas, others more calm and slow, and who, it may be, in common estimation, are accounted dull, search for, and discover truth, with far greater certainty.

He never, therefore, aimed at that "dispatch" which Lord Bacon reprobated; he bore with the meanest, and gave to every man full scope.[94] Lest, when addressing a jury, any thing material should, through inadvertence or forgetfulness, escape him, he constantly required the Bar, without regard to the temporary delay, to interrupt, and remind him of it.

The whole demeanour of Lord Hale was grave and dignified, and calculated to inspire respect. He was, at the same time, far from any thing gloomy, or repulsive; the very solemnity of his magisterial character was relieved, by occasional effusions of innocent humour. His pleasure in rising merit he manifested by the most encouraging acknowledgments; by those good-natured graces, and delicate compliments which, while they so eminently adorn talent, excite laudable ambition, and bind the recipient, in ties of deep, and grateful obligation.

He discerned at an early period the professional skill of Mr. (afterwards Lord Keeper) North, and he seized an opportunity, when the court was crowded, to declare it. Observing Mr. North with difficulty pushing in, he desired that way might be

[94] See Note F F F.

made for " the little gentleman ;" adding, " he will soon make way for himself."[94]

In proof of the delight it afforded him to *commend* what he approved, whether in books or men, and alike irrespective of place, station, and time, let a few instances be considered. Plato he quotes largely, as a " great master :"[95] his scholar, Aristotle, he preferred.[97] He designates both of them " masters of learning and reason ;"[96] but upon the latter, he *heaps* epithets of commendation. He styles him " the great master in natural philosophy ;"[99] " the great master of reason ;"[100] and " the great priest of nature."[1] Suarez he represents, as " acute and judicious."[2] The folio of Censorinus de Die Natali he mentions as a golden book.[3] Galen de Usu Partium, he refers to as a divine work[4]. Lord Bacon he calls the " great Verulam ;"[5] the great inquisitor into nature.[6] Noticing the tract, de Naturæ Substantia Energetica of Doctor Glisson, he mentions him as " our learned countryman ;"[7] nor does the treatise of Bodies, by Sir K. Digby, meet with less favour ;[8] and in one of his allusions to Helmont, he says, " I shall not be ashamed to own him for my instructor, because

[94] Life of North, vol. i. p. 84.
[96] Prim. Orig. p. 219.     [97] Ib. p. 221.     [96] Ib. p. 221.
[99] Observations and Remarks, p. 5. See also his Letter of Advice, p. 107.
[100] Preface to Rolle's Abridgment.
[1] Observations and Remarks, p. 104.
[2] Prim. Orig. p. 81.     [3] Ib. p. 99.     [4] Ib. p. 49.
[5] Observations and Remarks, p. 44.
[6] Ib. p. 105.     [7] Ib. p. 130.     [8] Ib. pp. 60, 130.

he speaks with great evidence of reason."[9]   While
engaged in controversy with Dr. Henry More, he
mentions him as the " learned remarker," and the
" learned author ;" and, after prominently exhibiting a cavil made by him against one of his own
positions, he says, with his accustomed mildness,
" What I have written in my observations upon
Remark 17, &c. I think sufficiently discovers the
impotence of this objection ;"[10] a method of treating that celebrated opponent the more worthy of
notice, because so complete a refutation of Roger
North's malicious charge,—that Sir Matthew was
habituated not to bear contradiction, and that he
had no value for any one who did not subscribe to
him.[11]

Such, indeed, was his *moderation* and catholic
charity, whatever the condition of others, or how
greatly soever their sentiments differed from his
own, that when that " wise and religious " person,
John Bunyan, (so he is called by Dr. Southey),
was harassed for nonconformity ;[12] though unable
to give the relief he evidently designed to do, he
communicated, in open court, such counsel, and
treated the young and afflicted wife of the impri-
soned saint, with such gentleness, and sympathy, and condescension, as to reflect upon him
everlasting honour.[13]

In reference to the validity of an indictment

---

[9] Observations and Remarks, p. 8.        [10] Ib. p. 256.
[11] Life of Lord Guilford, vol. i. p. 118.
[12] See Note G G G.
[13] See Ivimey's Life of Bunyan, pp. 199—245.

against a celebrated Quaker, he showed the same lovely spirit; for when, on the proceedings being quashed, some enemies of the accused moved the judges, with strong insinuations, that the oaths might be tendered; instead of joining in the general hue and cry, he only remarked, that he had heard some such reports of George Fox, but he had also heard more good reports of him.[14]

The deliverance from custody under a defective warrant of the Rev. Robert Seddon (another seceder from the Established Church) is ascribed in part to the "justice of worthy Judge Hale."[15]

With these things in view, the clerical author of the Pleas for the Nonconformists, already quoted, in one of his Prefaces,[16] thus addressed "all entrusted with the administration of justice, and conservation of the peace, by what title soever they were honoured:"—"Your place and office requireth wisdom. And I may be bold to say, that the renowned Sir Matthew Hale was as wise, as strict, as just, as able a lawyer as the ablest of you all: it is no disparagement to the learnedst and gravest of you, to take him for an example, whose *moderation* towards Dissenters is a part of his noble character."

*Nobleness* was, truly, a prominent feature in his lordship's moral physiognomy. So completely was

[14] Gough's History of the Quakers, vol. ii. pp. 377—391; Neal, pp. 5, 255.

[15] A Breviate of the Life of Margaret, the Daughter of Francis Charlton, of Apley, in Shropshire, Esq., and Wife of Richard Baxter, p. 57, 4to. 1681.

[16] The Second Plea. 4to. 1682. 2d edition.

he elevated above every thing *like* bigotry, and narrow-mindedness, as to spurn away from him what was contrary to the " charity which Christ left, not only as his command, but as a kind of discriminating property of true believers."[17]

He, in short, regarded the religion that is genuine, as more than notion, or profession, or form : as consisting, in such great and plain things as are *necessary* ;[18] and wherever he saw *them* in operation, there he recognized " the secret and invisible church" of the most high God ; *the* church, constituted of *all*, who " by faith in Christ ; and by the participation and energy of the Spirit of Christ, are united to *him*."[19]

It is no wonder, therefore, that the estimate he formed of his fellow-men, and his conduct towards them, had little to do with a formal consent in opinions or ceremonies ;[20] or that he considered [21] those persons, whatever their rank, or party, or pretences, who strove for " collaterals, " rather than the " great and weighty" truths, in which Christians *agree*, as actually *injurious ;* as obstacles to the success of the gospel ; and, by " widening" instead of healing, " the wounds of religious discord," as the upholders of the " devices of vain-glorious, covetous men ;"[22] not to say of profaneness, and infidelity.

[17] Hale, Orig. MS.
[18] See *ante*, pp. 190, 191 ; and Note HHH.
[19] Hale, Orig. MS.
[20] See Note III.
[21] See *ante*, pp. 190, 191.
[22] See Note KKK.

L

To this class he assigned Dr. Patrick's[23] "Friendly Debate," and the "Ecclesiastical Polity" of the notorious Bishop Parker;[24] "Martin Mar Prelate," and White's "Centuries."[25] He regarded them, and all books of the same description, as *contrary* to "that spirit which Christ brought with him into the world;" as just such a manifestation of fierce ambition, and unconcern about consequences, as proved, that if the pride, or spleen of the writers could be gratified, the end really designed was answered.

Many appropriate remarks upon topics like those alluded to, enrich his unpublished manuscripts, as well as the Discourse upon Religion.[26] The latter, in this aspect of it, to mention no other, may, indeed, be pronounced one of the most valuable homilies in English theology. While setting forth (probably without design) his own character and principles, he *there*, after enumerating some of the "subtleties" of great scholars, and divines, shews, how the "contests" he had in view, instead of filling men's hearts with the intended effects of Christianity, have "blown up their fancies with speculations." He strips off the thin disguises worn by zealots; and unceremoniously ascribing their "marvellous fervour," to selfish designs,—to a perception, oftentimes,

[23] Bishop Patrick lived long enough to see his error, and had the candour publicly to acknowledge it. See his Life in the Biog. Brit. &c. &c.

[24] See *ante*, p. 191 ; and see Note LLL.

[25] Hale's Works, vol. i. p. 325. "A Discourse of Religion," pt. 3.

[26] See Note MMM.

of the road to preferment, or the "favours of great persons," lying that way,—explodes their worldly views, their specious appearances, and their insidious arts. The *causes*, in any party, of "severity," and "contempt," and "censoriousness," and "studied estrangings," upon points, on which upright and well-intentioned men may differ, are detected with amusing shrewdness; and dispassionately, but powerfully, exposed; while, as one "tender for the honour of God," and desirous of composing the dissensions unhappily subsisting among Christians, he excites to *mutual* compassion, forbearance, moderation, and love. The whole being free from a spirit of partizanship, is singularly adapted for edification. In that portion of the first part, wherein is discussed the way in which religion "teacheth, and tutors the soul;" and the last paragraph of the second, in which he shows that it is *another* thing from "ceremonies" —"at the best its dressing and trimmings,"—he uses a style of eloquence scarcely less impassioned, or less persuasive, than that of Tully himself.

Nothing can be plainer, than that attainments, such as those described, must have been the prize of no common efforts; of an unceasing "discipline, both to religion and reason:"[27] a discipline involving prayer; constant observation of himself; absolute dependence upon divine grace; the most solemn conviction of the nearness, and reality of eternal things; the self-denial inculcated in the

---

[27] Works, vol. ii. p. 115.

" Contemplations ;"[28] and a steady regard to the promised crown. And this, habitually, and very eminently was the case.

Lord Hale represented himself as naturally passionate, but the propensity appeared only in the occasional rising of his colour ; his nearest observers felt justified in affirming, that they never saw him, even amidst trials the least easily borne, disordered with anger. His exemplary practice, renders the testimony he has borne on the subject of meekness, doubly striking. "When," he writes, " I first read the saying of our Saviour, ' Blessed are the meek, for they shall inherit the earth,' I looked upon it as a mere paradox, if applied to the comforts of this life ; and thought it must be merely, and only, intended of that ' new heaven and new earth, wherein dwelleth righteousness.' But upon deeper consideration, I found it in a great measure true, also, of the former."[29] So fully was he impressed with the importance of the duty thus commended, as, in the " Letter of Advice," to propose *rules* for duly regulating the passions. One of them is to learn by heart, and privately repeat, the four passages of scripture there mentioned.[30]

Injuries he had learned, he thanked God, to forget. Burnet, narrating a case in which he had overlooked a heinous offence, and cordially shown the offender professional kindness, adds, " he had

---

[28] Works, vol. ii. p. 550, &c. It was a favourite saying with him that *Perimus licitis*,—we perish by [the abuse of] things allowable. See *ante*, p. 8.

[29] Works, vol. ii. p. 155. " On Humility."

[30] Prov. xiv. 29 ; xvi. 32 ; Matt. v. 44 ; and Rom. xii. 19.

the soul of a gentleman, for he refused the money offered for his services."

He exemplified, in *afflictions*, of whatever kind, the same subdued temper, and the devoutest acquiescence, also, in the Divine will. The tenderness of his spirit made him keenly alive to trouble; but such was his regard to the wisdom, and providence of God, that he considered so much as expostulation, "rebellion."[31] A friend, offering condolence upon the loss of one of his sons, under circumstances peculiarly grievous,[32] he satisfied himself with remarking, that "those were the effects of living long; that such must *look* to see many sad, and unacceptable things;" and then proceeded, with his ordinary freedom, to other discourse.

"I will look upon my children," is his language, after a bereavement in his family, "and all other outward comforts, as lent me by the Lord. I will not set my heart upon them: but, whenever the God of the spirits of all flesh calls for *their* spirits, I will most cheerfully submit to his will; from him I received them, and he is still the Lord of them; and shall he not 'do what he will with his own?' 'The Lord gave, and the Lord hath taken away; blessed be the name of the Lord.' He knows what is fittest for me to have, or want.

[31] Works, vol. i. p. 209. The Second Letter.
[32] Bishop Burnet, in his Preface to the Judge's Life, alludes to some "particular exercises" he had for patience in his domestic concerns; and he designedly drew "a veil over" them; "since, though in these he was a great example, yet it signifies nothing to the world."

I will make *his* will mine; not by a necessary submission to what I cannot help, but by a voluntary resignation of my will to his. Why should not I desire what is best for me; and who knows better what is best for me than he that made me; my most wise, and merciful, and bountiful Lord, and Father? All things, even those that seem most harsh, are managed by his most wise counsel, for the *best*. I will, by his grace, diligently observe the consequents of this affliction, and I doubt not but to find that promise, even in this particular, made good unto me. It may be, he will recompense this loss with some outward blessing more than answerable to it. And if he do *not*, yet I am confident that his grace will so work upon my heart, even by this affliction, that I shall find more comfort and content with my loss, than I had by my enjoyment: so that I shall conclude with David, ' It was good that I was afflicted.' "[33]

With such themes, so well calculated to mitigate, if not to prevent, the excesses of sorrow, his thoughts were perpetually occupied. Trials were, in his estimation, " the school of wisdom : "[34] he considered them as messengers from heaven ;[35] his chief anxiety, therefore, was to "learn the message ; and to improve it to that end for which God, who is most wise and bountiful, sent it ; and thus to be delivered, from the evil of the evil."[36]

[33] Hale, Orig. MS.                    [34] Orig. MS.
[35] Works, vol. i. p. 210. Second Letter, vol. ii. pp. 219, 222. " On Afflictions."
[36] Ib. vol. ii. p. 570. " Meditations upon the Lord's Prayer ;" and also the Letter of Advice, p. 58.

Upon God, his eye, in every occurrence, was fixed; and of his *goodness*, he cherished the most exalted ideas. The deluge itself, he regarded not only as an act of vengeance upon the wicked, but, possibly, as an act of bounty, and benevolence to the constitution of the inferior world.[37] And in the Tractates on afflictions, and true wisdom, he shows, how " right considerations concerning Almighty God, " were brought to bear upon his habits; how they "converted" his civil employments into a kind of *"continual course of religion:*[38] a circumstance deserving especial notice; and one which will call forth admiration, in proportion as the character of the times (an awful picture of which he has drawn in the " Letter of Advice ") is duly contemplated. The floodgates of iniquity, after the " Restoration," were thrown open. An honest follower of the Saviour, though never so sober-minded, became the object of general odium, as well as courtly disdain. Yet—*then* it was that Hale, under the influence of motives generated by Divine revelation, was found faithful: like another Enoch, he " walked with God," and " delighted himself" in him.

Hence, his great wisdom, and the *stability* of all his purposes. Feeling as if surrounded with Deity; acting in reference to the accredited will of the Most High; and his heart being " established with grace;" he was impervious alike, to the fickleness of the " unstable;" the vagaries of deluded

[37] Prim. Orig. p. 188.
[38] Discourse of the knowledge of God and ourselves. Pref. 1688.

"prophets;"[30] and the agitations of rash, and presumptuous speculators. Neither the one nor the other, was able to disturb his composure, or to make the slightest inroad upon his understanding.

In the year 1666, a notion was started that the world would then end; whether it originated with astrologers, or with those who pondered "the number of the Beast," or with men of ill designs to disturb the public peace, is now of little consequence: but it spread among the people. He was at that time Chief Baron, and took the western circuit: while upon the bench, a storm arose, accompanied with thunder and lightning, so exceedingly loud and vivid, as to occasion a whisper that the time predicted was come. Great consternation followed, and the majority of those who were present, regardless of every secular concern, betook themselves to prayer. A gentleman of no common resolution and firmness, confessed, as he related the matter to Bishop Burnet, that the scene made a powerful impression upon himself; but that the judge was not at all affected. In spite of the general confusion, he attended to the ordinary business of the court, so as to make it evident, that if the world really had then ended, it would have given him no considerable disturbance.

That Lord Hale was an enlightened and consistent Protestant, must have been obvious to the most superficial observer; but it may be added, that when, in subversion of the doctrines of human infallibility,[40] he declared, "the Scriptures" to be

"the rule, the *only* rule to attain our chief end;"
a rule by which we must try other men's books
and sermons, yea, "the very Church itself;"[41] he
proclaimed, though in other words, the very sentiment which has rendered Chillingworth immortal.

In his second Letter to his children, as also in
the "Discourse of Religion," besides other parts
of his works, he has given prominence to his preference for the Anglican Establishment. He was
a true son of the Church of England. The legal
reader will probably bear in mind, as closely connected with it, his Lordship's representation (when
pronouncing judgment in an information for blas-
phemous words) of Christianity, as a "parcel of
the laws of England; and that, therefore, to
reproach the christian religion, was to speak in
subversion of the law."[42]

Baxter, who wrote from observation, has told
us[43] his demeanour at church; and when directing
his grandchildren, the judge himself writes as
follows:—"At church, let your carriage be decent
and reverend; sitting at sermon with your hat off;
kneeling upon your knees at prayers; and standing up at the Creed, and Gloria Patri; and at the
reading of any part of the Canonical Scripture.

[41] Works, vol. ii. p. 318.—"Of the chief end of Man:" and at
p. 319, there follow some important deductions from the principle
above-mentioned.

[42] Ventris's Reports, p. 293, part 1. In the King v. Bosworth,
Lord Chief Justice Lee referred to that case, and to a manuscript
which he had seen of Lord Hale's to the same effect. See Strange's
Reports, vol. ii. p. 113. 3d ed. 8vo. 1795.

[43] See *ante*, p. 185: and see also his "Directions for keeping
the Lord's day." Works, vol. i. p. 202.

This hath been my custom for forty years, in all times."[44]

It is in *secret*, however, we must, after all, look for the steady support that flame received which, ascending from "the love of God shed abroad in the heart" of this eminent man, "by the Holy Ghost," shone before others with such brilliance. And it is worthy of observation, how, in the "Letter of Advice" (to say nothing of what is disclosed by the "Contemplations") he not only urges private exercises, in spite of every hindrance; but expresses the distrust he had been accustomed to entertain as to any business, undertaken *before* he had been so employed.

That these employments included the reading of the Scriptures, is a matter of certainty, as well from the counsel[45] he administered, as from his own declaration in "the Good Steward:" after representing *him* as setting apart some portion of his time for prayer, and reading God's word, he is made to say,—"I have constantly, and peremptorily observed" this course, "whatever occasions interposed, or importunity persuaded the contrary."[46]

The Christians of that age, *generally*, abounded in the quiet, unostentatious, but soul-invigorating duties of the closet; in the culture of the heart and of home; in calm and prolonged thought upon

[44] See Letter of Advice, p. 76.
[45] Works, vol. i. p. 238; Fourth Letter; and vol. ii. p. 20. "Of Wisdom and the Fear of God."
[46] Ib. vol. ii. p. 271. See also the Letter of Advice, p. 65.

Divine truth; in that observance of God's hand which is inseparable from acknowledging him in all our ways; and' in the vigorous outgoings of the soul towards him, as the infinitely blessed Jehovah. An example shall be selected from Lord Hale's papers.

" My intensest love to God is my duty. I cannot exceed my proportion: it is my wisdom, for I fix my heart upon that which is more than worthy of my love. It is my happiness: for I am joined to that which is the choicest good. The best of creatures is too narrow for the compass of my love. There is not fulness enough in it to answer my desire; it is too short and temporary. It will die when my soul, and the motions of it, will live, and so again want that upon which to fix. But in my love to GOD, I shall find an overflowing fulness, that will fill up the most capacious, and intensest gaspings, and outgoings of my love: a fulness that will continue to all eternity; a fulness that will satisfy my soul, and yet increase my love. New and higher discoveries will *eternally* be let in unto me, which my soul shall everlastingly *pursue*, and, in pursuing, enjoy with delight and blessedness."[47]

The following passage is not less impressive, whether considered with regard to the Divine faithfulness, or to the directions, and encouragements it furnishes to other Christians. " I can call *my own experience* to witness that, even in

[47] Hale, Orig. MS.

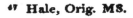

the external actions, occurrences, and incidents of my whole life, I was never disappointed of the best guidance and direction, when in humility, and a sense of my own deficiency, and diffidence of my own ability to direct myself, or to grapple with the difficulties of my life, I have, with humility and sincerity, implored the secret direction and guidance of Divine wisdom and providence. And I dare therein appeal to the vigilant and strict observation of any man's experience, whether he hath not found the same experience in relation to himself, and his own actions and successes; and whether those counsels and purposes which have been taken up, after an humble invocation of the Divine direction, have not been always most successful in the end."[48]

Much of the interest of such paragraphs as the foregoing (and it is the case with most that were written by Lord Hale) arises, from their having been designed solely for his own use; and being incapable, therefore, of any construction foreign to unaffected piety. It is heightened, moreover, by association with a care, bordering upon excess, to elude observation as to every thing connected with his Christianity. It is difficult to say, whether constitutional temperament, or known instances of the "shipwreck of faith and a good conscience," had most power, in producing such a state of mind, and feeling: but it pervaded all his doings. Our

[48] Hale's Works, vol. ii. p. 141. "Of Humility." See also p. 31 of the same volume, "Of Wisdom and the Fear of God;" and his "Discourse on the Knowledge of God and Ourselves," pp. 324—327.

Saviour's directions, with regard to making feasts, he understood, as we have seen, in the most *literal* sense; and some other rules of christian duty were similarly interpreted. It, consequently, is the less surprising that he *hid* all he could, as the Hon. Robert Boyle is said to have done, both his piety and charity.[49] Such was his uncommon humility; such the particular and entire distrust he cherished of himself; and, may it not be added, such his concern for the Divine glory; that he expressed his dread, lest, at any time, he should do some enormous thing, which, if he were looked upon as a very religious man, might cast a reproach upon his profession, and give advantage to blasphemers.[50]

This will account for that reserve upon religious subjects which served to create, for a time, in the mind of the ardent and open-hearted Baxter, " one fear, or suspicion concerning him;"[51] and though " but one," the circumstance, unless attributed to christian love and vigilancy, must appear strange, whether we consider the testimony of Baxter himself elsewhere, or the uniform conduct of the judge. " Those, " — they are Baxter's words, — " that take no men for religious who frequent not private meetings, &c. took him (Lord Hale) for an excellently righteous man; but I that have heard, and read his serious expressions of the concernments of eternity, and seen his love to all good men, and

[49] Sermon for the Hon. Robert Boyle, by Bishop Burnet, p. 34. 4to. 1692.
[50] See Note P P P.          [51] See *ante*, p. 186.

the blamelessness of his life, &c., thought better of *his* piety than my own."[52]

Every thing connected with the history we have examined, evinced a *religious* character; and not a few things gave vastly more proof of it, and involved more genuine principle, than any indulgence in the kind of conversation Baxter referred to,[53] great as the duty of such communications, properly regulated, may, and ought to, appear.

There was, remarkably conspicuous, in Lord Hale, what Hooker designated, with such beauty, "the *behaviour*" of humility; one, in itself, of the most indubitable tokens of piety, and often best expressed by speaking sparingly of God, and divine things.[54]

Besides what has been stated, there was his deportment in a prosperous condition. Not only, unlike many who, in the "warm beams and sunshine," cast off their innocence, as the traveller in the fable, his cloak,[55] did *he* hold fast his integrity; but, he manifested that weanedness from the world, and indifference to its trifling vanities, which must, of necessity, be enumerated among the surest proofs of godliness. The lowliness of his mind, instead of being diminished, seems to have increased with the accumulation of honour; and riches, used by him with the moderation which is divinely enjoined, so far from being trusted in,

[52] Reliq. Baxter, part 3, p. 47.
[53] See *ante*, p. 186.
[54] See Note QQQ.
[55] Works, vol. ii. p. 146.   "On Humility."

gave frequency, and solemnity to his anticipations of a final account.[56]

Then, there is the high, and sacred regard he paid to the Lord's day. His attachment to *it* was, as we have seen, supreme; and lay, undoubtedly, at the foundation of the varied, and attractive excellencies we have admired. Its power was such as to overcome, even the distrust and love of secrecy which have been noticed. As early as the year 1651, when suddenly called upon, in the capacity of counsel for Mr. Love, he shrank not, like a true-hearted follower of Christ, from avowing, as the reason of his unpreparedness, that " it was Saturday night late before he had notice of" the engagement; " and the next day was not a day, to think of these things."[57] In harmony with this conduct were the minute directions he gave to his children; and, besides what has already appeared,[58] the very striking passage which occurs in his " Discourse of the Knowledge of God, and Ourselves."[59]

But, instead of extracting further from the collected works, or from the volume just quoted, a few paragraphs shall be introduced from a manuscript preserved in the British Museum, first made known by the Christian Observer,[60] and since published.[61]

[56] Works, vol. ii. p. 146, &c. "On Humility."
[57] Trial, p. 98.
[58] See *ante*, p. 146.
[59] Pp. 432, 433, 8vo. 1688.
[60] For 1813, vol. xii. p. 16.
[61] See *post*, chapter XIII.

It will not fail to be observed, how he appears literally, as a " witness for God," testifying from his own experience the inviolability of those numerous promises and instructions, which stand connected, in the Divine Word, with the observance of the Lord's day.

" I will acquaint you with a truth, that above forty years' experience, and strict observation of myself, hath assuredly taught me. I have been near fifty years a man as much conversant in business, and that of moment and importance, as most men, and I will assure you I was never under any inclination to fanaticism, enthusiasm, or superstition.

" In all this time I have most industriously observed in myself, and my concerns, THESE THREE THINGS :—

1st. That whensoever I have undertaken any secular business upon the Lord's day (which was not absolutely and indispensably necessary) that business never prospered, or succeeded well with me.

" Nay, if I had set myself that day but to forecast, or design any temporal business to be done, or performed afterwards, though such forecasts were just and honest in themselves, and had as fair a prospect as could be effected, yet, I have been always disappointed in the effecting of it, or in the success of it. So that it grew almost proverbial with me, when any importuned me to any secular business that day, to answer them, that if they expected it to succeed amiss, then they might desire my undertaking to it upon that day : and this was so certain an observation of me, that I feared to *think* of any secular business that day, because the resolutions then taken would be disappointed, or unsuccessful.

" 2dly. That always the more closely I applied myself to the duties of the Lord's day, the more happy and successful were my businesses, and employments of the week following. So that I could, from the strict or loose observance of that day, take a just prospect, and true calculation of my temporal successes in the ensuing week.

" 3dly. Though my hands and mind have been as full of secular business, both before, and since I was a Judge, as, it may be, any man's in England, yet I never wanted time, in my six days, to ripen and fit myself for the businesses, and employments I had to do, though I borrowed not one minute from the Lord's day to prepare for it, by study, or otherwise. But, on the other hand, if I had at any time borrowed from this day any time for my secular employments, I found it did further me less than if I had let it alone ; and, therefore, when some years' experience, upon a most attentive, and vigilant observation, had given me this instruction, I grew peremptorily resolved never in this kind to make a breach upon the Lord's day, which I have strictly observed for above thirty years. This relation is most certainly and experimentally true, and hath been declared by me to hundreds of persons, and now I declare it to you."[62]

But, notwithstanding the noble combination of

[62] Letter of Advice, pp. 72—74.

virtues which has been exhibited, and the sources
of which, to a certain extent, have been traced,
it would be a great mistake to suppose that Lord
Hale was free from *imperfection;* and it has been
already shown that he did not escape censure.
There are limitations, of necessity, to all human
excellence; and although Mr. Curran eloquently
described the errors of such men as "Hale and
Hardwicke," as "only the specks that arise for
a moment upon the surface of a splendid lumi-
nary,"[63] they still serve the purposes of malicious
spirits; nor can learning or piety, be the forms
of their manifestation ever so lovely, prevent it.
Lord Hale mentioned it, as a thing too plain
for dispute, "that he who has the greatest name
is most exposed:"[64] a saying never, perhaps, more
verified, than when the Abbé St. Real, "in the
wantonness of idle ingenuity," attacked Atticus;
unless it was, when Roger North published, concerning Hale himself, long after he had rested in
the tomb, a series of calumnies, too familiar to
need verbal repetition; and furnishing one testimony more to the thousand instances that may be
cited, of the depth and acuteness of Tacitus, when
he remarked that — hatred is sharpest, where it is
most unjust.

Mr. Hargrave bestowed upon those calumnies
due attention, and commented upon them with his
usual ability and elegance; leaving, in short,
nothing necessary unsaid. The spirit those obser-

[63] Speeches, p. 33, 8vo. 1808.
[64] Works, vol. ii. p. 207. "Of Afflictions."

vations breathe; their triumphant exposure of the slanderer's absurdities; their mild dignity; and their virtuous enthusiasm; are adapted to interest, as well as satisfy, every intelligent reader; and being far less known than the libels refuted, they shall conclude the summary of the judge's " habits and character."

" A sensible and pleasant, but very prejudiced, writer, the Honourable Mr. Roger North, whose Life of his brother, Lord Keeper North, is full of interesting anecdotes, about the principal lawyers in the reign of Charles the Second, and on that and other accounts, deserves to be read by all students of the law, has anxiously laboured to depreciate the character of Lord Hale, with posterity. Into this invidious office he seems to have been precipitated by two very powerful influences over the human mind,—one was of an amiable kind, being an extreme affection for his brother, the Lord Keeper, whose pretensions to fame were, beyond all doubt, very high, but whom he wished to lift into rivalship of character with Lord Hale himself. The other was an over-violent party zeal, which ill suited with Lord Hale's temperate line of conduct, in the contentions between the crown and people. Mr. North was what he describes his brother, the Lord Keeper, to have been, a monarchist declared; in consequence of which he was far too indulgent to excesses of royal authority. But Lord Hale, though sincerely hostile to all irregularities attempted against the crown, was, at the same time, so averse to all encroachments under the sanction of prerogative, that he could neither be awed nor won, into any compliances having that tendency. Being so swayed into a sort of enmity towards Lord Hale, the agreeable biographer to whom I allude, exhibits a very injurious portrait of our most reverend judge ; for such a colouring is given to this great and inestimable man, that all his numerous good features are endeavoured to be spoiled or obscured, and the few imperfections incident to him are multiplied, and exaggerated. Thus we see his abundant piety degraded into the lowness of an excessive puritanical prejudice ; his extreme humbleness of mind distorted into self-conceit and vanity ; his manly independent spirit as a judge, sunk into a mean and fearful courting of popularity. We see, also, his private weaknesses commemorated with triumph, and his writings, out of the line of the law, especially his famous treatise on the Origination of Mankind, extravagantly ridiculed and despised ; and, as to his steady and uniform attachment to the real constitution of his country, it is confounded with the wild enthusiasm of those who blindly, or corruptly aimed, to extirpate the monarchy,[65] and to establish on its ruin, the specious tyranny of pretended republicanism ; or, to introduce the still greater calamity of successive anarchy. Nay, his most exemplary justice is not spared ; in arraigning which, however, the honourable writer's prejudice betrays him into the most palpable

[65] See Note RRR.

inconsistency. For in many passages the reader is instructed to consider Lord Hale as an inveterate enemy to the crown, and as seldom impartial where the anti-court party was concerned in a cause. Yet in one place of the same book we are told that ' when he knew the law was for the king, as well he might, being acquainted with all the records of the courts, to which men of the law are commonly strangers, he failed not to judge accordingly ;' and, in another place, Lord Keeper North is made to say, that ' whilst Lord Hale was Chief Baron of the Exchequer, by means of his great learning, even against his inclination, he did the crown more justice in that court than any others in his place had done with all their good will, and less knowledge.'

" But notwithstanding the shafts of invective thus industriously thrown at Lord Hale, enough has escaped from their singular author concerning his lordship, to confirm the unqualified eulogiums heaped upon him both as a judge, and a law writer, by his other contemporaries, and so to convert the enemy of his high fame, into the most convincing witness of its having been both fully possessed, and superabundantly deserved. The passages to be met with in justification of this remark, are occasionally interspersed ; but, being collected into one point of view, must, I think, strike the most insensible reader. It is part of the biographer's own representation of Lord Hale, that ' his opinions were by most lawyers and others, thought incontestible ;' that ' the generality, both gentle

and simple, lawyers and laymen, idolized him as if
there never had been such a miracle of justice
since Adam ;' that ' his voice was oracular, and
little less than adored ;' that ' he was allowed, on
all hands, to be the most profound lawyer of his
time ;' that ' even Lord Keeper North revered
him for his great learning in the history, law, and
records, of the English constitution ;' and, further,
that ' his collections and writings of the law were
a treasure, and being published, would have been
a monument of him beyond the power of marble.'
To these testimonies from Mr. North himself,
should be added the two passages I before appealed
to ; according to the obvious construction of which,
it is manifestly confessed not only that Lord Hale
was better qualified than any other judge to
explore the rights of the crown, but that he always
declared them when the law warranted it, and that
thus, by the union of superior knowledge with the
severest impartiality, he had actually done more
for the crown, in that respect, than any of his
predecessors, the most devoted to the claims of
regal prerogative, with all their partiality, had
been able to effect. All these passages, even in
spite of the wishes of the writer, whose declared
object was to lessen the estimation of Lord Hale,
tend to fix the character given of him by his
warmest admirers, or rather to elevate it above
their description, if, in truth, there was room for
higher encomium than they have bestowed. But
what seems most remarkable in these testimonies
for Lord Hale from the foe to his fame is, that

one part of the merits conceded to him obviates the chief objection made to his judicial character, to sink which was clearly one great motive to the attack of him. The leading feature of Lord Hale, as a judge, which his censurer strives to impress upon his readers as a genuine characteristic, most certainly imports, that, in the exercise of his judicial function, he was greatly and continually under the dominion of an obstinate prejudice against the court, and of a proportionable predilection for the opposite party. But, surely, this impression cannot have long currency with any considerate reader, when the same person, in effect, tells us that, where the crown was concerned, Lord Hale sought to find what the law was, and, having found, declared it accordingly. As I construe these two representations, it is imputing the grossest partiality in principle, and the purest impartiality in practice, to the same judge, almost in the same breath ; and if this inconsistency be fairly chargeable, the destruction of character intended may be said to operate like a strong poison, accidentally so combined with, and qualified by, antidotes, as to become a most salutary medicine."[66]

[66] Collection of Tracts, Preface, pp. vi.—ix.

# CHAPTER XIII.

## SOME ACCOUNT OF HIS GENIUS, LEARNING, AND WRITINGS.

AFTER what has appeared, no doubt, it is thought, can reasonably exist as to the early cultivation of Lord Hale's mind, any more than as to its capaciousness.

Burnet alleged, and upon his authority the statement has been retained,[1] that during the latter part of his abode at college, he almost wholly *forsook* his studies: but Mr. Stephens denied the charge, and asserted that the judge was as hard a student *there*, as he was, afterwards, at London.[2]

That the good bishop was too honest, and too much prepossessed in Hale's favour, intentionally to misrepresent him, is certain. The allegation, therefore, if to any extent incorrect, which Bishop Jebb does not admit,[3] could have arisen only from

[1] See *ante*, p. 4.
[2] Disc. on the Knowledge of God, &c. Pref.; and see Note SSS.
[3] Burnet's Lives, p. 14.

the report of others. Without, however, attempting very nicely to adjust a matter so unimportant ; or to estimate the *amount* of interruption his love to the theatre might, at one time, have occasioned to his studies ; it shall suffice to observe, that the education he received was sound, and religious ; that his acquirements were respectable ; and that his reputation for wisdom, is too firmly established, to render belief possible, that it could have rested on any basis less solid, than corresponding culture, and proficiency. Dr. Parr often spoke of his writings, in terms of high commendation : he said that he was, " *all* mind and learning."[4] In the works, too, of that pre-eminent scholar, Lord Hale is alluded to, invariably, with epithets of special honour.

" Who," it is asked, " would dare to dispute his erudition, his integrity, or his wisdom ? "[5] And, after elsewhere quoting him as a " great writer," it is added — " These are the words of a judge, who, to legal knowledge, and legal experience, such as have rarely fallen to the lot of man, united the most various erudition, and the most exemplary probity."[6]

The fact of Lord Hale's younger days having been spent among such, as were then called Puritans, sufficiently accounts for attempts at his disparagement. It has been fashionable to load the persons alluded to, and all associated with them, because of the extravagances of *some* of their

---

[4] Butler's Reminiscences, vol. ii. p. 252.
[5] Dr. Parr's Works, vol. iv. p. 181.
[6] Ibid. vol. v. pp. 505, 506.

number, with obloquy. It, nevertheless, is demonstrable, that the Puritans, to mention no other grounds of respect,[7] ranked among the best scholars in the nation ; that they were all members of the Universities ; and that, as a body, they were the patrons of sound literature. It cannot be denied that, generally, they were inattentive to the elegancies of composition ; perhaps culpably so ; but they were renowned for piety, and diligence ; they will ever be numbered among the best preachers ; their writings, never yet surpassed, possess an " unequalled unction ; " and to them belongs the praise, of having originated the first general movement to secure a learned ministry.

So far back as the year 1658, they established an education society ; and the list, containing the names of the founders, includes, besides six and thirty laymen, Matthew Poole, Richard Baxter, William Bates, Thomas Manton, and twenty more of their brethren.[8]

That Hale's early training, whether styled " Puritanic " or not, was *beneficial* to him,[9] as well at College as before he went there, to say nothing of after-life, the narrative places beyond dispute. Nothing, indeed, can be plainer, than that it was when the influence he received in his pupillage was, for a season, *weakened*, and only then, that

[7] See Note TTT.
[8] See Note UUU.
[9] I gladly embrace this opportunity to remark, that the allusion at p. 120, *ante*, as to the " moral respectability " of Hale, ought to have been restricted to his " patronage of the Nonconformists." This oversight was not discovered until after the sheet was struck off.

consideration and restraint were thrown off; and that he had to mourn, because of idleness, seeing plays, and " many youthful vanities." With the *exception* of that period, he was distinguished by the sedate gravity of his deportment; by his indifference to time-wasting amusements; by his devotedness to study ; in a word, by those very things that could promote his own satisfaction, increase his knowledge, and recommend him to wise observers. The Prefacer of the " Discourse on the Knowledge of God and ourselves," aware, from a perusal of it, that the judge must have been acquainted with the " schoolmen ; " and aware, also, of his extraordinary application to legal studies ; desired to know from himself, *when* he could have found leisure for such pursuits, and what authors he had read ? At Oxford, was the reply ; and that he there read Aquinas, Scotus, Suarez, and others, whom he particularly named.[10]

How resolutely good dispositions and habits, were carried with him to Lincoln's Inn, has been shewn : the consequences, too, were equally manifest ; not only in the discharge of daily duties, but the pursuits of scholarship, and science.

In the prosecution of his literary inquiries, he spared neither labour, nor expense. He collected the best mathematical instruments ; he employed himself in curious experiments ; and every new book, on philosophical subjects especially, was eagerly procured, and critically examined. It was

[10] Discourse on the Knowledge of God, &c. Preface, 8vo. 1688.

M 2

a veteran in letters, who remarked, that " the *elegant* studies " of Lord Hale, " than whom English jurisprudence boasts no brighter ornament, are universally known."[11]

At one time, as several of his works shew, he bestowed attention upon the Greek philosophers ; but, subsequently, he relaxed those pursuits, and actually apologized[12] for using the Latin translation, in his transcripts from such authors as Plutarch, Plato, and Aristotle.

Although he had no acquaintance with the Hebrew language, his frequent conversations with Selden, rendered rabbinical learning familiar to him.

His fondness for antiquarian pursuits, is apparent every where ; and when the celebrated Countess of Pembroke enriched Appleby Castle with inscriptions and pedigrees, he is said greatly to have assisted her, as well by needful transcripts, as by the perusal, and arrangement, of her numerous muniments.

The expensive collection of manuscripts, which he bequeathed to Lincoln's Inn, and several of his printed productions, likewise, evince the attachment referred to. In the " Primitive Origination," he discovers, but without parade, how vigilantly he had traversed the most remote, if not the dustiest, regions of antiquity.

Like many other great men, Lord Hale courted the Muses ; but, as might be expected from one so

[11] Reminiscences, by C. Butler, Esq. vol. ii. p. 8.
[12] See Note XXX.

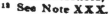

entirely devoted to the substantialities of truth, he was less successful in this, than in any other of his pursuits. He had no fondness even for music; and notwithstanding a love to *it* may exist, apart from the genius of poetry,[13] yet it not often happens that a poet, any more than Milton, is *without* relish for what Herbert has styled, happily enough, the " sweetest of sweets."

Who, besides one combining the two affections, *could* have described the " Jubilee "—

> " Where the bright seraphim, in burning row,
> Their loud up-lifted angel-trumpets blow,
> And the cherubic host in thousand quires
> Touch their immortal harps of golden wires ? "

The souls of Milton and Herbert responded to the spirit-stirring impulses of a choir; and so enamoured with it was the latter, that he usually " went twice every week to Salisbury," affirming, " that the time he spent in prayer, and cathedral musick, elevated his soul, and was his heaven upon earth."[14]

Hale, though not of opinion that singing, " as used in our cathedrals,[15] with instruments and select voices, is unlawful;" has recorded the " disadvantage, and discomposure," it occasioned himself. He conceded, however, that, in the case of some persons, it *improved* their *devotion*, and that the sensible help of church music raised up their hearts

---

13 See Note YYY.
14 Life by Isaac Walton, pp. 44, 45, ed. 1674.
15 See Note ZZZ.

with much advantage ; for, says he, but the statement savours of the coldness of scepticism,—" I have heard men profess it, and charity commands me to think they speak true, unless I knew the contrary."[16]

Nor was he destitute only of love to music ; the " *acer spiritus et vis*," so indispensable to the writer of verse, were, unless the assertions of a noted astrologer [17] be credited, *wanting*.   That individual, zealous, either for his lordship's honour, or his own profit, having ludicrously analysed the judge's character, instanced, as one of its perfections, an " admirable acquaintance with the rules and measures of poetry ;" and appealed to " his many Divine poems, made upon the *birth* of our ever blessed Saviour's *birth*-day," as " a testimony, and proof, how excellently well he understood that seraphique science."[18]

One of the best examples of Lord Hale's efforts at rhyme, is entitled, " Changes and Troubles."[19] It occurs at the end of his " Thoughts on a good Method to entertain unstable and troublous Times :" but, even that, how illustrative soever it may be of " poetical piety,"[20] is totally destitute of

[16]  Hale, Orig. MS.            [17]  See Note AAAA.

[18]  The just and pious Scorpionist;  or the Nativity of that thrice excellent Man, Sir Matthew Hales, late Lord Chief Justice of England, who was born in the Year of our Lord 1609, on Wednesday, November the first, 7ʰ 8′ mané under the celestial Scorpion : astrologically considered, by John Gadbury, Student in Physic and Astrology, p. 7. 4to. 1677.

[19]  Works, vol. ii. p. 237.

[20]  Wrangham's British Plutarch. Life of Hale, vol. iv. p. 79.

inspiration. All his other pieces were commemorative of Christmas Day, and are exhibited together at the close of the "Works—moral and religious."[21]

It is worthy of remark, nevertheless, that, unblessed as he was himself with poetic fire, he was, it is more than probable, instrumental in fanning it into flames elsewhere. A passage, in his tract on "the Redemption of Time,"[22] wherein he amplifies such casualties, and uncertainties as proclaim the preciousness of the fleeting treasure, if compared with the nineteenth and fifty-fifth hymns in Dr. Watts's Second Book; and the description[23] of the soul sitting upon the lips, when death looks in, with a "sight of heaven in sickness," in the Doctor's Horæ Lyricæ; will serve for illustration.

When studying a subject, Lord Hale first prepared a plan, to which he strictly adhered; he took nothing for granted; and he pursued his inquiries with equal caution, and ardour. Having drawn the scheme, or as much of it as he then intended to consider; sometimes upon a loose piece of paper, at others upon the corner, or margin, of that upon which he wrote; he, to borrow his own phrase, "tapped his thoughts, and let them run:" they, usually, flowed as fast as his hand, ready as it was, could secure them. Often he wrote two sheets at a time; seldom less than between one and two; and the gentleman, from whom this testimony is borrowed,

[21] Vol. ii. p. 581—614.
[22] Works, vol. ii. p. 251.
[23] Ibid. vol. i. p. 270. "Seasonable Considerations for cleansing the Heart and Life."

states,—that, when reading in the same room with him, he has known him to continue writing in that proportion for hours together.[24]

So extreme was his love of method, as to lead him to endeavour the reduction of every thing with which he meddled, to scientific principles: and once hearing it remarked, how incapable the common law, by reason of its undigestedness, and the multiplicity of cases, was of *being* systematised, he not only expressed a different opinion, but speedily prepared that wonderful outline of it which formed, at a subsequent period, the basis of Blackstone's Commentaries; and the use of which, even that immortal work has failed to supersede.[25]

Every part of Sir Matthew's character was marked by features of comprehension, extensiveness, and strength. Baxter testifies that he was, to the last, most diligently and thirstily learning.[26] No narrow circle restricted, either his meditations, or his reading. He had, as a matter of course, his favourite topics, and these are sufficiently visible: but he did not confine himself to them. If he cherished a fond attachment for the ancients, he neither neglected, nor overlooked such writers as were later, and contemporary. Hence his works, though evincing so much intimacy with Plato and the great Stagyrite, with Lucretius, and with Seneca, discover no less familiarity with the

[24] Preface to the Discourse of the Knowledge of God and Ourselves.
[25] Collection of Tracts, by Hargrave, pp. xi. xii.
[26] Hale's Works, vol. i. p. 88.

" learned" Drs. Harvey and Hakewill ; Ben Jonson, and Dugdale ; " that excellent person Sir Francis Bacon ;" and the " ingenious" Mr. Ray.

Some of his works, as for instance, his " Observations and Remarks," and the " Primitive Origination," place him before us as a *naturalist*. See especially the ninth chapter of the volume last mentioned.

In another part of the same book, he so mentions finding, when a youth at Kingscot, a quantity of petrified cockles ; and so notices the alterations observable in river fish, such as trout and flounders, when put into ponds ; as to give us an idea of the minuteness, as well as the range of his observations. Similar impressions are produced by his mention of the " works of creation," in " the Good Steward ;" while the accompanying reflections ; his allusion to the spider and the ant, in the same piece ; and his remark, in " the Knowledge of Christ Crucified," upon the grain of corn dying before it is quickened,[27] give prominence to some, at least, of the happy effects.

The Honourable Roger North would have it supposed, that Lord Hale emulated the character of a " profound philosopher ;" but the insinuation is totally destitute of support. His philosophical papers are noticed by himself, merely as pamphlets ; collected partly in his youth, and partly for recreation ; as having been unostentatiously published ; as marked by uninviting titles ; and, moreover,

[27] Part II., 8vo. 1700, p. 39, &c.

anonymous, because he thought them *trifles;* and, because unworthy also, in his own estimation, of the perusal of the learned; a " divertisement," at best, for the leisure hours of young students.[28]

The truth is, that while " philosophy herself seemed naturally to reside" in the mind of Hale, he was as far from thinking too highly of its attendant pursuits, or of his own attainments in them,[29] as he was of using them for purposes of gain, vanity, or ambition. He carefully guarded *against* such an estimate, and such an application. He mentions his judgment of discourses of the nature referred to, as not a very profitable expense " of time in the writers or readers; yet as innocent diversions to both; and such as may be of some use in the indagation of natural causes, and effects."[30] And when " two of the most learned masters in philosophy, and mathematics, that this latter age hath yielded," did him the unexpected honour, to peruse, and examine, and make remarks upon, what he had printed, he would still call what he had written, only " Nugæ."[31] This delicacy, this genuine, unpretending lowliness, so confounding to his malevolent, though " honourable" slanderer, evidently commended him to Dr. Henry More; it increased the high estimate that great and good man, though in some things his opponent, set upon him.[32]

[28] Observations and Remarks—The Epistle to the Reader.
[29] See the Tract on " Humility." Works, vol. ii. p. 164.
[30] Observations and Remarks—Epistle to the Reader.
[31] Ibid.
[32] See Note BBBB.

For the metaphysical jargon of the schools, Lord Hale certainly had a taste; he shews it in " the Good Steward,"[33] and in other parts of his writings, also; how it was fostered we have seen by his conversations with Baxter; and as it is kept in view, it prevents surprise, either that Dr. More's Enchiridion Metaphysicum, should have attracted his notice, or that it should have provoked the controversy which followed. Some of the hypotheses of that celebrated man, struck him as " hazardous;" and he was not more favourable to the " philosophy of Lucretius, Epicurus, and Democritus," as reassumed, and reformed by Gassendus, and Des Cartes:[34] the last named philosopher, and " his too adoring followers," he has mentioned, indeed, in rather strong terms.[35]

The main point at issue between Hale and Dr. More, and the writers of the Platonic School, respected what was called the Principium Hylarchicum, or Spirit of Nature. Lord Hale did " not conclude it impossible," that there *might* be such a kind of common spirit of nature, as Dr. More would have, and not much unlike the Archeus of Helmont, (which he puts into a middle office between the soul and body,) or the Colcoda of Avicen.[36] But it seemed to him, that the erudite author of the " Remarks," out of zeal to assert the existence of incorporeal spirits, a truth not

---

[33] Works, vol. ii. p. 278.
[34] Observations and Remarks—Epistle to the Reader.
[35] Magnet. Magnus. p. 61.
[36] Observations, &c. p. 282.

questioned, had gone further than was needful, or fit, in the attribution of those phenomena whereof they had been debating, to the immediate operation of an incorporeal, vital spirit, designated by him the *spirit of nature;*[37] such phenomena being, in Hale's apprehension, reasonably solved by the mechanism of bodies, and the most wise order, institution, and laws settled by the great Creator; in other words, by the laws of nature.[38]

Complete as is the proof, thus furnished, of Lord Hale's talents and learning,[39] a circumstance which occurred in connexion with his survival of the illustrious Selden, cannot be omitted; for, besides displaying, in very strong colours, the love of literature, already noticed, it makes equally conspicuous that disinterestedness, that acumen, and that veneration, also, for departed excellence, which, on all occasions, distinguished him. It is entitled to the more especial notice, since, but for its occurrence, the Bodleian Library would, probably, have been deprived of one considerable portion of its treasures.

The case was this : Selden, who had intended to bequeath his noble collections to the University of Oxford, being required to give security, for the safe return of a MS. he wished to borrow from its celebrated depository, was so offended (though without good reason, the statutes prohibiting even a *book* to be carried away upon any other terms) as, in anger, to expunge the bequest; and he left

[37] See Note CCCC.      [38] Observations, &c. p. 285.
[39] See Note DDDD.

the whole (some Arabic works on medicine, which he bestowed upon the College of Physicians, excepted) to his executors; desiring them, however, " rather to part them among themselves, or otherwise dispose of them, or the choicest of them, for some public use, than put them to any common sale;" and suggested " some convenient library, public, or some college in one of the universities."[40] His executors, among whom was Lord Hale, honourably interpreting his general and obvious intention to be, that a present should be made of them to one or more public bodies, and regarding themselves as the executors of his *will*, and not of his passion, resolved to carry into effect the original design.

The bringing in of the books was carefully noted by Anthony Wood, and appears in the journal of his own life; in connexion with which record, may be seen the history of the whole transaction, and the " conditions " also, signed by three of the four executors, upon which the donation was ultimately made. The catalogue enumerated more than eight thousand volumes, and the apartment allotted to them still bears an inscription in honour of the former celebrated possessor.[41]

The value Lord Hale placed upon books and manuscripts, exceeded his estimate of any other earthly treasure; nor was the evidence of it, though that is clear, confined to the admirable conduct

---

[40] Seld. Oper. by Wilkins, vol. i. p. lv. fol. 1726.
[41] The Lives of Leland, Hearne. and Wood, vol. ii. p. 131 ; and Ath. Oxon. vol. i. pp. xxxvii. xxxviii.

just narrated : it was declared to be the *ruling passion*, by the stores he amassed relating to the laws of England, at an expense, notwithstanding the narrowness of his fortune, and the largeness of his family, of about 1500*l.* ; a sum, since he left property of barely 900*l.* a year,[42] equal, according to the probable price of land, at his death, to a considerable part of his whole estate.[43]

Those rich fruits of forty years' " care and toil " he bequeathed [44] to the Library of Lincoln's Inn ; not, however, without pronouncing them (and it further illustrates this part of his character) a rare collection ; a treasure worth having and keeping ; and not fit for every man's view. The catalogue will have already attracted notice ;[45] and should further information be desired, it may be obtained from the Hon. Silvester Douglas's (afterwards Lord Glenbervie) account, in the Appendix to the Report on the Public Records of Great Britain ; a document preserved, also, in Savage's Librarian.[46]

Lord Hale left many MSS. of his own composition, and they shall be here enumerated. Some of them have, since Burnet's time, been printed.

1. Concerning the Secondary Origination of Mankind, fol.

[42] Burnet says, " a very considerable part of this came in by his share of Mr. Selden's estate." Life, p. 93 ; and see Reliq. Baxter, part 3. p. 176.

[43] Mr. Hargrave—Collection of Tracts, pp. x. xi.

[44] See the Will, *post.*

[45] In the Will.

[46] Vol. i. pp. 183—190, 225—238. 8vo. 1808. See likewise Herbert's Antiquities of the Inns of Court, pp. 303—308. 4to. 1804.

2. Concerning Religion, 5 vols. fol. viz.

> (1.) De Deo, Vox Metaphysica, Par. 1 & 2.
> (2.) Par. 3. Vox Naturæ, Providentiæ, Ethicæ, Conscientiæ.
> (3.) Liber Sextus, Septimus, Octavus.
> (4.) Par. 9. Concerning the Holy Scriptures, their Evidence and Authority.
> (5.) Concerning the Truth of the Holy Scriptures, and the Evidences thereof.[47]

3. Of Policy in Matters of Religion, fol.

4. De Anima, to Mr. B. fol.

5. De Anima; Transactions between him and Mr. B. fol.

6. Tentamina,[48] de ortu, natura et immortalitate Animæ. fol.

7. Magnetismus Magneticus. fol.[49]

8. Magnetismus Physicus. fol.[49]

9. Magnetismus Divinus.

10. De Generatione Animalium et Vegetabilium. fol. Lat.

11. Of the Law of Nature. fol.[50]

12. A Letter of Advice to his Grandchildren. 4to.[51]

13. Placita Coronæ. 7 vols. fol.[52]

---

[47] A portion of this MS. is at Cottles.

[48] See note EEEE.

[49] These are mentioned in the Preface to the Magnetismus Magnus, *post*, but it should seem have never been published.

[50] See Note FFFF.

[51] See *post*, and Brit. Mus. Bibl. Harl. 4009. Plaut. lxii. D.

[52] Printed, see *post*.

14. Preparatory Notes concerning the Right of the Crown. fol.[53]

15. Incepta de Juribus Coronæ. fol.[54]

16. De Prerogativâ Regis. fol.[55]

17. Preparatory Notes touching Parliamentary Proceedings. 2 vols. 4to.[56]

18. Of the Jurisdiction of the House of Lords. 4to.[57]

19. Of the Jurisdiction of the Admiralty.[58]

20. Touching Ports and Customs. fol.[59]

21. Of the Right of the Sea,[60] and the Arms thereof, and Customs. fol.

22. Concerning the Advancement of Trade. 4to.

23. Of Sheriffs' Accounts. fol.

24. Copies of Evidences. fol.

25. Mr. Selden's Discourses. 8vo.

26. Excerpta ex schedis Seldenianis.

27. Journal of the 18th and 21st, Jacobi Regis. 4to.

28. Great Common-place Book of Reports, or Cases in the Law, in Law French. fol.

### IN BUNDLES.

On quod tibi fieri, &c. Matt. vii. 12.

Touching Punishments in relation to the Socinian Controversy.

Policies of the Church of Rome.

Concerning the Laws of England.[61]

[53] See Note GGGG.

[54] See Hale's Jurisdiction of the Lord's House, Pref. pp. lxxx. n. and ccxi.

[55] See Note HHHH.

[57] See Note KKKK.

[59] See Note MMMM.

[56] See Note IIII.

[58] See Note LLLL.

[60] See Note NNNN.

[61] See Note OOOO.

Of the Amendment of the Laws of England.[62]
Touching Provision for the Poor.
Upon Mr. Hobbs's[63] Manuscript.
Concerning the time of the Abolition of the Jewish Laws.

### IN QUARTO.

Quod sit Deus.
Of the State and Condition of the Soul and Body after Death.
Notes concerning Matters of Law.

In addition to the foregoing, may be noticed, as in Mr. Hale's possession, at Cottles, and entirely in Lord Hale's handwriting, a folio volume, containing " The Confession and Reason of his Faith;" " Matters Chronological;" and, " A Dissertation on the Book of Job;" a quarto volume on theological subjects, commencing with remarks upon Phil. iii. 8, " Yea, doubtless," &c.; besides a considerable variety of detached, and important papers.

The Memoir of the Life and Writings of " that hermit of literature," the Rev. Thomas Baker, B.D. by Robert Masters, B. D. 8vo. 1784, gives a catalogue of Mr. Baker's manuscript collections. Among them is a volume, the sixth deposited in the British Museum, containing, "Reasons for the Universities being exempt from a Metropolitan

---

[62] This has been printed, see *post*. The Orig. MS. is at Cottles.
[63] See Note PPPP.

Visitation, with some Letters of Archbishop Laud, and his Answer in support of his Power of Visiting; with *Reasons and Authorities, also to that Purpose, from MSS. of Lord Chief Justice Hale.*"

Well might Lord Erskine, when shown, by a learned gentleman at the bar, Mr. Hardinge, but a *part*, in his own hand, and scarcely legible, of Sir Matthew's relics, express not surprise only, but declare, that his name would " live to all time!"[64]

Before proceeding to the printed works of Lord Hale, it may be well to notice, that two, though ascribed to him, have been *omitted*. The reasons governing that omission shall be stated.

One of the publications alluded to, is entitled, the " Original Constitution and Jurisdiction of Parliament, with a Declaration of the House of Lords, concerning their Privileges." London, 1707. 8vo. Mr. Hargrave, in the copy he possessed, and which is now in the British Museum, has carefully marked several lengthened, and very gross *piracies* in it, from Lord Coke's First Institute; he observes, too, that there is no such piece in the list of Hale's writings, by Burnet; nor yet amongst the MSS. in the possession of the family. Besides which, he says, at p. 101, at the commencement of Part II. " I have a MS. of this part, including all to the end of the volume, and my copy mentions the book as Herbert's;" or, as he has put it, in the title-page, " a Mr. Herbert."

[64] See Hardy's Trial. Cited in Hale's Works, vol. i. Preface, p. xviii.

The other volume referred to, as here omitted, is also preserved in the British Museum, and was part of the king's library.   The title runs thus :—" The Harmony of the Four Evangelists ; or, the History of the Incarnation, Miracles, Doctrine, Sufferings, and Ascension of our Blessed Lord and Saviour, Jesus Christ ; being a Collection of the Four Evangelists, Matthew, Mark, Luke, and John, into one continued History." It was printed in 1720, and is a thin folio, with a long dedication to " Her Royal Highness the Princess ;" signed, " John Coren." That gentleman says: " When this piece came first into my hand, from the library of a learned man, after his death, I laid it up amongst the choicest of my little collection, as a curiosity only ; but, being told (from a tradition in the family whence it came) that its author was the Lord Chief Justice Hale, (a name eminent in the lists of piety and virtue,) I perused it with more care, and found it a jewel of inestimable value, too bright to lie concealed in a corner," &c.

Such is the *editor's* statement ; but very slight attention to what follows, in the form of a pre-fatory address, by the *author*, will make the mistake, it is thought, sufficiently manifest.

It will be observed, that the style is unlike Lord Hale's ; that the tone is still more at vari-ance with his manner ; that the historical fact does not correspond with his history ; and that his MSS. furnish no clue whatever to such a produc-tion.  " Possibly," is the language, after explain-ing the nature of the undertaking, " some may

think me unworthy to meddle with so sublime a
subject as this is, my practice and profession being
otherwise engaged. Indeed, I may well think so
myself; but, in vindication of my thus doing, I
shall only, in short, tell you that being, in my
former years, somewhat atheistically inclined, but
since, many ways, convinced of my mistakes,
especially by one miraculous favour from the
Divine bounty, for which I shall never be able to
render thanks sufficient, and of which (in regard, I
am a professed enemy to enthusiasm, will not,
therefore, in the least, give any occasion to any to
think I intend to advance my own reputation by
any such means) I shall say nothing whilst I live, but
leave it amongst my faithful notes, after my decease, to be either published or destroyed, as shall
please Providence and my survivors, when neither
applause or disparagement, renown or dishonour,
can signify any thing, in the least to me. Considering with myself what return I should make in
gratitude for so great a favour, I could not find
any thing in my power, or custody, to offer a
present that might, in the least, render it worth
acceptance with so infinite, omnipotent, and immense a God, was willing therefore to sit down
quietly, and contemplate the ever to be adored
love, humility, doctrine, and life of the most holy
Jesus, our only Mediator and Saviour."

In ignorance of the real author, it is difficult even
to hazard a conjecture. The indications, however,
seem to favour the " Mr. Saunders," to whom,
Dr. Watt, in his Bibliotheca, has attributed a

folio, published in 1682, entitled, " A View of the Soul ;" a volume, not only full of interesting matter, and including several epistles to Dr. Tillotson, then Dean of Canterbury, but, sometimes announced as Lord Hale's ; although, from the publisher's address, as well as the author's account of himself, with the most palpable incorrectness.

The notices now to follow, will place Lord Hale's publications before the reader chronologically.

*London Liberty ; or, a Learned Argument of Law and Reason.* 1650.

It was reprinted in 1682, under the title of " London's Liberties ; or, the Opinions of those Great Lawyers, Lord Chief Justice Hale, Mr. Justice Wild, and Mr. Serjeant Maynard, about the Election of Mayor, Sheriffs, Aldermen, and Common Councilmen of London, and concerning their Charter."

*A Preface* (to Sir Henry Rolle's Abridgment of Cases and Resolutions in Law) *addressed to the Young Students in the Law of England.* fol. 1668.

This admirable address, of which some account

has already been given, was introduced into a valuable collection of tracts relative to the law and constitution of England, entitled " Collectanea Juridica," Vol. I. p. 263. 8vo. 1791.

Sir Thomas Reeve, Lord Chief Justice of the Common Pleas, writing to his nephew, on the study of the law, referred to that preface, as the best directory then extant. Coll. Jurid. Vol. I. p. 80.

*An Essay, touching the Gravitation and Non-Gravitation of Fluid Bodies, and the Reasons thereof. 8vo. 1673.*

*Difficiles Nugæ; or, Observations touching the Torricellian Experiment, and the various Solutions of the same, especially touching the Weight and Elasticity of the Air. 8vo. 1674.*

This work, and the preceding one, gave rise to a small volume, by Dr. Henry More, under the title of " Remarks upon two late ingenious Discourses; the one, an Essay, touching the Gravitation and Non-Gravitation of Fluid Bodies; the other, touching the Torricellian Experiment, so far forth as they may concern any passages in his Enchiridion Metaphysicum." 12mo. 1676.

Some copies, with occasional additions, are dated 1675. See Wood's Ath. Oxon. Vol. III. p. 1092.

*Contemplations, Moral and Divine, with Meditations on the Lord's Prayer.* Parts I. & II. 8vo. 1676, 1677.

The circumstances attendant upon this publication have been already noticed; and all the pieces contained in it, form a part of the Rev. T. Thirlwall's collection of the " Works."

Many of the tracts having been found in the hands of the judge's children, and his servants, in a neglected state, and in danger of being lost, were published together in the year 1679.

Job Orton, in his Letters to a Young Clergyman,[85] recommended them.

By means of the " Select Christian Authors, with Introductory Essays," published by Mr. Collins, of Glasgow, a further reprint has obtained circulation.

The Preliminary Disquisitions, by the Rev. David Young, of Perth, 8vo. 1828, and Dr. Chalmers, will amply reward the reader.

*Contemplations, Moral and Divine,* the III[d]. Part. *By Sir M. Hale, Knight, some time Chief Justice of the King's Bench.*

A second edition, with large additions, to which was added, the Life of the Author, by Bishop Burnet, appeared in 8vo. 1700.

[85] Vol. i. p. 151. 2d Edition.

All the papers contained in this volume, except the first, namely, the second part of the tract on the Knowledge of Christ Crucified, are included in Mr. Thirlwall's edition of the works. The tract so omitted, is, nevertheless, one of the best of his Lordship's productions. It is chiefly devoted to the contemplation of the state, and condition of the soul and body after death; and the privilege, that with, and by Christ, the Christian will then receive.

*The Primitive Origination of Mankind, Considered and Examined according to the Light of Nature.* fol. 1677.

In addition to the account before given of this able, but uncouth volume, it may be mentioned, that it appears in the list of books upon " First Principles," referred to by Robert Nelson, Esq. in his Address to Persons of Quality and Estate, 8vo. 1715, p. 5; that Dr. Wotton thought it well worth reading; see his Thoughts concerning a Proper Method of Studying Divinity, p. 19, 8vo. 1734: and that it is found among the books recommended by Dr. Cleaver, the Lord Bishop of Chester. List, p. 16. 8vo. 1792. 2d edition.

In the year 1683, a translation was published in another language, in a handsome folio, embellished with a rich frontispiece, and a copy of the judge's portrait. The following letter, written by Sir Robert Southwell, (whose name has been frequently mentioned,) and yet preserved at Cottles, needs no comment, and will best narrate the circumstances.

" Sr.

" I am sorry my short stay now, in the country, allows me not time to wayt on you, and to desire your acquaintance and friendship, such as I had with your renowned grandfather.

" However, I have sent you a token, which you may properly place among your bookes, it being a translation, into High Dutch, of his last worke, the Origination of Mankind.

" It was, in 1679, that King Charles the Second sent me to the Elector of Brandenburg. This prince, though very warlick, was a lover of learning, and, asking me after the famous men of England, I told him so much of your dead grandfather, and of a book of his, which was then my best compaynion, that he requested it of me; and, for the benefitt of the German nation, caused it to be put into High Dutch. Dr. Schmettaw, one of his chaplains, that had studied at Oxford, and knew English, was imployed herein. He made one dedication of the booke to his own prince, and another to King Charles, and sent two of them over to me, whereof one was placed in the King's Library, at St. James's, and this other may not be unworthy of your closet; for 'twill put you in mind how that excellent man, did not onely serve his generation while alive, but does it now, being dead. And, I confesse, I was zealous for his

N

fame, and for the honour of our nation, that the world abrode might know, what a treasure we once had.

"I shall be glad to see you in London, and ever to be,

"S<sup>r</sup>·

"Your most affecti. and humble servant,

"ROBERT SOUTHWELL.

"FOR MATTHEW HALE, ESQ.
"*At Alderly.*"[65]

*Observations touching the Principles of Natural Motion, and especially touching Rarefaction and Condensation; together with a Reply to certain Remarks, touching the Gravitation of Fluids. By the Author of Difficiles Nugæ. 12mo. 1677.*

These were intended as a reply to Dr. H. More's Remarks, *ut supra.*

*The Life and Death of Pomponius Atticus, written by his contemporary and acquaintance, Cornelius Nepos, translated out of his Fragments; together with Observations, political and moral, thereupon. 12mo. 1677.*

This, like the preceding volume, was published anonymously; but was soon known and noticed, as Lord Hale's. See Sir Philip Warwick's Memoir

[65] Orig. MS.

of the Reign of King Charles the First, p. 441.
8vo. 1702, (reprint.)

The defects of this translation, elicited Roger
North's utmost asperity : it was too excessive,
however, to be efficient ; being done in the spirit,
rather of " an affected pedant, and haughty critic,"
than of either a scholar, or a gentleman. Mr.
Thirlwall properly noticed the subject,[67] nor was
it overlooked by the Rev. Edward Berwick, in his
elegant translation of the Life of Atticus, 12mo.
1813.

*Pleas of the Crown ; or, a Methodical Summary
of the principal matters relating to that subject.*
8vo. 1678.

This volume was afterwards continued by Jacob,
and reprinted in 1716. To this edition is often
added the Treatise of Sheriffs' Accounts—the Trial
of the Witches—and the Provision for the Poor.
The " Summary" has passed through seven
editions, the last in 1773, 8vo, with many
additions, new references, and an improved table,
to the whole. It was not, however, considered by
the author as a complete work ; but intended as
a plan only for his Historia Placitorum Coronæ.[68]

Sir Michael Foster remarked, that it is a very
faulty, incorrect piece, never revised by Lord Hale,
and not intended for the press.[69]

[67] Works, vol. i. p. 165.
[68] See Bridgman's Legal Bibliography, pp. 143, 144. 8vo. 1807.
[69] Report, *ut supra*, p. 32.

An account of an interleaved copy of it, with MS. corrections and additions, is prefixed to East's Pleas of the Crown, vol. i. p. xiii.

*Jura Coronæ; His Majesty's Royal Prerogatives asserted against Papal Usurpations, and all other Anti-Monarchical Attempts and Practices. Collected out of the Body of the Municipal Laws of England.* 8vo. 1680.

*Judge Hale his Opinion on some Select Cases.* 8vo. 1680.

This production extends but from pp. 247 to 262, of a volume entitled, " The Excellency and Pre-eminence of the Law of England, above all other Human Law in the World, asserted in a Learned Reading upon the Statute of 35 Henry VIII. c. 6, concerning Trials by Jury of Twelve Men, and Tales de Circumstantibus, by Thomas Williams, late of the Inner Temple, Esquire, sometime Speaker of the Commons House in Parliament."

The volume is divided into four parts. The first has been stated ; the second contains Mr. Risden's reading upon the statute of 21 Henry VIII. c. 19, of avowries ; the third, Hale's opinions as above ; and the fourth, certain cases which have been formerly mooted by the Society of Gray's Inn.

In the preface the writer says, "The third and fourth parts are genuine and authentique copies of some select cases of the late Lord Chief Justice Hale, in which he gave his opinion when at the Bar : as also of several moot cases, called the cases of Gray's Inn. I conceive it would be both vanity and presumption in me, to offer any encomium upon the first set, least I should injure the manes of that reverend person, whose learning and integrity, not only now flourishes in the memories of, but is never to be forgotten by, the gentlemen of the long robe."

That part of the above volume which pertains to Lord Hale, is in French, and has this title prefixed: " L'Opinion en ascun Select Cases del trèsgrand et érudite Sage de la Ley Matthew Hale, jadis Chief Justice d'Angleterre."

No. 150 of the Hargrave collection, Catal. p. 42, contains " Cases in C. B. in 1656 and 1657 ; also from the 12th to the 19th Charles II. by Henry Darell, Esq., *with Cases and Opinions of Hale*, Maynard, Finch, &c., relating to wills and settlements. At the end of the book is the record of the proceedings in the writ de ventre inspiciendo in Willoughby's case, 39 Eliz. fol. on paper."

*A Discourse, touching Provision for the Poor.* 12mo. 1683.

This little tract—one of whose leading objects was the supply of the poor, by industry and labour—Mr. Nelson alluded to, in his "Address,"[70]

[70] *Ut supra*, p. 264.

with great approbation; and not without observing, "how preferable it would be, to all the gibbets and whipping-posts in the kingdom."

It was reprinted in 1684, with "Several Tracts;" it has been frequently associated with the work next to be mentioned—the Treatise concerning Sheriffs' Accounts—and now has a place in the "Works, Moral and Religious."

*A Short Treatise, touching Sheriffs' Accounts, written by the Honourable Sir Matthew Hale, Knight. To which is added a Trial of Witches, at the Assizes held at Bury St. Edmund's, for the County of Suffolk, on the 10th of March, 1664, before the said Sir Matthew Hale, Knight. 8vo. 1683.*

The time when this treatise was *written* does not appear; but from the hints that are scattered over its pages, there can be little doubt it was penned shortly after the Restoration. In the epistle dedicatory, Sir Matthew alludes to the "late distraction;" and, at p. 89, says, still more plainly, "In the times of the late troubles, viz. 6 Julie, 1650, there was an order made," &c.

There is a copy of it in the British Museum, with MS. notes by Mr. Hargrave. In Manley's addition of Cowell's Interpreter, folio, 1701, it is used as authority, sub. voc. Vicontiel rents.

Although the Trial of the Witches is noticed by Watt, as having appeared in quarto, in 1664,

I have been unable to discover an earlier edition than that of 1683; and the "address to the reader" favours the opinion, that it was then first printed,—as an addition to the Treatise touching Sheriffs' Accounts. Wood, however, says it was published by itself, in 1682.[71]

A reprint, of both the books, was issued in 1716, 8vo, together with the "Provision for the Poor." They are usually found connected with the octavo edition of the Pleas of the Crown.

*The Judgment of the late Lord Chief Justice, Sir Matthew Hale, of the Nature of True Religion, the Causes of its Corruption, and Church's Calamity, by Men's Additions and Violences, with the Desired Cure. In Three Discourses, written by Himself, at several times. Humbly dedicated to the Honourable Judges, and learned Lawyers, who knew and honoured the Author, because, in their true sentiments of religion, and its depravations, and the cure, the welfare of England, under His Majesty, as well as their own, is eminently concerned. By the faithful publisher, Richard Baxter. To which is annexed, the Judgment of Sir F. Bacon, Lord Verulam, St. Albans, and Chancellor of England; and somewhat of Dr. Isaac Barrow, in the same subject. 4to. 1684.*

[71] Ath. Oxon. vol. iii. p. 1093.

Mr. Baxter's preface to this admirable tract, after adverting to the direction in Lord Hale's will, which said that he would have no writings of his published but what, in his lifetime, he gave to be published ; and alleging that this tract was not, in his lifetime, given to him ; and that, till very lately, no price could have hired him to publish it ; thus states the case : —

" When he was gone from us, in great weakness, to the place of his death, in my last letter to him, I told him how much good the Lord Bacon's book, called *Considerations of Matters Ecclesiastical,* had done with many that too justly suspect clergy-contenders of partiality ; and that the honour, and just esteem, that God hath given him with all sorts of men, he owed to the service of him that gave it : and, therefore, knowing the doleful case of this land, as divided and striving about religion, I intreated him, that he would write his judgment briefly and freely, of the cause and cure ; the rather, because his *Contemplations* were so acceptable to many.

" In his last letter, answering this, he professeth that those Contemplations were printed without his purpose, knowledge, or consent ; but thanks God, if they did good, though beyond his intent. But though the rest be full of kindness, I will not publish it, least, really, it should violate his will. But when he was dead, he who published his Contemplations shewed me a bag of his manuscripts— small occasional tractates ; and gave me out these three, saying that they were directed [for Mr. Baxter], by which I knew they were by him given me,

in answer to my foresaid letter, which craved the
publication of his judgment of our divisions.   But
I conjecture they had been long before written by
him, at several times, and much to the same purpose ; and so, I suppose, that he gave them me,
and left the use of them to my discretion.   Now,
say these learned lawyers, 'A man may have several
wills, in writing, in reference to several things,
not repugnant, but consistent, and all shall stand
and be taken as his last will, and may make several
executors, and give them several distinct powers ;'
and, *clausula generalis non porrigitur ad ea, quæ
specialiter nominantur ;* and this direction to you
on that occasion, maketh it a legacy bequeathed
to you ; and the answering your letter by it,
sheweth to what use ; and his after liking of the
publishing his Contemplations, sheweth that he
was not utterly against appearing in print.

" By this, and much more, they satisfy me, that
it was my ignorance that made me resolve to conceal them.   I confess the deliverer thought it best
for me to make one treatise out of them all, because, not being intended for publication, at the
writing of them, the same thing is repeated,
especially in two of them.   And that repetition,
and the brevity made me long undervalue them.

" But I take it as an intolerable *piaculum*, to
put any altering hand of mine to the writings of
such a man ; which I profess I have not done, in
adding, expunging, or exchanging one word (save
some false spelling of the scribe, for only the Latin
verses, and an interlining or two, are his own hand,

which I know by many a sheet that I have had from him).

" And, as long as the occasion of the writing them is known, I think it no dishonour to them to have these repetitions; at least, not so much as my alterations would be : yea, it is useful; 1. as fully shewing the readers, that these are no hasty, crude conceptions; but matters that long, and deeply, dwelt in his heart. 2. And great matters, especially to dull, or unwilling, or negligent readers or hearers, must be oft repeated; for a transient touch passeth away from such, without any effect. O that the matter of these three papers were written, and spoken, an hundred times, if it would make rulers, and teachers, and people, once truly to consider and receive them, as they deserve."

Thus far Baxter. The late Rev. W. Orme, in his Life of Baxter, pp. 610, 611, after noticing the fine illustration the publication now under consideration afforded, of the wisdom and moderation of its author, added,—" it shews, that, were all religious men like Sir Matthew Hale, there would be no oppression on the one part, or unnecessary quarrels on the other; so that peace and love would prevail."

The same year, the " Discourses " were reprinted, in small 8vo, with the treatise touching provision for the poor, accompanied by the " Letters to his Children on their Speech," and to " One of his Sons, after his recovery from the Smallpox," under the title of " Several Tracts ;" which.

probably, led Wood to notice them, by mistake, as two distinct works. See the Ath. Oxon. vol. iii. p. 1093.

The " Judgment of Religion," has been lately edited by E. H. Barker, Esq. of Thetford ; 8vo. 1832.

*A Letter from Sir Matthew Hale, Knight, some time Lord Chief Justice of England, to his Children, advising them how to behave themselves in their Speech. 8vo. 1684.*

This formed part of the " Several Tracts."

*A Letter from Sir Matthew Hale, Knight, some time Lord Chief Justice of England, to one of his Sons, after his recovery from the Small-pox. 8vo. 1684.*

This formed part of the " Several Tracts."

*A Discourse of the Knowledge of God and of Ourselves ; 1st. by the Light of Nature ; 2d. by the Sacred Scriptures. Written by Sir Matthew Hale, Knight, late Chief Justice of the King's Bench, in his younger time,[72] for his private Meditations and Exercise. To which are added, Sir Matthew's brief Abstract of the*

[72] About thirty, or one and thirty. Pref. to the vol.

*Christian Religion, and his Considerations, seasonable at all times for the cleansing of the Heart and Life.* 8vo. 1688.

To this valuable work is prefixed, a " Preface concerning its Author." The volume, as the prefacer remarked, demonstrates " the true principles of the judge's worth, and those great and generous actions which have made him so famous in his generation, and like to be so in future ages."

*A Collection of modern relations of matter of fact, concerning Witches and Witchcraft upon the Persons of the People. To which is prefixed a Meditation concerning the Mercy of God in preserving us from the Malice and Power of Evil Angels. Written by the late Lord Chief Justice Hale, upon occasion of a Tryal of several Witches before him. Part I. London. 1693. 4to.*

This tract is entirely confirmatory of the representation given in a former chapter, as to Lord Hale's sentiments upon witchcraft, harmonizing with those which were entertained, both by his predecessors and contemporaries. It shews, moreover, that, how mistaken soever the opinions alluded to were, they were, to a considerable extent, identical with a belief in Christianity.

The " Meditation " is announced as one, " though

not finished, of that no less wise, profound, sagacious, and ingenuous, than just and good man, the late Lord Chief Justice Hale ; and as written by him at Cambridge, the next Lord's day after his trial of the witches." The publisher remarks, that he printed it, " not only for the use which well-disposed people may make of it, but also as an evidence of the judgment of so great, so learned, so profound, and sagacious, so cautious, circumspect and tender a man, in matters of life and death, upon so great deliberation (for he knew, by his kalender, beforehand, what a cause he was to try, and he well knew the notions and sentiments of the age); and, upon so solemn an occasion, to check and correct the *impiety*, the vanity, the self-conceitedness, or baseness, of such witch advocates as confidently maintain, that there are no witches at all," &c.

The " Trial" before noticed, is alluded to in the preface as having been written by the judge's marshal ; which, the anonymous writer adds, " I suppose is very true, though, to the best of my memory, not so complete as what he [query Lord Hale] related to me at his return from that circuit. But that he was well satisfied in it, may be perceived by his writing this ' Meditation' so immediately upon it."

*A Treatise shewing how useful, safe, reasonable, and beneficial, the enrolling and registering of all Conveyances of Land may be to the Inhabitants of this Kingdom. By a person of great learning and judgment.* 4to. 1694.

The reprint, in 1710, states that it was written by Sir Matthew Hale.

It was again printed in 1756. To the latter edition was prefixed, the draft of an act for a county register, by the Lords Commissioners Whitlock and Lisle, Lord Chief Baron Lane, Mr. Attorney Prideaux, and Sir Anthony Ashley Cooper, &c. The whole volume is entitled, " Two Tracts on the Benefit of registering Deeds in England."

*Magnetismus Magnus : or Metaphysical, and Divine Contemplations on the Magnet, or Loadstone. 8vo. 1695.*

While the nature and properties of the magnet are so explained, and evidence of the " existence of the glorious God, and his vast perfections, is so associated with the magnetical parts of the universe, as to confound infidelity," the general subject, without any thing like overstrained analogy, is made the occasion of a beautiful, and very solemn appeal upon the actual state of mankind.

It is shewn that " this pitiful inconsiderable mineral, the magnet, in all *his* motions and affections, regularly and exactly follows, those laws and directions that are implanted in his nature. But if we cast our eyes, or thoughts, upon the children of men, and *their* ways and walks, we shall, for the most part, find it quite otherwise ; they imbase their souls and faculties with poor, sordid, vanities and trifles, and *neglect* that wherein their perfection and happiness consists.[73]

A brief Meditation upon Psalm lxxxvi. 8, " *Neither are there any works like thy works*," closes the Volume.

*Two Arguments in the Exchequer, by Sir Matthew Hale, when Lord Chief Baron.* folio. 1696.

These arguments were in the cases of Sir Robert Atkyns *v.* Holford Clare, undersheriff of the county of Gloucester ; and in Collingwood *v.* Pace, in the Exchequer Chamber: they appeared at the close of the First Part of the Reports of Sir Peyton Ventris, Knight, one of the Justices of the Common Pleas.

*Tractatus de Successionibus apud Anglos ; or, a Treatise on Hereditary Descents.* 8vo. 1700.

Reprinted with a different title in 1735. It formed also chap. xi. of the History of the Common Law. See Bridgman, p. 145.

*The History of the Common Law of England, divided into Twelve Chapters ; together with an*

[73] Magnet. Mag. pp. 143, 144.

*Analysis[14] of the Law, being a Scheme or Abstract of the several Titles and Partitions of the Law of England, digested into Method. By Sir Matthew Hale, Knight, late Lord Chief Justice of the Court of King's Bench. Second Edition, corrected, with the addition of an Alphabetical Table. 8vo. 1716.*

This copy is in the British Museum, and contains the MS. notes of Mr. Hargrave.

The first edition, Mr. Bridgman states,[15] was printed without a date; and seemed, as a tract, only a design for the larger work bearing the same title, which passed through several editions, and appeared, in 1794, in 2 vols. 8vo; edited, for the second time, by Serjeant Runnington, with considerable additions, notes, and references.

The Analysis appeared in 1739 as a separate publication, but was intended by its author as a concluding chapter (the 13th), to the history. In a MS. folio of the work, kindly lent me by Mr. Joshua Wilson, bearing the date of Oct. 16, 1696, and transcribed " from the Bishop of Worcester's copy, that was taken after the original under my Lord Chief Justice Hale's own hand, before it was *abused*," the title of the whole is —" The History and Analysis of the Common Law of England."

What is referred to by " abuse" is not exactly known; but it is conjectured to be, the freedoms

---

[14] See *ante*, p. 248.     [15] Legal Bibliog. p. 146.

manifest, on a comparison of the printed copies with the MS. : they consist of verbal alterations ; the omission of illustrations ; and transpositions. The original publisher was, perhaps, inimical to the exercise of the imagination upon legal subjects ; for any approach to the use of that faculty is vigilantly guarded. Thus, for instance, at the close of chap. vii. he has omitted the following sentence, with which in the MS. that chapter concludes ; and it is one of two reasons (one only of which has been printed), our author assigns for greater brevity in the succeeding parts of his work—"because the law began now [in the time of Edward I.] to grow more voluminous every king's reign, nay, almost every year ; increasing, as it were, the torrent, by continual accessions of new rivulets, till it is now come to the larger channel, that it now possesseth."

The Brit. Mus. Bibl. Harl. 7160, Plut. XXXIII. E. contains a transcript of "the History and Analysis of the Common Law of England, copied from the original of the Lord Chief Justice Hale, in his own hand, lent to Sir Robert Southwell, by his Grandson Matthew Hale, Esquire, of Lincoln's Inn, October, 1690."

Another copied from the original is in the Bibl. Harl. 711, Plut. XLI. F.

In the Hargrave collection, too, is a copy No. 140, Catal. p. 38, having the following title—"The History and Analysis of the Common Law of England. Written by the Lord Chief Justice Hale. Folio, on paper." It contains also the following memorandum :—" 20 November, 1786. I this day was favoured with this book as a present from Charles Butler, Esq. He tells me that it formerly belonged to Orby Hunter, Esq. F. Hargrave."

*The New Natura Brevium, by the most Reverend Judge, Mr. Anthony Fitzherbert ; with a Commentary, containing curious Notes and Observations, by the late Lord Chief Justice Hale. 4to. 1730.*

The latest edition of this standard work, with the Commentary by Lord Hale, appeared in two volumes, 8vo. 1794.

*Historia Placitorum Coronæ : The History of the Pleas of the Crown, by Sir Matthew Hale, Knt., some time Lord Chief Justice of the Court of King's Bench ; now first published from his Lordship's original MSS., and the several references to the records examined by the originals, with large Notes. By Sollom Emlyn, of Lincoln's Inn, Esquire. 2 volumes, folio. 1736.*

A vote passed the House of Commons so far back as 29th November, 1680, that the executors of the judge should be desired to print his MSS. relating to the crown law ; and it referred the superintendence to a committee then appointed : but that parliament being soon after dissolved, the design dropped."[76]

Mr. Emlyn effected the desired object, and dedicated the work to Sir Joseph Jekyll, Knt., the Master of the Rolls, because to *him* it was that we, after all, are indebted for " rescuing this valuable book from the obscurity wherein it had long lain." It was cordially hailed, and the writer of a brief review of it in the " Republic of Letters," for September, 1736, vol. xviii., remarked, that " whoever is in the least acquainted with the extensive learning, the solid judgment, the indefatigable labours, and above all, the unshaken integrity of the author, cannot but highly esteem whatever comes from so valuable a hand." P. 255.

In the preface to the able work before cited,[77] Sir Michael Foster made some free observations to the prejudice of Mr. Emlyn, in reference to a statement by the latter gentleman as to the MSS. he used : but in an " advertisement" which followed that preface, he acknowledged his mistake, and thus established the authenticity of the edition, and, consequently, of those which have succeeded, as grounded upon it.

The last and best, was published in two volumes, royal 8vo, by Thomas Dogherty, Esq.

A writer in the " Legal Observer" has properly

---

[76] The preface to the Histor. Plac. Cor. by Mr. Emlyn, vol. i. p. xv.

[77] Report, *ante.*

entitled this work " the great text book of criminal law."[78]

In the Hargrave collection, No. 258—264, Catal. pp. 75, 76, the MS. bears the following title, and is attended by the following information, in the hand-writing of Mr. Hargrave,— " Historia Placitorum Coronæ. The History of the Pleas of the Crown, in seven volumes, folio, on paper."

" This, and the six succeeding volumes, are a transcript of Lord Hale's History of the Pleas of the Crown, from the original MS. in his own hand-writing. The printed book was from the latter, with such corrections as appear in this transcript to be in the hand-writing of Lord Hale. In respect of these corrections, Mr. Emlyn, the editor of the printed work, considered this transcript as the original, finished and perfected. I bought this transcript in seven small folio volumes of Mr. Deighton, the bookseller ; and he bought them of the personal representatives of the late Mr. Lockyer Davies. What is now become of the volume containing the original MS. I have not yet heard."

" My friend, Mr. Henry Brown, of Liverpool, since the date of the above-written memorandum, accidentally met with the original MS. of Lord Hale's History of the Pleas of the Crown, at a shop for books, near Mr. Brooke's, in Bell Yard, Temple Bar, Fleet Street, and bought it for the trifling sum of 10*s*. 6*d*. F. H."

[78] Vol. v. p. 341.

*The Power and Practice of the Court Leet of the City and Liberties of Westminster displayed.* 8vo. 1743. *A Pamphlet.*

*A Treatise on the Management of the King's Revenue.* 4to. 1787.

'This formed a part of a volume published by the Honourable John St. John, entitled Observations on the Land Revenue of the Crown; containing the Origin and Sources of the Land Revenue of England; with an Appendix, containing Manwood's Project for Improving the Land Revenue, Norden's Project, Lord Hale's Treatise, &c. It was reprinted in 8vo, in 1790, and again in 1792. See Reed's Bibliotheca, p. 87.

1. *Treatise, in three Parts. Pars Prima, " De Jure Maris et Brachiorum ejusdem." Pars Secunda, " De Portibus Maris." Pars Tertia, " Concerning the Custom of Goods imported and exported." By Lord Chief Justice Hale.*

2. *Considerations touching the Amendment or Alteration of Lawes. By the same.*

3. *A Discourse concerning the Courts of King's Bench and Common Pleas. By the same.* 4to. 1787.

The above-named learned disquisitions were printed by F. Hargrave, Esquire, in a volume,

" Notes" are both acknowledged, and shewn, in Mr. Butler's elaborate preface to the 13th edition of the Institute in question.

*The Jurisdiction of the Lords' House of Parliament considered, according to the ancient Records. By Lord Chief Justice Hale.* To which is prefixed, by the Editor, Francis Hargrave, Esquire, an Introductory Preface, including a Narrative of the same Jurisdiction, from the Accession of James I. 4to. 1796.

Of this profound, and ably edited volume, a good and full account, appeared in the Monthly Review for 1800, vol. xxxiii. pp. 382—393.

*The Works, Moral and Religious, of Sir Matthew Hale, Knight, Lord Chief Justice of the Court of King's Bench. The whole now first collected and revised. To which are prefixed, his Life and Death. By Gilbert Burnet, D.D. And an Appendix to the Life, including the additional Notes of Richard Baxter. By the Rev. T. Thirlwall, M.A.* 2 vols. 8vo. 1805. pp. 1180.

The contents are as follows :—

VOL. I.

The Life and Death of Sir Matthew Hale, by Bishop Burnet. — A Catalogue of Sir Matthew

Hale's Works.—An Appendix to the Life and Death of Sir Matthew Hale, by the Editor.—Additional Notes on the Life and Death of Sir Matthew Hale, Knight, written by Richard Baxter, at the request of Edward Stephens, Esquire, Publisher of his Contemplations, and his Familiar Friend.—A Continuation of the Appendix, by the Editor.—Four Letters of Sir Matthew Hale to his Children; viz. Letter I. Directions touching the keeping of the Lord's Day; Letter II. Directions touching Religion; Letter III. Concerning their Speech;[81] Letter IV. To one of his Sons, after his recovery from the Small-pox.[82]—A brief Abstract of the Christian Religion.—Considerations, seasonable at all Times for cleansing the Heart and Life.—A Discourse of Religion, in Three Parts.[83] Part I. The Ends and Uses of it, and the Errors of Men touching it. Part II. The Life of Religion; and Superadditions to it. Part III. The Superstructions upon Religion, and Animosities about them.—A Discourse on Life and Immortality—on the Day of Pentecost—concerning the Works of God—of doing as we would be done unto.—-The Life and Death of Pomponius Atticus, written by his Contemporary and Acquaintance, Cornelius Nepos; translated out of his Fragments:

[81] The first impression I have met with of this Letter is in a volume entitled, " Several Tracts, written by Sir Matthew Hale, some time Lord Chief Justice of England," 12mo. 1684; and it is in the British Museum. It forms part iii. of the volume.

[82] This forms part iv. of the "Several Tracts."

[83] This forms part i. of the "Several Tracts."

together with Observations, political and moral,
thereupon.—A Discourse touching Provision for
the Poor.[54]

VOL. II.

Of the Consideration of our Latter End, and
the Benefits of it.—Of Wisdom and the Fear of
God, that is true Wisdom.—Of the Knowledge of
Christ crucified.—The Victory of Faith over the
World.—Of Humility:[55] its opposite Vices: Benefits and Means to acquire it.—Jacob's Vow; or,
the Modesty and Reasonableness of Jacob's Desire.—Of Contentation, and the Motives to it, both
Moral and Divine.—Of Afflictions; the best Pre-
paration for them, and Improvement of them, and
our Delivery out of them.—A good Method to
entertain unstable, and troublesome Times. —
Changes and Troubles; a Poem.—The Redemp-
tion of Time: how and why it is to be redeemed.—
The Great Audit: with the Account of the Good
Steward.[56]—An Inquiry touching Happiness.—Of
the chief End of Man: what it is; and the Means
to attain it.—On remembering our Creator in the
Days of our Youth. Of the Uncleanness of the
Heart, and how it is cleansed.—The Folly and
Mischief of Sin.—Of Self-denial.—Motives to
Watchfulness, in reference to the good and evil
Angels.—Of the Moderation of the Affections.—
Of the Vanity and Vexation that ariseth from

[54] This formed part ii. of the " Several Tracts."
[55] See Note QQQQ.
[56] See Note RRRR.

Worldly Hope and Expectation.—Of the Instability and Vicissitude of our present Condition.—Of Contentedness and Patience.—Of Moderation and Anger.—A Preparative against Afflictions; with Directions for our Deportment under them, and upon our Delivery out of them.—Of Submission, Prayer, and Thanksgiving.—Meditations upon the Lord's Prayer.—The Lord's Prayer paraphrased.—Poems upon Christmas Day.

*A Letter of Advice to his Grandchildren, Matthew, Gabriel, Ann, and Frances Hale.* 12mo. 1816. Second Edition. 1823.

This was printed with great care, from an ancient copy of the MS. in the British Museum.

The authenticity of the book was doubted by the British Critic; but in the remarks prefixed to a second edition, those doubts were satisfactorily answered.

The " Letter" furnishes Lord Hale's matured " advice " upon the following interesting topics :—

The danger of the times in relation to religion—Dangers incident to your age—Dangers that arise to you from your condition and relations—Dangers that may arise from your constitution and complexion.—Religion in general—The christian religion.—Directions concerning prayer—Reading of the Scriptures, &c.—Observations of the Lord's day.—Ordinary religious conversation—On the sacrament—Moral and civil conversation, and

actions in general.—Moderation of the passions—
Idleness and employment — Ordinary employments — Employment of young gentlewomen —
Company, and the choice of it — Recreations—
Eating, drinking, and sleeping—Apparel and
habit—Carriage to your inferiors, superiors, and
equals—Single life, and marriage.

In proportion as the Catalogues which have now
been exhibited are *considered*, will be the reader's
amazement, notwithstanding the detail before given
of diligent habits, how one individual, who died,
it should be remembered, at the age of sixty-seven,
should have achieved so much; how he should, in so
short a space, and amidst avocations so important and
pressing, have acquired a *variety* of knowledge quite
extraordinary, and in sciences, too, and upon subjects, supposed to demand, in other cases, constant
leisure and application. But can *any thing*, it may
be inquired, successfully oppose itself to endowments like his, when united with the same unre-
mitting ardour, the same indefatigable industry,
and a mind so habitually serene, as to convert into
*aids* for study, those very troubles which, commonly, are the greatest hindrances ?
Lord Hale, it has been noticed, discovered, now
and then, a vein of playful humour upon the judgment-seat : the reader will perceive the same propensity, occasionally, in his writings, and a turn,
also, for satire. The former, however, never put
in jeopardy the respect his station and conduct
commanded ; and the latter, so great were his

charity and humility, and " the depth and fervour," likewise, " of his religious feelings," was kept constantly in check.

In the utterance of a virtuous indignation, he shewed a less degree of delicacy. Besides those instances which have been adduced, of an oral nature ; and his aversion, already narrated, to the tempers too often manifested in controversy ; that example in the last chapter of the Treatise on the Jurisdiction of the Lords,[87] which attracted the notice of Mr. Hargrave, cannot but be adverted to. There, notwithstanding the placid dignity of his disciplined mind, Sir Matthew appears quite roused by claims, which struck him as unconstitutional, and arrogant.

Trained to habits of nice discernment, logical correctness, and a careful inquisition into facts, those habits were transfused into his writings ; hence the *methodical* mode of treatment which is every where conspicuous, marking, not the process of his mind only, and the love of system before instanced,[88] but the mechanism, also, of composition ;[89] and hence, too, that impressive gravity and regard, moreover, to the simple truth, which are too invariable to be overlooked.

The tendency to dry discussion which, more or less, is visible in all Lord Hale's writings, is, at times, relieved in those upon theological subjects, by bursts of sacred feeling, evidential of a mind

[87] Pref. p. ccxxii.
[88] P. 248.
[89] See the Works, vol. ii. p. 180, &c.  " On Contentation."

entirely captivated with its subject; and so communicating its conceptions and anxieties as, almost irresistibly, to produce conviction. When he gives directions, pertaining, immediately, to the life to come, the "*power*" of that world is actually felt; and such arguments are furnished against evil, as (the expression is his own) carry "thunder in them." The avenues to a diversion of thought from the main object, whether in the shape of speculation or ornament, are stopped up. Nor has the reader to encounter any of that affected obscureness and mystery, by which the style of otherwise great men, has been marred. We uniformly perceive the same regard to plainness,** and strictly business-like procedure, which we have noticed in his living, furniture, and attire.

The *illustrations* employed, where his lordship intended to be most impressive, partook of the same plainness, as well as adaptation. An instance relating to his profession, occurs in the case, before cited, of Sir Robert Atkyns *v.* Clare; but an example shall be selected, as still more appropriate, from the " Contemplations."

In the "Discourse of Religion," having noticed what " a pitiful thing" it is to " see men run upon the mistake" there exposed,—namely, the confounding of religion with systems and ceremonies,—he likens them to " a company of boys that blow bubbles out of a walnut shell. Every one runs," said he, " after his bubble, and calls it religion; and every one measures the religion, or

** See Note SSSS.

irreligion of another, by their agreeing with, or dissenting from them, in these or the like matters;" whereas, "at best, while we scramble and wrangle about the pieces of the *shell*, the kernel is either lost, or gotten by some, that do not prize any of" such " contests."[91]

A too minute formality has already been alluded to: but since it disfigures, not only his lordship's productions as a lawyer, but those which relate more immediately to theology, it seems necessary to give additional prominence to it; for, in the class last named, the objectionableness is even greater than in the former, the custom being less useful, and more striking. It partly arose, no doubt, from the extent of his perceptions; and, in part, from a wish to insure accuracy of comprehension in others. But, be the cause what it may, it, more or less, pervades *all* his works. In those affecting the law, it clearly possessed some advantages; and the eloquent author of the " Commentaries," has shewn how capable they were of being improved. But in such compositions as he was most fond of, the benefit is not so obvious. In fact, all the ends might have been attained, even better, *without* so full a display of numerical divisions, as occurs, for example, in the tract on " Doing as we would be done by:" and *without* the metaphysical dryness which mars the concluding paragraph of the " Contemplation," on

---

[91] Works, vol. i. pp. 315, 316. " A Discourse of Religion." See also vol. ii. p. 372. " Of the Moderation of the Affections." And see Note TTTT.

the works of God. The fault, at the same time, it should be borne in mind, was, to a great extent, the fault of the age : an age which, though fertile in writers of intellectual strength, was an age neither of refinement, nor taste.

In Lord Hale's *phraseology*, as in that of most of his contemporaries, there were, also, almost as a matter of course, great blemishes ; awkward and undignified sentences ; useless expletives ; and words inelegant, latinized, and low. Their effect occasionally is repulsive, so much so, as to create sensations, not unlike those produced by the sudden appearance of a reptile in a well-ordered garden. Some of them seriously reflect upon the judgment and care of Mr. Stephens, the original editor ; but others discover, in the judge himself, a culpable indifference, comparatively, to every thing beyond the announcement of his thoughts, in such words as first presented themselves. He closes his " address to the reader" in his Primitive Origination, with an *apology* extending—to "faults or mistakes in syntax ;" and " language, either improper, or obscure."

The redeeming points in his writings are many. There is discoverable, every where, eminent candour ; remarkable seriousness ; and those amiable courtesies, by which his general demeanour was distinguished. Keen as was the sense he entertained of human folly, he never suffered it to excite emotions of unkindness, or malevolence ; and evils, to which many would have applied the harshest epithets, he designated *mistakes*. In short, he avoided every thing, even when his reprehension was most pointed, that he considered contrary to " a spirit of love, and sweetness of disposition." [92] He remarked, that he never knew any man converted by a passionate, angry, railing adversary. [93]

Nor must the *unambitious* character of his compositions be disregarded. It will be found, that all he says is unassuming, and well digested; marked, when least attractive, by strong sense, and enlightened piety. He, habitually, pursues his course, whether of didactic or illustrative instruction, with the most imperturbable calmness. The weight of those materials which he had been so long, and so gradually accumulating, never seems to have oppressed him; the variety of his employments produced no distraction; and if he is inferior to an Alleine, or a Hopkins, in burnishing the " hard sayings " of the New Testament (which stand like swords, appointed for defence, across the narrow way), to brightness,—the earnestness of his manner, the lucid and convincing light in which he places truth before the mind, compensates the lack. What can be more adapted to set the pulse of the soul in motion, than the momentous thoughts (not to extend allusions) which enrich his tract on the " Consideration of our Latter End;" and the eleventh section on the " Redemption of Time?"

To urge such excellencies in *justification* of the carelessness already noticed, would be absurd; but

[92] Works, vol. i. p. 325. " Discourse of Religion."
[93] Ibid. p. 328.

they certainly may be pleaded in extenuation ;
and as a reason, also, for fixing the eye upon what
is in itself entitled to praise. And here, his lordship's *imagination* will claim a due share of notice ;
for, although less vivid than that of some illustrious
writers, it occasionally demonstrated the ease, had
such been the object, with which, in the exercise
of it, he might have summoned to his assistance,
the most attractive graces of composition. On
those occasions we may discover, in the selection
of his language, considerable judgment : his
thoughts are decked in pleasing imagery ; and
there is the occurrence of such felicities of diction,
as to make regret the more deep and constant,
that the deformities which have unavoidably been
alluded to, were not fewer ; that he had not written less, that he might have written better. What
can be finer than his representation of eminent
humility, operating on the minds of others by
" a kind of secret magnetism ? "[94] or, than his illustration of " the rhetoric of lusts ? "[95]

The *plainness* of Lord Hale's illustrations has
been already the subject of remark ; but injustice
would be done to him, were we not to advert further to their propriety ; to their approach, sometimes, to elegance.

Having mentioned, in his Primitive Origination,
" flies and worms," as not without their worth and
use, seeing that in the least of them, " the curious
wisdom, skill, and power of the great Maker of all

[94] Works, vol. ii. p. 154. " On Humility."
[95] Ibid. p. 340. " On Cleansing the Heart."

things, is conspicuous;" he adds, " though they are but *little rills*, yet if closely followed, they are, and may be, manuductions to lead us to that great ocean of wisdom, power, and goodness of the God of nature, from which they had their original." [96] To the same class belongs his description of the fear of God, as "*walking through the soul*, and pulling up those weeds, and roots of bitterness and folly, which infect, disquiet, disorder, and befool it." [97] The first three paragraphs of the second part of his Discourse on Religion furnish another example: and so does the second part of the Knowledge of Christ Crucified. But to multiply citations would be tedious. To instance, there-fore, all in one; nothing for an impressive combination of appropriateness, wit, and beauty, can exceed his exposure of those hypotheses which philosophy, in her most preposterous moments, invented, respecting the eternity, and original of the universe. [98]

If *sententiousness* cannot be mentioned as descriptive of his lordship's *manner*, there are, in his publications, examples, and not unhappy ones, of that once popular mode of instruction; and although the passages alluded to are, comparatively, thinly scattered, they are worthy of association with the best apophthegms of antiquity; because, leavened by Christianity, they surpass them.

A few specimens must suffice :—

[96] P. 4.
[97] Works, vol. ii. p. 27. "Of Wisdom and the Fear of God."
[98] Prim. Orig. pp. 340—342.

" There is no more of good in the creature than what God lends it." " They that are rich are *stewards* of their wealth, and they that are wise are *stewards* of their wisdom—unto that great Master of the family of heaven and earth, to whom they must give an account." " I will learn contentment by considering others' wants and my enjoyments, and not learn discontent from others' enjoyments, and my own wants." " Integrity of conscience is a jewel that will make rich in the midst of poverty ; a sun that will give light in the midst of darkness ; a fortress that will keep safe in the greatest danger ; and that never can be taken, unless thou thyself betray it, and deliver it up." " Keep God thy friend in thy prosperity, and thou mayest with confidence resort to him, and rely upon him, in adversity." " Every increase of mercy, calls for an increase of duty." " A man never loseth by prayer."

In harmony with these sayings, and as further elucidating the merits of their author, may be noticed his frequent introduction of *soliloquies ;* or, to adopt his own words, " a practical supposition wherewith we are to entertain *ourselves.*" [99] Not only was the style of his address thereby agreeably diversified, but his skill in the difficult duty of meditation displayed ; his vivid perception of " that which is spiritual" made prominent : and those alternations of solicitude and joy which are peculiar to a disciple of Christ, so unfolded, as to promote the best interests of the reader. The

[99] Works, vol. ii. p. 209. " Of Afflictions."

instances in view are of frequent occurrence, which makes it unnecessary to do more than advert to a few of them; such, for example, as enrich the " Seasonable Considerations for cleansing the Heart and Life ;" the chapter on " Self-Denial," at the close; the " Preparative against Afflictions ;" and the " Discourse on the Knowledge of God and ourselves."

Nothing will strike an attentive reader of Lord Hale's *devotional* writings more forcibly, than the superlative regard he paid to the inspired oracles. He was attached to philosophy, and admired many of its sages ; but to display the *inferiority* of all systems, how captivating or popular soever, to the doctrine of the gospel, was his delight. His representation of the " pre-eminence of the Scriptures," in *contrast* with " the light of nature," [100] can hardly be surpassed.

This affection it was, pure and ardent like that of the king of Israel, that gave such artlessness to his thoughts ; that transfused such sobriety into his writings ; that dignified his conceptions ; that inspired his praise. " Blessed be God," he exclaims, " he hath given us the copy of his will in his great letter of declaration—the Books of the Old and New Testament. You must value it as the greatest jewel you can have." [101]

It is not, therefore, surprising, that his compositions should be impregnated with scriptural language ; with illustrations, derived immediately

[100] Works, vol. ii. pp. 321, 322.  " The Chief End of Man."
[101] Letter of Advice, p. 57.

from the Bible; bordering, at times, it must be
acknowledged, upon the quaintness which once
was fashionable; but, nevertheless, generally appropriate, and always instructive. Those "two
great experiments which God is pleased to use
towards the children of men—correction and deliverance"—are mentioned as his "rod and staff."[1]
The fear of the Almighty once put into the heart
is like, he says, "the tree put by Moses into the
waters: it cures the disorder and uneasiness of all
conditions."[2] Expatiating upon "a conscience
full of peace, and integrity, and comfortable attes-
tation," he styles it—a "*Goshen* to and within
itself, when the rest of the world without, and
round about a man, is like an *Egypt* for plagues
and darkness."[4] And—any solicitation to give
ease or deliverance by wounding conscience, he
compares to a design for clipping off "that lock
wherein, next to God, the strength lieth."[5]

But, notwithstanding this admirable regard to
divine Revelation—nay, *because* of it; and because
there is, also, in his lordship's writings so much,
to be extolled, and recommended; it becomes
the more needful to remark, though the duty
be unpleasant, that there *are* statements, occasionally, which, as fairly brought to the test of
God's word, seem objectionable. They were not
noticed, it is true, by the reverend Editor of the

[1] Fourth Letter to his Children. Works, vol. i. p. 224.
[2] Works, vol. ii. p. 30. "Of Wisdom and the Fear of God."
[4] Works, vol. ii. p. 234. "A good Method to entertain unstable, and troublesome Times."
[5] Ib. p. 234.

" Works," but they exist; they appear as un-
guarded axioms; and they convey impressions
contrary to the faith, " once delivered to the
saints."[6]

That which is alluded to is—a mode of statement
at all times adapted to afford aliment to a self-
righteous spirit: a careless phraseology, exposing
the author to the charge of being an upholder, in the
matter of a sinner's justification before God, of those
works of moral obedience, which, for *that* purpose,
are pronounced by the highest authority, unavailing.
Hence, occasionally, is discoverable a representation of an actually mercenary character, *as if*
the Saviour's merits, instead of being the sole
ground of Divine acceptance, were a sort of ad-
junct only, supplementary to the merits of the
redeemed.

The following selections will explain what is
meant. After noticing three classes of unfaithful
stewards, his Lordship says, that the third contains—

" Such as do make some use of their talents,
but do not produce an increase proportionable to
their stock: and so, though they are not debtors
for their whole talents, yet are in arrear, and
grown behind hand; and so upon the foot of their
account are found debtors to their Lord, which,
without faith in Christ, and his *merits coming
in to make up the sum*, will be enough to cast them
into prison, and there keep them to eternity."[7]

[6] See Note UUUU.
[7] Works, vol. ii. p. 255. " The Great Audit."

Again — on commencing his " account," the " good steward" is made to say, " I confess I have not improved my talents according to that measure of ability that thou [Lord] hast lent me ; I, therefore, most humbly offer unto thee the *redundant merit of thy own Son, to supply my defects, and to make good what is wanting in my account.*" [8]

Many of the learned, " because of the analogical ratiocination perceptible in brutes," have defined man a *religious* animal ; and, although Lord Hale would not stand to justify such an opinion in all particulars,[9] it is obvious that his " Contemplations" received a colouring, from the habitude of his thoughts upon it. It so affected some of his phrases as to render comprehensive explanation necessary ; and occasional association, also, with topics beyond a common ken, and far too speculative and metaphysical, for even uncommon minds. If he were not, in a degree at least, corrupted by it from the simplicity of Christ, it led him, sometimes, to keep apparently aloof from an unfettered avowal of that blessed doctrine—justification by faith *only* [10]—which Luther designated the *articulus stantis, vel cadentis ecclesiæ.*

[8] Works, vol. ii. p. 258. " The Account of the Good Steward."
[9] Ibid. p. 21. " Of Wisdom, and the Fear of God."
[10] " While *this* doctrine standeth, the Church shall stand and flourish. But when this doctrine faileth, the Church must needs fail and fall to ruin. This doctrine I do so often, and so diligently repeat, for that Satan desireth and seeketh nothing so much, as to pluck the knowledge thereof out of all men's hearts."—Luther, on the 130th Psalm, in his Commentary upon the Fifteen Psalms, called Psalms of Degrees, p. 222. 4to. 1577.

Whether the foregoing remarks are sufficient to explain the matter, or to account satisfactorily for what it seems impossible to defend; or, whether the knowledge we do not possess, as to the *times* when the several meditations were written, would lessen the difficulty; or, whether the language commented upon, was resorted to in avoidance of Antinomian heresy, or under the influence of Arminian apprehensions; or, whether any doctrine of analogy, in reference to human affairs, was uppermost in the judge's mind at the moment he wrote, (an idea, the plan of the " Great Audit" seems to favour) must remain a secret.

But be it as it may, the passages in question, and all of a similar kind, are capable of the most dangerous perversion : they stand in opposition to the writings of the Reformers; the Homilies and Articles of the Established Church; the whole body of the Puritans; and the first elements of the gospel. Instead of harmonizing with those convincing arguments, which were directed by the Apostle Paul, to the churches of Galatia and Rome, for the manifestation and overthrow of the self-same error; or the powerful appeal of the same infallible writer to the Ephesians; or his awakening and conclusive counsels to Titus; they savour, altogether, of those misty distinctions when treating upon " terms and qualifications," " conditional justification," and " the merit of works," which bewildered Bellarmine, and Aquinas, and even Baxter; and they are the rather to be deplored, because proceeding from one who, in other parts of his writings, expressed himself so very differently.

Thus, in one of his best pieces, Sir Matthew lays it down as a principle—that "*nothing* but the blood of the Son of God can countervail the weight of the least sin;"[11] that "forgiveness is an act of most free mercy, and nothing of merit in the person forgiven."[12] Elsewhere, he describes, with great energy and clearness, the work of the Holy Spirit in convincing the heart " of that sin, and that death which hath overspread the whole race of mankind; and of the truth, efficacy, and sufficiency of that redemption which came by Christ, and is published" in the word.[13] Faith he explains to be " that result of dependence upon, and confidence in, and adherence unto, *Christ*, which follows upon the sound conviction of the truth of God concerning him;" and the effects, he adds, are of two kinds.

" 1. In reference to God, our *justification;* God having, of his free goodness, exhibited the righteousness of Christ and his satisfaction to be theirs, that shall truly know it, and rest upon it. Rom. iii. 4, 5, &c.; Galat. ii. 16.

" 2. In reference to us, peace with God (Rom. v. 1,) in him that is our Peace-maker. Humility, because the righteousness whereby we are justified is none of ours. Rom. iii. 27. Where then is boasting ?"[14]

[11] Works, vol. ii. p. 484. " Preparative against Afflictions."
[12] Ibid. p. 532. " Meditations upon the Lord's Prayer."
[13] Ibid. p. 500.
[14] Disc. of the Knowledge of God, &c. p. 247.

But there is one passage in the Treatise " Of the Knowledge of God and ourselves," so very beautiful, as well as instructive ; and so showing man's affecting circumstances as a transgressor ; and how *alone* he can be accounted just with God ; as to preclude the necessity of further comment, or extracts, in contrariety to those which have been the subject of animadversion.

" We are encompassed every where with *guilt ;* and the avenger of blood pursues that guilt ; and we cannot by any means find any power in ourselves, or in any other creature, to escape it. The soul being seriously convinced of this, God presents unto it the satisfaction and righteousness of Christ ; his promise of acceptation of it ; and our deliverance from his wrath by it. And *now* the soul, like a man ready to be drowned, first lays hold of the cable that is thrown out to him, even before it hath leisure to contemplate the goodness of him that did it. So the condition of our misery teacheth us, first to clasp the promise of mercy and salvation in Christ ; and then, to consider and contemplate the great mercy and goodness of God, and to entertain it with love and thankfulness. An extreme exigence will give a man some confidence, to adventure upon a difficult, and unlikely occasion of deliverance ; because it is possible his condition may be bettered ; it cannot be made worse. (2 Kings vii. 4.) ' *Why sit we here until we die ? If we enter into the city, the famine is in the city, and we shall die there : if we sit still here, we die also. Now, therefore, let us fall into the host of the Assyrians : if*

is considered, that most of the publications which bear Lord Hale's name, were *posthumous*; and that nearly all of them were, in a measure, subjected to the inconveniences of posthumous authorship.[20] Mr. Hargrave earnestly desired to remedy these evils; and the attention, and learned toil, bestowed by him upon some of the manuscripts, make it the more to be regretted, that his avowedly favourite object—a complete edition of the whole works—was not accomplished. An imperishable monument would then have been raised to the memory of Hale, from materials of his own providing, and by just such an architect as he deserved.[21]

Lord Chancellor Northington, then Lord Keeper Henley, pronounced Sir Matthew "one of the ablest, and most learned judges that ever adorned the profession."[22] Mr. Justice Grose declared he was "one of the most able lawyers that ever sat in Westminster Hall:"[23] "as correct, as learned, and as humane a judge as ever graced a bench of justice."[24] Lord Kenyon said, that the operations of "his vast mind always call for the greatest attention to any work that bears his name."[25] In

---

[20] See Note YYYY.

[21] See Butler's Reminiscences, vol. i. p. 121, 3d Ed.

[22] Burgess v. Wheate, 1. Eden, vol. i. p. 252, and p. 211, *ut supra*, Note DDD. In the report of the same case, 1. Sir W. Blackstone's Rep. p. 182, there is a slight variation—"the ablest" is omitted.

[23] Doe dem. Duroure v. Jones, 4. Durnf. & East, p. 311.

[24] The King against Rice, 3. East's Rep. p. 582.

[25] Proceedings in the Court of K. B. in the case of B. Flower, p. 60, 8vo. 1800.

Herries *v.* Jamieson,[26] alluding to a case cited from Ventris in argument, the same great judge observed, " that it ought not to be treated lightly, or overturned without great consideration, because it had the sanction of Lord Hale's name :" and in the King against Suddis, he mentioned him as " one of the greatest and best men who ever sat in judgment."[27] Lord Erskine, in addition to his other frequent testimonies,[28] mentioned him as " the never-to-be-forgotten Sir Matthew Hale ; whose faith in Christianity is an exalted commentary upon its truth and reason, and whose life was a glorious example of its fruits ; whose justice, drawn from the pure fountain of the Christian Dispensation, will be, in all ages, the subject of the highest reverence, and admiration."[29]

A late Attorney General, Sir Samuel Shepherd, mentioned him as " the most learned man that ever adorned the bench ; the most even man that ever blessed domestic life ; the most eminent man that ever advanced the progress of science ; and, also, one of the best, and most purely religious men that ever lived."[30] Lord Ellenborough spoke of him as " one of the greatest judges that ever sat in Westminster Hall :"[31] as " venerable, as well for the sanctity of his character, as for the profundity of his learning."[32]

[26] 5. Durnf. & East, p. 556.   [27] 1. East's Rep. p. 314.
[28] See Note ZZZZ.
[29] Speeches, vol. ii. p. 198.
[30] The first Trial of Hone, p. 4.
[31] In the case of Wain *v.* Warlters, East's Rep. vol. v. p. 17.
[32] The second Trial of Hone, p. 44.

Mr. Dwarris, in his Treatise on Statutes, regards him as " a powerful," as almost " an insuperable authority."[33] And although Sir Michael Foster, in the volume before referred to, indulged in animadversion upon some things in his writings, relative to the principles upon which the Revolution was founded; yet, his remarks betray every symptom of conscious inability, adequately to pronounce his praise.

The name is mentioned as one " ever honoured, and esteemed;" he is styled, an author whose memory the writer *loved*; as the learned judge; as " very great in his profession; and, which raiseth even a great character infinitely higher in point of real merit and just esteem, as, in every relation of life, a *good* man." [34]

The leading characteristics, in a religious point of view, of the age of Hale, with respect, especially, to their influence upon his *theological* " remains," might be here prominently noticed, as has been done by an able reviewer of Mr. Thirlwall's edition of the " Works;"[35] and, after the same pattern, a comparison might be instituted, between that period and the present. Nor would proof be wanting, that the piety of the former era, in which Hale lived, though, of course, essentially the same, was yet less brilliant than that of later times. But it shall suffice to remark, that while the strictness,

---

[33] P. 16, 8vo. 1830.

[34] Report, *ut supra*, pref. p. vii.

[35] See the American Christian Spectator for Dec. 1831, vol. iii. p. 531.

and entire abstraction from the world, which a profession of religion then necessarily involved, can scarcely be estimated too highly, it cannot be denied, that there is *now*, a beneficial expansiveness in operation among Christians, which was *then*, generally, unknown ; there is *now*, as the result of increased illumination, a wider spread of liberality and knowledge ; and such active efforts, moreover, are at work for the diffusion of the gospel, as, compared with the period in which Hale lived, to occasion inexpressible pleasure. In the present day we witness, an emancipation from the dormancy and supineness, and, almost, monastic cast of Christianity, which formerly prevailed. Thomas Gouge once was a prodigy. Bible Societies, and Missionary Societies, and Tract Societies, had no existence : the population were literally untaught : a cloud of thick darkness hung over the Church, both with respect to christian operations, and christian liberty ; the ambition of one " *zealous* for the Lord of hosts" was ideal : nor does there seem to have been more than an individual, here and there, who had the slightest perception of what Locke and Lord Mansfield, have since so ably taught, and the legislature recognized,—that the extension of vital Christianity by secular force, is as impracticable, as the attempt is impolitic, and unrighteous. Upon this subject Hale himself had, to say the least, confused notions.

That he was in favour of an Act of Uniformity, and, consequently, yielded to the magistrate, power *in sacris* (at all events, as to things " indifferent,")

P

we have seen. His manuscripts, however, to say
nothing of what has been printed, and what he
did, show, how he shrunk from some of the consequences; and how, upon several collateral points,
he was perplexed. He saw difficulties in the very
onset, relating to the *determination* of the " indifferency of a thing indifferent:" and he could
not shut out those which attached themselves to
the penalty fixed upon disobedience : it might be
" too severe for the nature of the thing enjoined."
Obstacles, again, presented themselves in connexion with the abrogation of things offensive to
some consciences, when, in other instances, the
abrogation *itself* would become an offence. And,
when he adverted to the case of the magistrate's
*own* conscience being strongly persuaded, in opposition to the consciences of others, he was
any thing but relieved. In short, to avoid an
enumeration of all the nice questions, and distinctions, which are discussed in his papers, it shall
only be added, that he seems to have been completely puzzled, to make out, in some cases, *when*
" obedience, or non-obedience, would be sinful."
It is easy, therefore, to perceive, how such a state
of doubt, and uncertainty, combined with an opinion, nevertheless, then pretty generally prevalent,
that " legal coercion" in religion was not *unlawful*,
operated to the production of that quietude,[36] by

---

[36] In one of his manuscripts, he notices, with some compla-
cency, the *effects* of that spirit of ignorant, and unthinking acquiescence which it had been the policy of Charles I., as well as his
immediate predecessors, to produce, and maintain.

which *his* religious emotions, and those of the bulk of his contemporaries, were, in a great measure, repressed. For, it may be very confidently affirmed, from history, and observation,—from Protestant principles,—from the christian economy,—and from the casuistical exercises of Lord Hale himself, that it is, as mankind come in contact with Scripture verities, *apart* from external compulsion, from any dictation merely human, that the mind will acquire a proper tone of elasticity; and reasonings upon the topics which have been referred to, will become definite, and clear. It is as filled with celestial light and love, that the human heart expands; just as the " word" is glorified, when it has " free course." Christians submitting to the guidance of inspired truth alone, will rise superior to feelings of sectarianism, and " strive *together*" for " the faith of the gospel:" they will employ *arguments*, instead of pains and penalties: and labour, like the Apostles, and primitive believers, " to *convince* by sound doctrine;" and by " weapons not carnal," but, " through God, *mighty*,—to pull down the strong holds" of error; while, with all importunity, they will seek those heavenly influences, without which success is impossible.

But, to what extent soever the foregoing observations may, in the case of Lord Hale, be justified, his *honesty*, and *simplicity*, and *devout purposes*, are not so much as questionable. To be " serious, and circumspect, and strict, and holy," he accounted his business. Hence his numerous relics contain no unhallowed speculations; no

affected novelties ; and little, if any thing, that can
be termed mere abstract theory. The remarks he
makes upon the evidences, are associated with the
doctrines of revelation. In " moral reasons" he
abounds, and often assigns them *seriatim ;*[37] as
likewise, in the inculcation of duties.[38] Sometimes they appear together in a directive form.[39]
His theological writings are, actually, his own life
" epitomized."[40] They are full of discrimina-
tion,[41] and " experimental feeling :" they, every-
where, discover a spirit eminently penetrating, and
chastened ; and they " enter into the Christian's
daily life."[42]

Considerations such as these, have served to
hinder the introduction of more, on the present
occasion, than the summary disclosed by the *titles*
of our author's works ; and notices of a merely
*general* nature. Unlike the continuous argumen-
tations of Saunderson, and Barrow, and Howe,
they are, indeed, ill adapted for analytical dissec-
tion ; and, as plain, unpretending records, strictly
personal, and intended to have been private, it
would be unfair to subject them to it. The
reader's own edification, moreover, as well as

[37] Works, vol. ii. p. 182. " On Contentation." P. 217. " On
Afflictions." P. 250. " On Redemption of Time."
[38] See, for instance, the Works, vol. ii. p. 218. " On Afflictions."
[39] Works, vol. ii. p. 416. " A Preparative against Afflictions."
[40] " That of the Great Audit I look upon as his very picture."
— Mr. Stephens' Preface to the Contemplations. 8vo. 1679.
[41] See Note AAAAA.
[42] Rev. E. Bickersteth's " Christian Student." p. 527. 2d Ed.

acquaintance with Hale himself, will be most furthered, by a thorough perusal of them : it will then be perceived, in a way the least exception-able, why it was, that his lordship's views were so uniformly *practical :* why he habitually, and with " preparing seriousness," mused upon his future condition : why, amidst the enjoyments of his pros-perous circumstances, and necessary avocations, he solaced himself with the delights of holiness, and heaven.

So *entirely* practical were Lord Hale's habits, as to enable him, by a sort of blessed chemistry, to extract things salutary and useful, from truths, in appearance, perfectly barren : and, at the end of the first chapter on " Primitive Origination,"[43] he has given an interesting specimen of the process.

If he did not, with Baxter, value " all knowledge, by the *greatness* of the benefit, and *necessity* of the use,"[44] still, the more palpably useful any thing appeared, the more strongly did it commend itself to his attention : and, on the contrary, in proportion as he discerned the want of that charm, in the same proportion was it either abandoned, or slighted. Consequently, " many grammatical criti-cisms ; how this word was written by one author, how by another ; what fashioned clothes the Roman officers, military, civil, or sacred used ; and very many curiosities relating to languages ;" were classed by *him* among " mere impertinences." And he observed, that, although " great volumes

[43] De Homine, cap. i.
[44] See ante p. 176.

have been" compiled upon such matters—the knowledge, if attained, would be inapplicable to any purpose, at all corresponding with the toil of acquisition. "

No one acquainted with the history, or the writings of Lord Hale, will suppose, for a moment, that he was *indifferent* to science, to mental culture, to learning; "still less, that he wished to *put out* those lights; lights which adorn, and cheer the present beautiful world. The reverse is notoriously true. He did, however, wish and aim, to cast a shade over much that is " highly esteemed;" to show the folly of intellectual trifling; and—by exhibiting the utter insignificance, comparatively, of every thing besides—to display the importance of moral, and holy greatness. And his own conduct corresponded with his convictions so fully, as to lead Burnet to suggest, how easily any person might imagine, that the study of *theology* had occupied, *most* of his time, and thoughts.[47]

That his thoughts were occupied upon it, with habitual and intense satisfaction, is clear. Nor could it be otherwise. He was a *believer* in Christianity—not because he, happily, had been trained in the true faith; nor because others whom he esteemed, professed it; nor because it has a beneficial influence politically, upon observers:—but as a matter of *personal*, and everlasting concern; and,

" Prim. Orig. pp. 4, 5. See also the Works, vol. ii. p. 38. " Of the Knowledge of Christ crucified."

" In the J        Advice, p. 104, a whole chapter is devoted to the study        nts of both sexes.

" S

upon the most careful examination, and study.[48]
While, therefore, it taught him diligence in his
proper business, it made him, of necessity, fervent
in spirit, and so he served the Lord. Neither
fashion, nor ambition, and least of all, the thirst
of worldly gain, had any influence upon *his* "Contemplations." They were written—partly for his
own use; partly for the benefit of his household;
and, as we have seen, without the slightest design
of publication.

In this point of view their demand upon the
reader's attention is vastly increased. For, whatever anxiety some persons may feel, to impugn the
motives of a writer upon religious subjects, if he
be of the clergy; and, *therefore*, to cavil with him
on the score of interest, or craft; the writings in
question, more than those of most other laymen,[49]
defy such hurtful, and unworthy suspicions.

His Lordship's *modest diffidence* is admirably
adapted to overcome the prejudices, and to baffle
the suspicions, of the most sceptical. For, whatever the subject upon which his pen was employed,
assertions are never obtruded in the place of conjecture:[50] he never swells with arrogance; an
approximation to dogmatism, is not so much as
discernible. When *most* dissentient from others,
there is, quite after the pattern of apostolical

[48] Disc. of the Knowledge of God and Ourselves. Preface.

[49] " A Clergyman of the City of London," properly associated
Sir M. Hale with Newton, Boyle, and others, in a small publication entitled, " Remarks on the Religious Sentiments of learned,
and eminent Laymen." 12mo. 1790.

[50] See the Jurisdiction of the Lords' House. Pref. p. lxxx.

wisdom, the utmost delicacy of tone, and of language. Such phrases as — " I must confess I could never assent to," &c. — " for I have always thought," &c. — " It seems to me" — " I forbear, therefore, any opinion," &c. &c. — frequently occur: and illustrate, in the aptest manner, his true character.

The Reverend Editor of the works — " Moral and Religious" — has in two instances noticed, and commented upon, what he considers a failure, in Lord Hale's soundness of *reasoning*. But it may be observed, without any disrespect, that both the annotations[31] might have been spared. In fact, animadversion upon the brief and profound hints thus referred to, would have given employment to the mighty genius of President Edwards, and *he*, surely, would have justified them.[32]

Had Mr. Thirlwall made a remark upon the too lax, if not mistaken, statements of the judge, respecting the translation, and dispersion of the Bible ;[33] or, like Mr. Hargrave,[34] rescued him from the terrible clutches of Bishop Warburton, the work would have been a good one, and must have occasioned legitimate pleasure. The haughty prelate just mentioned, because of an opinion in one of Hale's manuscripts[35] concerning the bishops in parliament, not coincident with his own; instead of

See the Works, vol. ii. pp. 18, 19.
Note CCCC.
816, 317. " Of the Chief End of Man."
317.
Right of the Crown.

resting satisfied with contradiction, aspersed this " great man," " the most candid of all writers," (for so he designates him,) with unwarranted severity : he actually characterised, as " a piece of management, and argumentative finesse," the modest reasons Sir Matthew offered, to shew that the bishops of the English church, have *not* a seat in parliament as *Barons ;* that " they sit there, as a privilege, by usage annexed to the episcopal dignity."[56]

The foregoing remarks, it will be observed, have been confined, mainly, to Lord Hale's relics in *divinity.* This has happened, because, unlike his labours on legal subjects, *those* compositions have never before, been the theme of lengthened comment. It must, however, be noted that, in the line of his profession, such appropriate excellencies, with respect to *authorship,* as are dictated by good sense and religion, were invariably displayed by him. This, indeed, has been abundantly shewn.

Although he would have regarded it as an unhappy commendation, to be " a *better* lawyer than a Christian ; " he, assuredly, recommends Christianity, by *extending,* so far as he did, the " grave advice " of Littleton. That famous judge contented himself, with limiting his counsel to " good pleading ; " but Lord Hale, instead of following it literally, employed " his courage and care "[57] in *every* department of legal science. A

[56] Warburton's Alliance. Works, vol. vii. pp. 129—133, 8vo. 1811.
[57] Co. Litt. lib. iii. s. 534.

slight acquaintance with his Treatises, aided by the preliminary dissertations of Mr. Hargrave, will make this plain ; will shew, how large a debt of obligation the nation contracted by them ;[58] and will prevent the observation being thought presumptuous,—that if Cowper could, unoffendingly, avow, that he knew no greater names in divinity than Watts and Doddridge,[59] it may, at least, with equal impunity, be asserted of Hale, that no greater name is known in law.

Besides the luminous order he discovered in the distribution of his subjects ; his scarce and curious materials ; and his guarded reserve in offering opinions upon some great controverted points ;[60] there was a stoutness about his judgment, with respect to legal questions, which led him into paths, as unusual as they were bold. In the essay[61] prefixed to " the Jurisdiction of the House of Lords," several instances are enumerated, where the opinion of Lord Hale, on some of the nicest points, either then unsettled, or entirely mooted by himself, have, in subsequent periods of English history, received the sanction of the legislature. And it may be here observed, in further proof of his wisdom, that to *him*, in direct opposition to the authority of Coke,[62] the country is indebted for the admissibility in evidence, of all persons professing to believe in a God, though neither believing in

[58] See Note DDDDD.
[59] Life, by Hayley, vol. i. p. 173, 8vo.
[60] The Coll. of Tracts, by Hargrave, p. vi.
[61] Pp. ccxx—ccxxiv.
[62] Co. Litt. 6. b.

the Old, nor New Testament.[63]  He had remarked,
long before that important question was decided,
how hard it were "if a murder committed in
England, in presence only of a Turk, or a Jew,
that owns not the Christian religion, should be
dispunishable."[64]

Lord Hale's manner of speaking has been noticed : but, notwithstanding it was as described ;
and notwithstanding, he paid, perhaps, less attention to that department of his public duties than
any other, Lord Chancellor Nottingham declared,
that he was the greatest orator he had known : [65]
and Lord Ellenborough, at a still later period,
said, that he was " as competent to express, as he
was able to conceive."[66]  There is, oftentimes, in
his " Judgments," the utmost energy, both of
thought and language ; and always, that healthy
vigorous robustness, which has been styled, so feli-
citously, " massy English wisdom."[67]

His professional works, eminent alike for their
precision of sentiment,[68] their comprehensive learning, and their deep research, have, uniformly, associated him with the brightest luminaries ; not
excepting Coke himself, the mighty " Colossus of
our law ;"[69] and, so ably have they been charac-

---

[63] 1. Atkyns ; 25. The case of Omichund and Barker.
[64] Hist. Plac. Cor. vol. ii. p. 279.
[65] Works, vol. i. p. 54.
[66] East's Rep. vol. v. p. 17.
[67] Quart. Rev. vol. i. p. 80.
[68] Lord Erskine's Speeches, vol. iii. p. 370.
[69] Hale's Jurisdiction of the Lords' House.  Pref. p. lxxviii.
See Note EEEEE.

terised in the citations made, or referred to, as not only to account, for the comparatively little space devoted to them in the present volume, but to render observations superfluous. A comparison, however, between the two great judges thus brought together, may not, unfairly, be attempted ; and with that, the account of the " genius, learning, and writings" of Lord Hale, shall close.

Coke, with all his greatness, and there can be no motive to diminish it, was *merely* a lawyer ;[70] " the whole of his philosophy lay in the Statutes ;"[71] his notions, consequently, in spite of his regard for " the good education of youth,"[72] were narrow,[73] and confined. Hale, equally sagacious, and equally profound, was a philosopher likewise ; a man of general science, the advocate of " industrious education ;"[74] and a " very good divine."[75] Coke was not only subtle, but sometimes insolent, and even ferocious ; as in the case of Raleigh, and the state prisoners ; and always politic.[76] Hale, while capable of feeling intense indignation, discovered, almost invariably, consummate prudence, and self-control ; nor was he

[70] See Note FFFFF.

[71] D'Israeli's Cur. of Literat. 2d Series, vol. iii. p. 96. 8vo. 1824.

[72] Epilogue to the 3d Instit. fol. 1660.    [73] Note GGGGG.

[74] Works, vol. i. pp. 517, &c. &c. &c. " On Provision for the Poor."

[75] Life of Sir Eardley Wilmot, p. 37. 4to. 1802. He was ' one of the greatest lawyers, philosophers, and divines, that ever lived.'—The Rev. Mark Noble's Mem. of the House of Cromwell, vol. i. p. 432. 8vo. 1787.

[76] Note HH

ever so devoted to policy, as to yield his independence, or trifle with his honour. COKE wrote, and common-placed, with remarkable, if not infallible, accuracy. HALE discovered the same aptitude.[77] COKE, though using his eyes, and constantly accounting for things, with "uncommon and singular reasons,"[78] contented himself, with the preservation of what he found. HALE, on the other hand, deduced consequences, as well as ascertained principles, and impressed all his communications with his own mind. COKE, completely as he exhausted every subject, is utterly defective in order, and method.[79] HALE, while every where evincing the same thoughtful comprehension, arranged with an accuracy bordering upon excess. COKE is invariably slovenly, abounding in quibbles, and quaintness, and pedantry; is often insipid; and never bold. HALE, if deficient in elegance, is uniformly energetic, seldom trite, makes no effort to shine, and uses a style at once masculine, lucid, and convincing. COKE, notwithstanding his laudable conduct in the House of Commons, and occasional opposition to the chief executive magistrate,[80] leaned to the court, interfered with its intrigues, was among the highest prerogative lawyers,[81] and used, as in the case of Essex and

[77] Lord Northington styled him, an "accurate writer." 1 Eden. p. 252.

[78] Life of Coke, by the Society for Diffusion of Useful Knowledge, p. 25.

[79] This is specially noticed by Sir William Blackstone, Comm. vol. i. p. 72. Ed. 15.

[80] Godwin's Hist. of the Commonwealth, vol. iv. p. 29.

[81] Lord Erskine's Speeches, vol. iii. p. 343.

Southampton, the grossest adulation.[82]  The atmosphere of the court, HALE studiously avoided; he delighted in the shades of privacy; and not merely cherished a strong bias to the rights of the subject, but was even zealous against unlawful power;[83] and, with the most unflinching firmness, pursued his own straightforward course, with as little regard to frowns, as smiles.

In many respects they were *alike*.  Both were splendid examples of industry, and attainments.  Both rose, by gradual and meritorious stages, to the chief seat of justice.  Both achieved wonderful objects, amidst continual cares, and weighty occupation.  Both reasoned, and inferred, with an adroitness that is truly enviable.  Both delighted to immure themselves among ancient records, and the rarest manuscripts.  Both drew copiously from them, and with equal fondness.  The works of both are a vast mine of erudition; and, notwithstanding defects, chiefly incidental to their day, both will continue to be the beacons, and lights of all other lawyers.

[82] Note IIIII.
[83] The Law Magazine, vol. ix. p. 363.

# •THE WILL OF SIR MATTHEW HALE,

EXTRACTED FROM THE REGISTRY OF THE PREROGATIVE COURT
OF CANTERBURY.

IN the name of God, Amen.  I, Mathew Hale, of
Acton, in the county of Middlesex, Knight, Cheife Justice
of His Majesties Court of Kings Bench, being, I thanke
God, in perfect memory, doe hereby revoake all former
wills and testaments by me made ; and doe hereby make
and ordaiue my last will and testament, in writing, in
manner following :—And, first, I doe, with all humility,
resigne up my soule into the hands of Almighty God,
beseeching him, for the sake of his own infinite mercy
and goodnes, and the meritts and intercession of his
only Sonne our Lord Jesus Christ, and by the sancti-
fication and unsearchable operation of his blessed Spiritt,
to make me a partaker of the inheritance of his saints
in light and glory.  And, as touching my body, I co-
mitt it to the earth, in assurance of a happy resurrection ;
and I desire it may be buried in the church-yard of
Alderley, on the south side of the tomb of my former
wife, if it may be done without much inconvenience and
expence : but (if otherwise) then in the south side of
the church-yard of Acton, neare the outside thereof, on
the south side of the tombe of my first wife, and neare
unto it ; [1] and a marble grave-stone laid upon my body,
with the inscription onely of my name : but all to be

[1] See Note KKKKK.

done privately, without any funerall pompe ; and the whole charge of my funerall, grave-stone, and mourning, by noe means to exceed one hundred pounds. And, touching the temporall estate which the goodnes and bounty of God hath lent me, I doe declare that I have made severall settlements of the greatest part of my lands by acts executed in my life-time ; and, to avoid mistakes, I shall hereafter, in this my will, mention them. First, upon, or shortly after, the marriage of my daughter Mary to Edward Adderley, Esquire, since deceased, 1 did settle or cause to be secured unto them and the heires of the body of the said Mary, the tenement in Alderley, wherein my father lived and dyed, and wherein I was borne, and the lands thereunto belonging, Mawdlins tenement, Nowells Mill, Sam. Bences tenement, Baylyes cottage, and a little new-built house and two closes of pasture, late in the occupation of Nicholas Webb, and Fowlers Meadow, as by the writings and assignements thereof made may appeare ; which settlement I doe hereby ratifie and confirme. Item, upon, or shortly after, the marriage of my eldest sonne Robert Hale with Frances his late wife (both since deceased), by indenture tripartite, bearing date on or about the fower and twentieth day of January, in the sixteenth yeare of his now Majesties raigne, I did settle the mannor-house and greatest part of the demeasnes of Alderley, in such manner that the greatest part thereof is since come in hand to Mathew Hale, his eldest sonne, in tayle male ; and for want of issue male of Mathew, then the same is to come to Gabriel, his brother, in tayle male ; and for want of such issue, the same is to come to trustees, for raising of a portion of fifteen hundred pounds, to be divided among his daughters ; which are, Anne, Mary, and Frances Hale : and the residue of the

demeasnes are, after my decease, to come to the said
Mathew, my grandchild, in tayle male; and for want of
issue male of him, to Gabriel, in tayle male; and for
want of issue male of him, to my right heires, as by the
same conveyance and the fine thereupon levied for the
execution thereof may more at large appeare; which
settlement I doe hereby confirme, with such further dispositions as I shall make touching the fee simple ex-
pectant in me, as I have by subsequent settlements now
in force, or shall by this my will or some further conveyances thereof declare, devise, lymitt, or appoint.
Item, by indenture bearing date the one and twentieth
day of September, in the eighteenth yeare of his now
Majestie's raigne, the mannor of Tresham, and the severall tenements in Tresham and Alderley, or either of
them, then in the tenures or occupations of Humfrey
Pincott, Richard Gawen, Robert Browning, and John
Hyett, or any of them; and the grounds called Culver
Acre, Mare Pooles, Mare Pool Closes, the West Hills,
and alsoe the farme in Alderley, heretofore in the tenure
of Thomas Sloper, and afterwards of John Sealy; and
the new-erected messuage thereupon built, and the severall buildings, barnes, gardens, orchards, closes, lands,
tenements, meadowes, and pastures, and hereditaments
thereunto belonging; and all the lands, tenements, and
hereditaments, which are herein after recited, to be settled
upon my now wife, for her joynture, by the indenture
herein next following to be recited, were setled and
lymitted to the absolute use and behoofe of me and my
heires; and all the rest and residue of the said mannor
of Alderley, and my lands in Hillesly and Hawkesbury
were setled by the indenture of the one and twentieth
of September, upon myselfe, for my life, with such
powers as are therein declared and reserved; and, after

my decease, to my sonne Robert Hale, and the heires
male of his body issueing; and for want of such issue,
to the heires male of my body issueing; and for want
of such issue, to my owne right heires; with a provisoe,
that if I or the heires male of my body should, within
seaven yeares after the death of my said sonne Robert,
without heires male of his body, pay to the heires
female of his body, three thousand pounds; that then
the remainder lymitted to the heirs female of the body
of the said Robert Hale should cease, as by the same
indenture more at large may appeare.  Now, I Mathew
Hale, doe hereby ratifie and confirme the said settlement,
with such further dispositions, devises, and provisions,
as I shall hereinafter make touching the lands and tenements thereby lymitted to me in fee simple, and touching the revercion or remainder in fee simple of the
premisses in Alderley, Hillesly, and Hawkesbury, to
me lymitted by the same indenture.  And I doe farther
declare and exprealy signifie, that the summe of three
thousand pounds therein mencioned or provided to be
paid to the heires female of my sonne Robert, is intended to be over and above the said summe of fifteene
hundred pounds, secured to the daughters of the said
Robert by the said settlement made upon his marriage,
beareing date the fower and twentieth day of January,
in the said sixteenth yeare of his now Majesties raigne.
Item, I doe farther declare, that a little before the marriage with Anne, my now wife, and for the setling of a
joynture for her, by indenture bearing date the nyne
and twentieth day of September, in the said eighteenth
yeare of his now Majesties raigne, I did settle and
assure to the use of myselfe for life, without impeach-
ment of waste; and, after my death, to the use of Anne,
my  now  wife,  for  her  life,  if  she  should  soe  long

continue a widdow; the remainder to the use of the heires males of my body, on her begotten and to be begotten; the remainder to the use of the heires females of my body, on her begotten and to be begotten; the remainder to the use of the said Anne, my now wife, for her life; the remainder to the use of me and my heires, all that farme and tenement in Alderley aforesaid, then before in the tenure or occupation of Thomas Sloper, and after in the tenure or occupation of John Sealy, their or some of their assignes or under-tenants, and then in the proper tenure or occupation of me, the said Mathew Hale; and all that faire new messuage then lately erected upon part of the said farme, by me, and wherein I then dwelt; and all buildings, barnes, stables, courts, backsides, closes, gardens, orchards, lands, meadowes, pastures, and appurtenants to the same messuage, farme, and tenement, or any of them belonging or apperteyning, or accepted, reputed, or taken to be part of, or belonging to, the same; and all the walls, mounds, hedges, and fences, inclosing the same or any part thereof; and ten foote in breadth of the waste ground or highway adjoyneing, contiguous to the south and west sides of the walls of the courts and garden belonging to the same new-erected messuage; and all that little spott or hill of waste ground, planted with trees, extending itselfe from the court of the said new-erected messuage westward, in length fower-score foote, or thereabouts, and extending itselfe in breadth, from north to south, fower-score foote, or thereabouts; and all those closes or grounds in Alderley aforesaid, called or known by the severall names of Wynner Hill, Wynner Hill Field, Wynner Hill Closes, the Castells, otherwise Caswells, lately divided into two closes, and the river contiguous thereunto, the closes or grounds called

Sloper's Meadow, otherwise the Gaston Meadow, Narre Leazes, otherwise Narre Leazowes, formerly three closes, the Two Horse Crofts, Sloper's Homes, Sloper's Tenn Acres, Browning's Innox, Browning's Ragg; and all that great field of arable and pasture, in Alderley aforesaid, called or knowne by the name of Alderley's Field, or Alderley's Common Field, or Alderley's Home Field, or by whatsoever name or names the same is called or knowne, conteyning by estimation threescore acres, be the same more or less; and all that new inclosure, then lately begun by me, in the south side of the same field; and all lands lying within the precinct of the said great field or new inclosure, then or before belonging to the said farme or tenement, or to the tenements of Arthur Vizard, Giles Biddle, and John Sloper, or any of them; and all other lands, pastures, and feedings, lying within the precinct of the said great field and new inclosure, or either of them; and all that parcell of land called Colepitt Bottome, conteyning, by estimation, five acres, adjoyning to the north side of the said field called Alderley's Field, with their and every of their appurtenances, as by the said last recited indenture may more fully appeare: all which premisses in the said last recited indenture comprised, are such lands as by all former conveyances were still left in me, and setled in me in fee simple, att the time of the makeing of the said last mentioned indenture, and not any way intayled before the makeing of that indenture. And I doe farther declare, that, for the better strengthening of the joynture of my now wife by the last mentioned indenture, I did leavy a fine of the lands and premisses conteyned in the said last mentioned indenture unto Sr Thomas Beverley, Knight, and Thomas Jenner, esquire names in the said fyne, comprized in the terme of St. Michaell, in the one and twentieth yeare of his said now Majesties raigne ; and I doe declare, that the same fyne was soe leavyed for the confirmation and corroboration of the joynture of my said now wife, for terme of her life, absolutely for her joynture, and to cutt off and barre the estates tayle thereof, by that deed to me lymitted, because I then intended to lymitt a like estate to the heirs of my body on her begotten, which would countervaile that estate tayle, which I have accordingly done ; and for the further assureance thereof, I doe hereby declare, devise, lymitt, and appoint, that the said capitall messuage in the said last-mentioned indenture comprized, and all other the lands, tenements, and hereditaments therein comprized, are effectually settled, and shall be accordingly held and enjoyed by my now wife absolutely for her life, for her joynture and in full recompence of her dower. Item, I doe declare that by indenture bearing date the twelfth day of October, in the fower and twentieth yeare of the raigne of our now Soveraigne Lord King Charles the Second, betweene me of the first part, my second sonne Mathew Hale, since deceased, of the second part, and the said Thomas Jenner and my servant Robert Gibbon of the third part, and fyne thereupon leavyed by me the said Sir Mathew Hale, and Mathew Hale my sonne, of the mannor of Raingery, otherwise Rayngeworthy, and of the Grange of Bagston and other lands in the same indenture and fyne, comprized the mannor house and demeasnes of Raingery, late in the occupation of John Prigge, are setled unto my said sonne Mathew, for a terme of fower score yeares, from the five and twentieth day of March then last past, if my sonne Mathew Hale, or any woman that shall be his lawfull wife att the time of his decease, or any lawfull sonne or daughter of my said sonne Mathew Hale, shall so long live, the remainder to the use of myselfe and my heirs; and all the residue of the said mannors, grange, and premises in the last mentioned indenture and fyne comprised, are settled upon me and my heirs. Item, I doe declare that by indenture of grant and release, bearing date the eighteenth day of January last past, I have settled the freehold and inheritance of the said mannors of Raingery and grange of Bagston, and all my lands in Raingery, Thornsbury, Weekewarre, and Bagston, and Frampton Cotterell, soe as that they are to come to Mathew, the onely sonne of my said sonne Mathew Hale, and the heirs male of his body; charged nevertheless with a terme of one and twenty yeares to my loving friends Sir Robert Jenkinson, Sir Gabriel Low, and Andrew Barker, for the raising of portions for my grandchildren Anne Hale, Mary Hale, and Frances Hale, in such manner as in the same indenture is expressed, as by the same indenture relation being thereunto had may more att large and particulerly appeare; and I doe ratify and confirme the same indenture, and doe will and devise the lands therein comprised to be enjoyed accordingly. Item, I doe declare that in consideration of the marriage of my sonne Edward, and for other considerations expressed in the indenture next herein mentioned, by indenture bearing date the second day of August, in the five and twentieth yeare of his now Majesties raigne, I have settled the greatest part of my lands in Eweline, in the county of Oxon, (except as therein is excepted,) upon my sonne Edward for his life, the remainder to Mary his wife for her life for her joynture, the remainder to Robert their sonne and the heirs of his body, with remainders over, as by the same indenture may more att large appeare.

Item, I do declare that by indenture dated the fifteenth day of December, in the six and twentieth yeare of his now Majesties raigne, for the consideration therein mentioned, I did settle upon my sonne Thomas and his issue, the mills att Eweline and certaine lands and hereditaments in Acton, in the county of Middlesex, (except as therein is excepted,) for such estates and in such manner as is therein expressed, saving the reversion thereof in fee simple to me and my heires, with power for the said Thomas to make joynture for his wife for her life, which he hath accordingly made, and is since dead without issue, soe that the reversion, after the death of his wife, is fallen to me or some other person to whom I have settled and conveyed the same by the indenture next hereinafter mentioned. Item, I do declare that by indenture dated the fowerth day of January last past, for a further respective provision for my dear wife, and for my grandchildren, Gabriel Hale, Anne Hale, Mary Hale, and Frances Hale, and for my sonne Edward Hale and his children, I have conveyed and assured the reversion in fee of the premises in Acton and Eweline, settled upon my sonne Thomas as aforesaid, and the rest of my lands in Acton, in the county of Middlesex, the reversion of my wife's joynture in Alderley, the farme in Tresham, in Humfrey Pincott's possession, my lands and mills in Eweline, (excepted out of the settlement made as above upon my sonne Edward's marriage,) and two fee farme rents issuing out of Cottesmore Farme, and the cottage called the Forge, respectively, my lands in the county of Somersett, my fowerth part of the mannor of Chedull, in Staffordshire, and of a tenement called Dudmandale, in Lincolnshire, to the severall and respective uses in the same last mentioned indenture expressed, as by the said indenture may more at large appeare. Item, I do declare that all these severall settlements and assureances above recited stand in their full force, unrevvoked and unaltered; and I do ratify and confirme the same by this my will, and doe declare, devise, and appoint, that the severall mannors, messuages, granges, mills, lands, meadowes, pastures, and hereditaments, in the said severall indentures above mentioned comprized, shal bee, remaine, and continue to the respective use and uses of such respective persons, and for such respective estates, and in such manner and forme respectively, as in or by the same respective indentures the same are distributed, declared, lymitted, or appointed, except such further dispositions as I have made or shall make by this my will, of part of the mannor of Alderley. Item, whereas I am seized of some coppyhold land in Acton, in the county of Middlesex, which lyeth neare unto or within some part of the gardens and closes belonging to the dwelling-house in Acton, wherein I now inhabite, formerly purchased of John Humfrey and Elizabeth his wife, or one of them (although the said dwelling-house and the greatest part of the gardens and closes thereunto belonging are freehold or charterhold, at the common law); and upon my purchase heretofore of the coppyhold from the said John Humfrey and Elizabeth his wife, I surrendered all the coppyhold soe by me purchased, to the use of my will, I doe therefore devise all my coppyhold lands, tenements, and hereditaments in the parish of Acton, in the county of Middlesex, unto my dear wife Anne Hale, for and during the terme of her naturall life; and from and after her decease, to and to the use of the heires of my body, on her begotten; and for default of such issue, to and to the use of the said Gabriel Hale, and the heires of his body yssueing; and

for want of such issue, to his sisters, Anne Hale, Mary
Hale, and Frances Hale, their heires and assignes for
ever, with a power to my deare wife, by her last will in
writing, to dispose thereof in such manner and forme
as by the said last mentioned indenture, dated the said
fowerth day of January last past, the capitall messuage
in Acton aforesaid, wherein I the said Sir Mathew Hale
doe inhabite or dwell, is lymitted.   Item, I doe declare
that I have lately purchased of Sir Thomas Stephens and
Thomas Stephens, his sonne and heire apparent, and
of their wives, by fyne and other assureances, a certaine
farme, lands, and tenements called Old Sodburyes
Parkes, and certaine other lands in Old Sodbury, Little
Sodbury, and Chipping Sodbury, or some or one of
them ;  and by my deed dated the six and twentieth
day of July last past, I have conveyed the same to Sir
Robert Jenkinson and others for fifteene yeares, partly to
secure a thousand pounds belonging to my daughter
Adderley and her children, and the growing interest
thereof: and afterwards, for the payment of my just
debts and legacies, and for such other disposalls as I shall
make in my last will, and by my deed of bargaine and
sale for a yeare, bearing date the twentieth day of January ;  and by my release thereupon, beareing date the
one and twentieth day of January last past, I have
settled the inheritance thereof upon my grandchild Gabriel Hale, and the heires of his body ;  and for want of
such issue, to his elder brother, Mathew Hale, and the
heires of his body, with remainders over, as by the said
deed may more att large appeare.  Now I doe ratify and
confirme the same deeds and settlement, and doe will that
the said parks and farme in Old Sodbury, Little Sodbury, and Chipping Sodbury, or any of them, shal bee
enjoyed according to the purport and tenor of those

Q

settlements thereof; and I doe further will, that out of the proffitts thereof dureing the said terme of fifteene yeares, the said one thousand pounds due to my daughter Mary Adderley and her children, be paid; and out of the residue of the proffitts there be paid to my grandchild Gabriel, towards the makeing good of his maintenance hereafter mentioned, the summe of twenty pounds yearly, till his age of tenn yeares, and the summe of twenty pounds from thence till his age of fifteene yeares, and the summe of three score and tenn pounds from thence till the expiration of the said terme of fifteene yeares; and I doe farther declare that the residue of the said proffitts, dureing the said terme of fifteene yeares, shal bee applyed towards payment of such debts as I shall owe att the time of my decease, and of such legacies of money as I have given by this my will, or shall give by any codicill subscribed with my hand; and that the residue of the said profitts during the said terme (if any be) shal bee and remaine to such persons to whome the inheritance of the said premises in Sodbury shall belong. Item, I doe declare that my deed, beareing date the thirteenth day of January last past, and by fyne and lease and release, the mannours of Wortley, Hillesley, and Tresham, are lymitted to trustees, for certaine termes of yeares; the remainder over to my grand children, Mathew Hale and Gabriel Hale, sonnes of my eldest sonne Robert Hale, deceased, in such manner as in the said deed is exprest. Now I doe ratify and confirme the same deed, and I doe will and devise that the lands therein comprized shal bee enjoyed according to the lymittations therein exprest. Item, I doe devise and bequeath that all my lands, tenements, and hereditaments in Alderley aforesaid, that remaine in me in fee simple, or are subject to my disposal, shal bee and

remaine unto my grandchild **Mathew Hale**, eldest sonne
of my late eldest sonne Robert Hale, deceased, and to
the heires of his body issueing; and for want of such
issue, to his said brother Gabriel Hale, and the heires of
his body issueing; and for want of such issue, to such
uses and under such lymittations and provisoes as are
lymitted by the said indenture, dated the one and
twentieth day of September, in the eighteenth yeare of
his now Majestie's raigne, subject nevertheles to such
estates as I have formerly made to my now wife and to
my grandchild Gabriel Hale. And whereas, by the
settlements above mentioned, or some of them, there
are severall termes of yeares lymitted unto trustees,
in trust to be disposed as I shall by my will direct (that
is to say) fifteene yeares in part of the mannor of Wortley, thirteene yeares in other part thereof, and in the
mannor of Hillesley and Tresham, and ten yeares in the
mannor of Chedull and Calcutt, one and twenty yeares
in part of the mannor of Raingery, fifteene yeares in
my lands att Sodbury, and tenn yeares in the tenement
called Pincotts Farme, as by the said severall settlements
more certainely and att large may appeare. Now I doe
hereby declare that the said tenn yeares in Pincotts
Farme is soe lymitted in trust for my grandchild Gabriel Hale; the said fifteene yeares in my said lands att
Sodbury is soe lymitted, in trust for the payment of the
said summe of one thousand pounds to my daughter
Adderley's children, as in the deed thereof is exprest;
and the residue of the proffitts thereof, arising duering
the said terme, is to be imployed for the necessary maintenance of the said Gabriel Hale, according to the proportion and allotment hereinafter made to him; and the
surplusage (if any be) to be employed towards the raising
of a farther summe of twelve hundred pounds for my

Q 2

three grand daughters, namely, Anne, Mary, and Frances Hale, children of my said sonne Robert Hale, to be equally divided amonge them ; and the surplusage of proffitts thereof ariseing during the same terme, to be imployed towards payment of my debts and other legacies ; and afterwards for such uses as the inheritance thereof is lymitted by the deed of settlement thereof; and as to the rest of the termes of yeares above lymitted in trust as aforesaid, the same shall be, in the first place, for the raising of necessary maintenance for my grand daughters, Anne, Mary, and Frances Hale, and the surplusage to be imployed for the raising of portions for them, to be equally divided amongst them ; and further, I doe declare that the said severall portions shal be equally divided betweene my said grand daughters, Anne, Mary, and Frances Hale, att their days of marriage, or ages of one and twenty yeares (which shall first happen); provided that if any of them, the said Anne, Mary, and Frances Hale, shall happen to dye before her age of one and twenty yeares, and before her marriage, or if any of them shall in the life time of any of my executors hereafter named, and before her age of eighteene yeares marry, or contract herselfe in marriage, without the consent of my executors hereafter named, or one of them, first had and obtained, then the part or portion of money of her soe dyeing or marrying without consent as aforesaid, shall remaine to her other sisters.  Item, although I have chosen to settle my mannors and lands, by acts and conveyances executed in my life time, as is above expressed, rather then to leave them to a disposall by my will ; and although by the before recited settlements, I have made good provision for my deare wife and my children, and for the most of those grandchildren of myne that were espeacially cast upon my care, and stood most in need of it, or were not otherwise conveniently provided for, yet I doe thinke fitt now farther to make a disposition of the testamentary and personall estate which God hath lent me, and to leave such farther disposalls and directions as by the blessing of God may be convenient for those of my neare relations that shall survive me; and therefore, in the first place, in testimony of my great and deserved love to my deare wife, who hath beene a most dutifull and faithfull and loving wife to me, and a most tender mother to my children and a most tender and loving grandmother to my grandchildren; I say, I give to Anne, my now wife, two hundred pounds in ready money, to be paid to her and received by her upon the day of my death before any other legacy given to any other, and also the peeces of gold coyne which I gave to her owne hands in my life time, amounting to about one hundred pounds sterling money. Item, I give unto my said wife all my rings, clocks, watches, jewells, apparell, plate, brasse, pewter, lynnen, woollen, wheresover, and all my hangings, bedds, and houshould stuffe in my said house att Alderley, settled upon her for her joynture, and now in the occupation of John Clarke, and the usual furniture of her closett, the little parlor chamber, and hall chamber of my mannor house of Alderley (excepting onely ready money not before given her in this my will, and except bonds, bills, mortgages, writings, and evidences, and except books and papers other then such as are given her espeacyally by my will, and except such goods or things as I shall otherwise give or dispose by this my will.) Item, I give and bequeath to my said wife all those printed books of divinity, chyrurgery, phisick, or history, in English, which I have subscribed or shall subscribe with my hand, testifying such guift to her,

and alsoe all those papers of myne touching divinity
which I shall soe alsoe subscribe, or have soe subscribed,
to be given her. Alsoe I give her my little chariott,
my two coach horses, and my cowes. Item, I give to
my grandsonne, Mathew Hale, eldest sonne of my
deceased sonne, Robert Hale, and the heires of his body,
the remainder to my grandchild Gabriel Hale, and the
heires of his body; and for want of such issue, to the
heires male of my body, as heire loomes to be preserved
in my family, my mathematicall instruments, my load
stones, my magneticall instruments, my turquoys ring,
my great chests of drawers for holding writings, marked
G: and E: and my oaken chest bonded with iron,
marked B: both which are at Alderley, onely I will
have these things remaine in the custody of my executors, untill my grandchildren, Mathew and Gabriel Hale,
or one of them, attaine one of their ages of one and
twenty yeares. Item, I give unto my said grandchild
and heire, Mathew Hale, the houshold stuffe and pictures that were in the mannor house of Alderley, except
what are above given to my wife. Item, I give to my
daughter, Mary Adderley, my black serpentine cupp
with silver cover, and my middle silver bason, and I
remitt unto her all the money she owes me, and I give
to her eldest daughter, Mary Adderley, one hundred
pounds; to her daughter, Anne Adderley, one hundred
pounds; to her youngest daughter, Susan Adderley,
one hundred pounds; to her youngest sonne, Edward
Adderley, two hundred pounds; and these summes are
given to them in satisfaction of that debt by bond of
one hundred pounds due by me, and made over to me
among other bonds, by their father, Edward Adderley,
Esquire, deceased, in trust for his wife and children.
Item, I give to my grandchildren, Elizabeth Webb and

Edward Webb, children of my deceased daughter, Elizabeth, the wife of Edward Webb, tenn pounds apeice. To my grandchild, Robert Hale, sonne of my sonne Edward Hale, ten pounds. Item, to my grandchild, Mathew, sonne of my sonne Mathew, my chest of drawers marked T: and tenn pounds. Item, I give to my servants Thomas Sherman and Robert Gibbon, Thomas Shrewsbury and Phineas Unicum, twenty pounds apeice. To my servants Robert Langley and John Clarke, tenn pounds apeice. To my servants, Thomas Allen, Isaac Hoare, Anne Jones, and Joane Rymer, fifty shillings apeice. To Joseph Brooker, when he comes out of his apprentishood, to help to sett up his trade, forty pounds. To Mr. Richard Baxter[2] and to Mr. Griffith, minister of Alderley, forty shillings apeice. To the poore of Alderley, forty shillings. To the poore of Wortely, forty shillings. To the poore of Wotton Underedge, twenty shillings. To the poore of Ringswood, twenty shillings. To the poore of Raingery, twenty shillings. Item, I doe devise and bequeath the custody and education of my grandchildren, Mathew Hale, Gabriel Hale, Anne Hale, Mary Hale, and Frances Hale, children of my sonne Robert Hale, untill their respective ages of one-and-twenty years, and likewise the management and government and custody of their estates and portions, unto my dear wife Anne Hale, dureing her widdowhood, and to my worthy friends, Sir Robert Jenkinson of Walcott in the county of Oxon, Baronett, and my late servant, Robert Gibbons, of the Middle Temple, London, Esquire, and to the survivors and survivor of them; and I doe direct and appoint that they shall have the receiveing of the rents belonging to my said grandchildren, and the letting out and

2 See Note LLLLL.

improvement of their portions and the provisions that I
have made for the improvement thereof, for the use of
my said grandchildren ; but it is my will that the said
three girles shall continue in house with my wife, and
be under her care and inspection dureing my wife's
widdowhood, and dureing their respective nonage ; and
likewise that the two boyes shall remaine in house with
my wife, and remaine under her care and inspection
till they are sent abroad to schoole or to the University :
and that when upon occasion they returne home they
shall be under her care and tutelage, for I have had
abundant experience of her care of them, and for that
end I doe appoint a competent maintenance and allowance to be made for them all, as well when they are att
home and abroad (that is to say) unto my grandchild
Mathew Hale, out of the rents and revenues of the
lands to him belonging, twenty pounds yearly, untill
his age of tenn yeares, and thirty pounds yearly from
that age till his age of fowerteene yeares, and fowerscore
pounds yearly from that age till his age of one-and-
twenty yeares ; and to my grandchild, Gabriel Hale, the
abovementioned summes of twenty pounds yearly, till his
age of tenn yeares, and thirty pounds yearly from thence
till his age of fifteene yeares, and threescore and tenn
pounds yearly from thence till his age of one-and-
twenty yeares, out of the revenues of the lands by me
settled upon him, as is aforesaid ; and to each of my
said three grand daughters, Anne, Mary, and Frances
Hale, out of the proffitts of the lands and other provisions by me made for them, twenty pounds apeice yearly
for them, respectively, untill their respective ages of
fowerteene yeares ; and afterwards, an addition of tenn
pounds per annum apeice till their respective marriages
or ages of one and twenty yeares ; and those yearly

summes I would have constantly paid for their cloathes, dyett, washing, and lodging, and other necessaries relating to their education, quarterly, unto the hands of my said deare wife, to be issued, received, disposed, and imployed for them ; for I would have her to have an honourable and plentifull allowance, that she may be a gainer and not a looser by them, and that they may be decently maintayned and educated as becomes the orphans of my eldest sonne ; the surplusage of the rents and proffits that shall accrue to my said last mentioned five grand children, Mathew, Gabriel, Anne, Mary, and Frances Hale, over and above their said maintenance and education, I would have imployed and disposed according to their respective interests for the increase and advance of their respective portions and estates according to the discreation of their said guardians ; I would have the two boyes sent to schoole when they are fitt for it ; the eldest, who is but weakly, to be taught but gently, as he will take itt ; the younger may be kept closer to his booke, but without rigour ; my desire is, that Gabriel may have all advantages of a learned education, and (if it please God so to order it) to be of my owne profession. As touching the disposall of my bookes, which I esteeme to be a choyce collection (though not great) I dispose thereof as followeth. First, I give to my dear wife such English books of divinity, humanity, history, phisick, and chyrurgery, as I have subscribed, or shall for that purpose indorse or subscribe with my hand, that I have given her, and alsoe such manuscript paper books and collections of my owne that I have subscribed or shall subscribe to have given her. Item, I give to my grand sonne, Gabriel Hale, in case he shall follow the study of the common lawes of England, those bookes or reports of the common lawes or statutes of this kingdome hereafter following (viz.) all my Manuscript Reports of the Cases adjudged or argued in the raignes of Queene Mary, Queene Elizabeth, King James, King Charles the First, and King Charles the Second, the three yeare bookes of Edward the Third, the yeare books of Henry the Fowerth, Henry the Fifth, and Henry the Sixth, Edward the Fowerth, and Henry the Seventh; the three volumes of Justice Crooke's Reports; the Reports of Popham, Hutton, Noy, Lee, Latch, Leonard, Bulstrod, Sarjeant Moore, Stiles, Fitzherbert's Abridgment, Brook's Abridgment, the Old and New Bookes of Entryes, Plowden's Commentaries, Dalton's Justice of Peace, Pulton's Justice of Peace, Lambert's Justice of Peace, Pulton's Statutes at Large, Dyer's Reports, my Lord Cooke's Magna Charta, and Pleas of the Crowne, and Jurisdiction of Courts. Item, as a testimony of my honor and respect to the Society of Lincolne's Inne, where I had the greatest part of my education, I give and bequeath to that honourable Society the several manuscript bookes conteyned in a schedule annexed to my will; they are a treasure worth the haveing and keeping, which I have beene neare forty yeares in gathering with very great industry and expence, my desire is that they be kept safe and altogether in remembrance of me; they were fitt to be bound in leather, and chained and kept in archives. I desire they may not be lent out or disposed, onely if I happen hereafter to have any of my posterity of that Society that desires to transcribe any booke, and gives very good cautione to restore it againe within a prefixed time, such as the Benchers of that Society in councell shall approve of, then and not otherwise onely one booke att one time may be lent out to them by the Society, soe that there be noe more but one of those bookes abroad out of the library att any one time. They are a treasure that are not fitt for every man's viewe, nor is every man capable of makeing use of them ; onely I would have nothing of these bookes printed, but intirely preserved together for the use of the industrious learned members of that worthy Society. Item, I give to my grand child, Gabriel Hale, when he shall attaine the age of twenty yeares, in case hee shall follow the study of the common law, all the rest of my books and Reports of the Common Laws of England, as well printed as manuscript, not before herein bequeathed, and all my books of the Statutes of England, Scotland, or Ireland, not before herein bequeathed, and particularly the coppy now transcribed by Mr. Allen, of my great manuscript collection of the new or written law, digested under titles or heads ; my Abridgments of Dyer, Henry the Sixth, the Booke of Assizes, my Great Collections, touching ports and customes, and Pleas of Crowne and Liberties ; those I will shall remaine under the safe custody of my executors without dissipation, or lending them out until my grand child Gabriel come to his age of one and twenty yeares, if he live soe long, and then to be delivered to him: if he study the law, and if he dye before that time without issue, or doe not apply himselfe to the study of the law, then I give the same to his brother Mathew Hale ; all the rest of my bookes, as well printed as written either by myselfe or any other, together with my mathematicall and magneticall instruments, I will shall remaine as a kind of heireloome in my family, and therefore, I will and devise that the same shall remaine either at Acton or Alderley, carefully looked to and kept together, locked up till my grand child Mathew Hale, or my grand childe Gabriel Hale, shall attaine his age of one and twenty yeares, and then I will the same books and all my mathematicall and magneticall instruments, loade stones, and mathematicall scales, weights, and glasses, shall remaine to my said grand child Mathew Hale, eldest sonne of my deceased sonne Robert Hale, and the beires of the body of the said Mathew Hale, the grand child; and for want of such issue to my said grand child Gabriel Hale, and the heires of his body issuing, and for want of such issue to such person and persons as should be inheritable to an estate lymitted to me and the heires male of my body; and I doe expressly declare that I will have nothing of my owne writing printed after my death, but onely such as I shall, in my life time, deliver out to be printed.' Item, as touching all the rest and residue of my debts, credits, and personall estate, not before herein bequeathed, and remaining after my debts and legacies paid; I will that two third parts thereof shal bee and remaine unto and amonge the children of my sonne Robert Hale, and the remaining third part to be to the younger children of my daughter Mary Adderley; and lastly, I doe hereby nominate and appoint my said deare wife Anne Hale, and the said Sir Robert Jenkinson, and my servant Robert Gibbon, to be executors of this my last will and testament; and I do declare that my executors shall have a full allowance of their charges and expences in and about the executeing of this my will, and the trusts in them, by this my will, reposed; and I do give to the said Sir Robert Jenkinson and Robert Gibbon, twenty pounds apeece, in witnesse whereof, I have subscribed, sealed, and published this my will, conteyneing seaventeene sheets, every sheete subscribed with

See Note MMMMM.

my hand, this third day of February, Anno Domini, 1675, and in the eight and twentieth yeare of the raigne of our Soveraigne Lord, King Charles the Second.

MATHEW HALE.

Subscribed, sealed, and published, on the said third day of February, 1675, in the presence of ROBERT GYBBON, ROBERT LANGLEY, GEORGE WEBBE, ROBERT HYDE, CLEMENT ARMITAGE, TRIAMOR BALDWIN.

### A SCEDULE of the Books given to Lincolnes Inne,[4] by the Will annexed.

Plita de Tempore Regis Johannis sticht, one volume.

Plita coram Rege E. 1st, two, volumes.

Plita coram Rege E. 2d, one volume.

Plita coram Rege E. 3d, three volumes.

Plita coram Rege R. 2d, one volume.

Plita coram Rege H. 4. H. 5th, one volume.

Plita de banco E. 1st, ab anno $1^{mo}$. ad ann. $21^{o}$. one volume.

Transcripts of many Pleas coram rege et de banco E. 1st, one volume.

The Pleas in the Exchequer, styled Communia, from $1^{o}$. E. 3d to $46^{o}$. E. 3d, five volumes.

Close Rolls of King John, verbatim, of $y^{e}$ most material things, one volume.

The Principall matters in the Close and Patent Rolls of H. 3, transcribed verbatim from the 9th H. 3. to 56 H. 3. velome, marked K. L, five volumes.

The Principal matters in the Close and Patent Rolls E. $1^{mi}$ with severall coppyes and abstracts of Records, one volume, marked F.

A long booke of Extracts of Records by me.

Close and Patent Rolls from $1^{mo}$. to $10^{mo}$. E. 3d, and other Records of $y^{e}$ time of H. 3d, one volume, marked W.

Close Rolls of 15 and 51 E. 3d, with other Records, marked N, one volume.

[4] See Note NNNNN.

Close Rolls from 17 to 38, E. 3d, two volumes.

Close and Patent Rolls from 40 E. 3d to 50 E. 3d, one volume, marked B.

Close Rolls of E. 2d, with other Records, marked R, one volume.

Close and Patent Rolls, and Charter Rolls in y^e time of King John, for y^e Clergy, one volume.

A great volume of Records of severall natures, marked G.

The Leagues of the Kings of England, Tempore E. 1st, E. 2d, E. 3d, one volume.

A Booke of Antient Leagues and Military Provisions, one volume.

The Reports of y^e Iters of Derby, Nottingh. and Bedford, transcribed, one volume.

Itinera Forest. de Pickeringe et Lancaster, transcript ex originali, one volume.

An antient reading, very large, upon Carta de Forestâ, and of y^e Forest Laws.

The Transcript of the Iter Forestæ de [Dean] one volume.

Quo warranto and liberties of the County of Gloucester, with the Pleas of y^e Chase of Kingswood, one volume.

Transcripts of the Black Booke of y^e Admiralty, Laws of y^e Army impositions, and several Hon^rs, one volume.

Records of Patents, Inquisitions, &c, of the County of Leicester, one volume.

Musters, and Military Provisions of all sorts, extracted from the Records, one volume.

Gervasius Tilburiensis, or the Black Booke of the Exchequer, one volume.

The King's Title to y^e Pre-emption of Tynne, a thynne volume.

Calendar of the Records in the Towre, a small volume.

A Miscellany of divers Records, Orders, and other things of various natures, marked E, one volume.

Another of the like nature, marked X, one volume.

Another of the like nature, in leather covers, one volume.

A Booke of Divers Records and Things, relateing to y^e Chancery, one volume.

Titles of Honour and Pedegrees, especially touching Clifford, one volume.

History of ye Maerches of Wales, collected by me, one volume.

Certaine Collections, touching Titles of Honour, one volume.

Coppies of severall Records, touching Premunire, one volume.

Extract of Commissions, tempore H. 7, H. 8, RR. and ye proceedings in ye Court Military, betweene Ray and Ramsey, one volume.

Petitions in Parliament, tempore E. 1, E. 2, E. 3, H. 4, three volumes.

Summons of Parliament, from 49 H 3, to 22 E 4, in three volumes.

The Parliament Rolls from ye beginning of E. 1st to ye end of R. 3, in 19 volumes, viz.—1 of E. 1st, one of E. 2d, with ye ordinations, two of E. 3, 3 of R. 2d, 2 of H. 4, 2 of H. 5, 4 of H 6, 3 of E. 4, 1 of R. 3 ; all transcribed att large.

Mr. Elsing's Booke, touching ye proceedings in Parliament, one volume.

Noye's Collection, touching ye King's supplies, stitched, one volume.

A Booke of various Collections out of Records, and ye Register of Canterbury and Claymes, at ye coronation of R. 2, one volume.

Transcripts out of Bishop Usher's Notes,[s] principally concerning Chronology, three large volumes.

A Transcript out of Doomsday Book of Glocestershire and Herefordshire, and of some Pipe Rolls and old Accounts of the Customes, one volume.

Extracts and Collections out of Records, touching Titles of Honour, one volume.

Extracts of Pleas, Patents, and Close Rolls, tempore H. 3, E. 1, E. 2, E. 3, and some old Antiquities of England, one volume.

Collections and Memorialls of many Records and Antiquities, one volume, Seldeni.

[s] See the Life of Usher, by Parr, p. 108.

Calendar of Charters and Records in y^e Tower, touching Gloucestershire.

Collection of Notes and Records of various natures, marked M, in one volume. Seldeni.

Transcript of y^e Iters of London, Kent, Cornwall, one volume.

Extracts out of the Leiger Books of Battell, Evesham, Winton, &c. one volume. Seldeni.

Coppies of the principall Records in y^e Red Booke in the Exchequer, one volume.

Extract of Records and Treaties, relateing to sea affaires, one volume.

Records touching Customes and Ports, Partition of the Lands of G. De Clare, &c.

Extract of Pleas in the time of R. 1st, King John, E. 1st, &c. one volume.

Cartæ antiquæ in the Tower, transcribed, in two volumes.

Chronologicall Remembrances, extracted out of y^e Notes of Bishop Usher,[b] stitched, one volume.

Inquisitiones de Legibus Walliæ, one volume.

Collections or Records, touching Knighthood.

Titles of Honour. Seldeni, one volume.

Mathematicks and Fortifications, one volume.

Processus curiæ militaris, one volume.

A Booke of Honour, sticht, one volume.

Extracts out of the Registry of Canterbury.

Coppies of severall Records, touching proceedings in the Military Court, one volume.

Abstracts of Summons and Rolls of Parliament, out of the Booke Dunelm, and some Records alphabetically digested, one volume.

Abstract of Divers Records in the office of First Fruits, stitched, one volume.

Mathematicall and Astrologicall Calculations, one volume.

A Booke of Divinity.

[b] See his Life, by Parr, p. 108.

Two Large Repertories of Records, marked A and B.
    (All those above are in folio and in paper.)

The proceedings of the Forests of Wyndsor, Deane, and Essex, in quarto, one volume.

        (Those that follow are most of them in velome or parchment.)

Two Books of Old Statutes, one ending 3 H. 7, the other 2 H. 5, with ye summes, two volumes.

Iter Northon. Nott. et Derby, one volume.

Five last yeares of E. 2, one volume.

Reports, Temp E. 2, one volume.

The Yeare Booke of R. 2, and some others, one volume.

An Old Cronicle from ye Creation to E. 3, one volume.

A Mathematicall Booke, espeacially Optiques, one volume.

A Dutch Booke of Geometry and Fortification.

Murti Benevenlani Geometrica, one volume.

Reports tempore E. 1st, under titles, one volume.

An Old Register and some Pleas, one volume.

Bernardi Braytrack Peregrinatio, one volume.

Iter Cantii et London, and some Reports, tempore E. 2, one volume.

Reports Tempore E. 1st, and E. 2d, one volume.

Leiger Booke Abbatiæ de bello.

Isidori Opera.

Liber altercationis et Christianæ Philosophiæ, contra Paganos.

Historia Petri Manducatorii.

Hornii Astronomica.

Historia Ecclesiæ Dunelmensis.

Hollandi Chymica.

De Alchymiæ Scriptoribus.

The Black Booke of ye New Law, collected by me, and digested into alphabeticall titles, written with my owne hand, which is ye originall Coppy.

      MATHEW HALE.      MATHEW HALE.

                  *Secundo die Novemb.* 1676.

I, Mathew Hale, knight, doe hereby republish, ratifie,

and confirme my Will hereunto annexed, as if the same were originally made this second day of November, Anno Domini 1676, but with these additions and alterations in this my codicil expressed. I doe declare that very lately since the making of my Will hereunto annexed, I have purchased of Christopher Parnels in the East Field of Wortley, and of Mr. Richard Thynn, and his wife, their messuage, lands, and tenements, in Wortley and Wotton Under Edge, part whereof they held in fee simple, or for some other estate of inheritance, under the devise of Robert Hopkins, deceased, late husband of Mrs. Thynn, and the residue thereof was held under a demise made by me to the said Richard Thynn, and I have laid a meadow ground neare Resty, a parcell of arrable land called Cucko Pen another parcell of inclosed land called Fryer's Hill, and all the arrable lands soe purchased of Mr. Thynn and his wife, lying dispersedly in the East Field of Wortley, upon and beneath the hills, and Hopkins Batswell Tayleamore, and Mr. Purnel's land in the East Field, unto the demeasnes of Wortley, now in the occupation of John Shrewsbury and his mother or one of them, and I have lett the same parcells together with the rest of the demeasnes unto John Shrewsbury, for two yeares from the 25th of March next, att the yearly rent of one hundred and twenty pounds. I doe hereby devise farther, that the said purchased lands soe by mee annexed, added or demised with the demeasnes of Wortley, shall be and remaine to such uses, estates, trusts, intents and purposes, and with such respective limitations as are by me made touching the farme and demesnes of the mannor of Wortley, by the indenture of settlement thereof above mentioned, beareing date 13 January Anno Domini, 1675, and that the residue of the lands by

mee purchased of Mr. Thynn and his wife, or by them
or either of them granted or surrendered to mee, shall
be and remaine to the same uses, intents, purposes, and
lymittations, as the residue of the mannor of Worteley is
thereby lymitted by that indenture of settlement, and
because the revenue of Wortley and the lands therein
setled will be of a good value and perfectly in my owne
disposall, and soe in time make a faire accession and
increase of my heires estate and revenue which will be
alsoe considerably improved by this purchase from Mr.
Thynn, I doe declare that the settlement of my lands,
comprized in the deed of 13th January, Anno Domini
1675, and alsoe this bequest of this new purchase, must
and shall and do go in discharge of all arreares of rent
or other accounts for any rents due to my heire, upon
or before this present second day of November, Anno
Domini 1676, and well it may, for it amounts to above
five times the value of the same arreares, besides my
great charge in buildings and in providing portions and
revenues for his sisters and younger brother.   Item, I
doe hereby appoint my servant, Thomas Sherman, to be
the generall receiver of the revenues that are to come to
my said grandchildren, the children of my eldest sonne,
Robert Hale, deceased, and to be accountable for the
same, and to pay the same in to my executors twice in
the yeare (viz.) about Michaelmas and Lady Day, or
oftener if there shall be occasion ; and I doe appoint him
to receive out of the revenues by me settled by will or
otherwise upon or in trust for my said grandchildren,
the yearly summe of twenty pounds, to be by him ratably
discounted upon their respective revenues.   Item, I doe
appoint Charles Crew to be tutor and instructor in learning of my grandchilde and heyre Mathew Hale, and
Gabriel his brother, during their respective minorities,

though possibly when Gabriel is about nyne yeare old he may be sent abroad to schoole, Mathew being more weakly, shall remaine under the instruction of Charles Crew, and in recompence thereof he shall have out of the revenue that will come to my grandchild and heire, the yearly summe of twenty marks and a chamber, lodging, washing, and diett, in my mannor house of Alderley. Item, although I have provided a good joynture and joynture-house at Alderley, and another house att Acton for my dear and deserving wife, yet it is my desire that she would make my manor house att Alderley the place of residence of her and my five grandchildren, children of my sonne Robert, for I would have that place their common home, that they may bee under the care and inspection of my deare wife, of whose prudence and love I have had abundant experience, and therefore I do devise and bequeath that the household stuffe in the mannor house of Alderley, above by me bequeathed, shall remaine in my executors' hands, for the reception of my wife and five grandchildren, and their necessary servants, till they are growne up to be otherwise disposed or provided for. Item, I doe hereby remitt and forgive my sonne Edward, and my daughter Mary, all debts and summes of money due from them to mee respectively. Item, because Phineas Unicum is destitute of friends, I give him the farther summe of twenty pounds besides the legacie of twenty pounds above by my will given to him, and this in full of all wages or other expectances by him from mee ; onely if I might presume soe much I should desire one of my worthy successors in the office of Cheife Justice or Cheife Baron, to bestow some employment in clerkshipp upon him for his better subsistence, if it stand with their convenience. Item, I give Mr. Edward Stephens, of Cherrington, tenn pounds.

Item, whereas it may so fall out that some books of my own wrighting as well touching the Common Law as other subjects [may be published] and for that purpose one Booke *de Homine* is now in the presse, for which the stationer, William Shrewsbury, hath contracted to pay twenty pounds, and twenty pounds more for a second impression, whereof five pounds is paid I doe appoint that the rest of the money comeing for that booke shal be equally divided betweene Thomas Sherman, Thomas Shrewsbury, Charles Crew, and Phineas Unicum; and if any other bookes shall happen to be printed, I would have William Shrewsbury to have the coppy and impression giveing, in reason as another stationer will give for it; and the money arising by such contracts to be divided into ten equall shares or parts, whereof two shares to goe to Mr. Edward Stephens for his care about the impression, one share to Mr. Allen, my amanuensis, for his care and assistance in examining the coppy and impressions, one share among my mayd servants equally to be divided, fower shares to be to Thomas Sherman, Thomas Shrewsbury, Phineas Unicum, and Charles Crew, and the remaineing two shares to be equally divided amonge all my household servants. I further desire Mr. Nicholas Heskins, late mayor of Wotton Underedge, and Mr. Rowse of Wotton Underedge, attorney att law, to be adviseing and assisting to my executors att the auditing of accounts, when they can conveniently spare soe much time, and not disposeing of money or making contracts, but I meane it onely as an advice and assistance, and not to alter or abridge the powers, authorities, trusts and interests by my will or codicill or deeds therein mentioned given to my trustees or executors, neither shall the direction of those deeds or will, or the proceedings thereupon be suspended, declared or hindred by the death or absence of the said Nicholas Hoskins and Mr. Rowse, or either of them, neither shall they have any authority, but onely to inspect and advise; but the authorities given to my trustees and executors, to stand in all points as if those two assistants were not named; and I give to each of these two assistants tenn pounds a peice.

MATHEW HALE.

# NOTES.

# NOTES.

---

## NOTE A.—Page 5.

SIR JOHN GLANVILLE was, considerably, Hale's senior, and ranked, by his professional acquirements, among *able* lawyers. —See his Reports, first published by John Topham, Esq. 8vo. 1775. Preface, p. 1.

The Serjeant, during several parliamentary sessions, represented Plymouth, of which town he was Recorder; and became, at length, Speaker to the House of Commons. In the year 1661 he died. The following circumstance in his history, is remarkable: it shall be given in the words of Burnet:—

The Serjeant's "father, had a fair estate, which he intended to settle on his elder brother; but he being a very vicious young man, and there appearing no hopes of his recovery, he settled it upon him that was the second son. Upon his death, his eldest son, finding that what he had before looked on as the threatenings of an angry father, was now but too certain, became melancholy; and that, by degrees, wrought so great a change on him, that what his father could not prevail in while he lived, was now effected by the severity of his last will, so that it was now too late for him to change, in hopes of any estate that was gone from him. But his brother, observing the reality of the change, resolved within himself what to

R

# NOTES.

## NOTE A.—Page 5.

Sir John Glanville was, considerably, Hale's senior, and ranked, by his professional acquirements, among *able* lawyers. —See his Reports, first published by John Topham, Esq. 8vo. 1775. Preface, p. 1.

The Serjeant, during several parliamentary sessions, represented Plymouth, of which town he was Recorder; and became, at length, Speaker to the House of Commons. In the year 1661 he died. The following circumstance in his history is remarkable: it shall be given in the words of Burnet.—

The Serjeant's "father, had a fair estate, which he intended to settle on his elder brother; but he being a very vicious young man, and there appearing no hopes of his recovery, he settled it upon him that was the second son. But in truth, his eldest son, finding that what he had intended on him upon the threatenings of an angry father, was now set in earnest, became melancholy; and that, by degrees wrought so great a change on him, that what his father could not prevail in while he lived, was now effected in the severity of his last will, so that it was now too late for him to change it unless he set any estate that was gone from him. But his brother seeing the reality of the change, recovered within himself some

2

do. So he called him, with many of his friends, together to a
feast, and after other dishes had been served up to the dinner,
he ordered one that was covered, to be set before his brother,
and desired him to uncover it; which he doing, the company
was surprised to find it full of writings. So he told them that
he was now to do, what he was sure his father would have
done, if he had lived to see that happy change which they
now all saw in his brother; and, therefore, he freely restored to
him the whole estate."—*Life of Hale*, pp. 7, 8. 12mo. 1682.


### NOTE B.—Page 6.

Dr. Watts has noticed it, in the beautiful discourse he entitled " Death Improved to our Advantage," as having " laid
a foundation for the eminent virtue and religion, which have
rendered Hale so renowned."—*Dr. Watts's Works*, vol. i.
p. 589. 8vo.


### NOTE C.—Page 11.

He often said, that the true grounds and reasons of law
were so well delivered in the Digests, that a man could
never understand law, as a science, so well, as by seeking it
there; and, therefore, lamented much that the Roman law,
was so little studied in England.

A writer in " The Jurist," vol. i. p. 207, reviewing the
" History of the Roman Law in the Middle Ages," has noticed
this eulogium: well observing, that irresistible weight attaches
to the testimony, in consequence of our author's partiality for
the *common* law.


### NOTE D.—Page 13.

How far the celebrated Pieresc was affected by a like
influence, does not appear; but the lines of resemblance

between *him* and Atticus were strongly marked. See Gassendi's
Life of Pieresc, by Dr. Rand, pp. 244, 245; 8vo. 1657; a
work with which, it is probable, Sir Matthew Hale was
acquainted.


### NOTE E.—PAGE 14.

The whole covenant, the parliamentary exhortation respecting it, and the answers to objections, are preserved in
Rushworth's Collections, vol. v. See also Neale's History,
vol. iii. p. 59, &c. 8vo. 1822. In Mr. Lewis's valuable
Collection of Bishop Saunderson's Casuistical Lectures, 3 vols.
8vo. 1722, may be seen, in elaborate detail, the reasons upon
which the University of Oxford rejected the Covenant, vol. i.
p. 283, &c.


### NOTE F.—PAGE 21.

The reviewer of Mr. Thirlwall's edition of Lord Hale's
Works, in the Christian Observer, evidently discredited Wood's
statement, as to the solemn League and Covenant; and seems
quite dissatisfied with the apologetic tone of Mr. Thirlwall's
remarks. Were, indeed, the fact established by *proof,* instead
of mitigating censure, he would rather consider it, as " additional testimony to the Scriptural doctrine, of the corruption,
and blindness of our nature." vol. v. p. 565. Be it so. Yet
see the extract from Lodge's Illustrious Portraits, *ante,* [p. 20.]


### NOTE G.—PAGE 26.

See the Preface to Lord Hale's Jurisdiction of the Lords'
House, p. lxii. 4to. 1796. The fact is also stated in the
Biog. Britan. vol. iv. p. 2476. fol. 1767. And the Me-
morials of Archbishop Laud, p. 422, &c. are referred to.

## NOTE H.—Page 26.

Hist. of the Common Law, pp. v. and vi.
In the Trials of Charles I. and some of the Regicides, Family Library, No. XXXI. p. 33, the writer notices, that the course pursued by the king, in steadily denying the jurisdiction of the Court, is said to have been advised " by the celebrated Matthew Hale."

## NOTE I.—Page 30.

Godwin's History of the Commonwealth, vol. iii. p. 31. The reviewer in the Christian Observer, does not think Hale's taking the Engagement can subject him to much censure. It is there suggested, that his doing so might arise from an opinion, that the new constitution was so far established, as to render submission to it a duty. Vol. v. p. 565.

## NOTE J.—Page 30.

In Hale's Account of the Good Steward, there are passages having a direct reference, both to the Engagement, and the solemn League and Covenant, and fully confirming the statements in the text. See particularly pp. 261, 262, and 280, &c. Works, vol. ii.

## NOTE K.—Page 34.

Wood's Athen. Oxon. vol. iii. p. 1091. Siderfin, noticing the proceedings after the Restoration, namely, on the 22d of June, 12 Car. II., says of Hale and some of his brethren, " Ils appeare et fueront jure en le Chancery, et le prochein jour ils veign en lour veux Serjeants' robes et count en le common Bank en Francois lour nosme fueront, Witherington, Brown, Glyn, Earle, Barnard, Newdigate, *Hale*," &c.—— *Reports*, p. 3. fol. 1683.

## NOTE L.—Page 48.

The other county member was Edward Stephens. Parl. Hist. vol. iv. p. 4. The same person, no doubt, who, subsequently, published the " Contemplations." He is designated by Baxter, the Judge's familiar friend.

## NOTE M.—Page 48.

Baxter's account of this event is uncommonly interesting. Reliq. Baxter, p. 214. Mr. Orme, in his Life of Baxter, has made some valuable reflections upon it. Vol. i. p. 160, &c.

## NOTE N.—Page 63.

" I am very confident that, had the Bishops laid down some ceremonies that were of no great moment in themselves, yet too strictly and tenaciously imposed and maintained by them, the State, ecclesiastical and civil, had never felt those convulsions, nor episcopacy ever been brought into that loss, we have seen."—*Hale, Orig. MS.*

## NOTE O.—Page 87.

From some existing manuscripts, which I have seen, relating to Sir Thomas Rokeby, Knight, who was made a Judge in the year 1689, first of the Common Pleas, and afterwards, in the year 1695, of the King's Bench, it seems that, on his appointment to his high office, he " propounded" the Rules given in the text, for his own observation. It is hoped that a suitable Memorial of that very excellent man will, ere long, appear.

### NOTE P.—PAGE 87.

His sentiments on this subject will be best collected, from the following useful remarks upon the changes, which passed under his own eye, in many of the parties who were busied, in the affairs of the Commonwealth, and Restoration :—

" A man may see the great wisdom of God in destining and appointing, ordinarily, an afflicted, and a low condition to his church and people ; though we are apt to think, that such a condition is grievous, and unbecoming a people, to whom God confesseth his love; and of whom, he declareth his principal care. When, indeed, if it be duly considered, or if the experience of this and former times be duly weighed, we shall most easily see it is the greatest mercy, and an act of the highest love in the world. For, it is most certain, that there is a sea of corruption in the best of men ; and there is nothing under heaven that gives it that advantage to discover itself, as temporal advantages; and nothing under heaven so natural, and rational a means to suppress it, as a low, or afflicted condition. For instance ; there is a man that fears God, and hath given up his name to him, but it may be, he is naturally haughty, and highminded ; give him prosperity—pride shall endanger to undo him ; or, it may be, he is naturally choleric and froward— give him prosperity and power ; oppression or revenge shall endanger him ; or, he is naturally melancholy and suspicious —give him prosperity, he will endanger to be a projector of mischief; or, it may be, he is naturally of an airy temper— give him prosperity, 'tis a great danger, if vain glory do not undo him ; or, he is of a jolly merry temper—give him power and prosperity, 'tis a great hazard if luxury, excess, and intemperance, do not prevail upon him. Therefore, these corruptions and distempers, as they are under a check in adversity, and weakened thereby, so they are fed, and heightened by prosperity, success, and power. And if the power of grace have much ado with these corruptions, when they are *stripped* of the advantage of external supplies (as any man must needs find in himself it to be true) certainly, when these corruptions *have* the contributions of that, which feeds, and strengthens them, and gives them the opportunity more freely to act, the grace of God is endangered to be suppressed by it, in all human probability. And a little observation of our times, will make this truth legible, if we observe it, but in *one* sort and rank of men, who have, many of them, been much bettered by adversity, but undone by prosperity."—*Hale, Orig. MS.*

### NOTE Q.— Page 106.

This position is denied by Dr. Hutchinson. Historical Essay, p. 198, &c. Instead, however, of refuting Lord Hale's assertion, he only attempts to show, that the laws of all nations, have not been *like ours.*

### NOTE R.—Page 106.

A Tryal of Witches before Sir Matthew Hale, Knight, then Lord Chief Baron of the Exchequer, p. 58. 12mo. 1682. Mr. Cotton Mather printed this trial in his " Wonders of the Invisible World ;" and the Vicar of Walberton preserved it, in his celebrated work, as " a trial much considered by the Judges of New England." Turner's History of Remarkable Providences, p. 141. chap. xcii. fol. 1697.

### NOTE S.—Page 108.

On Dæmonology. Howell's Familiar Letters, vol. iii. p. 33. 8vo. 1655.
" Many deny witches at all, or, if there be any, they can do no harm. But, on the contrary, are most lawyers, divines,

physicians, philosophers."—*Burton's Anatomy of Melancholy.* fol. 1624. p. 47. part 1. s. 3.

A curious dissertation, entitled " The Witch," may be seen in Fuller's Holy State, b. 5. chap. 3. fol. 1663. 4th ed. p. 351.

### NOTE T.—Page 113.

" I must," (they are Baxter's words) " with a glad remembrance, acknowledge, that, while we were so unsuitable in places and worth, yet, some suitableness of judgment and disposition, made our frequent converse pleasing to us both. The last time but one that I was at his house, he made me lodge there, and in the morning, inviting me to more frequent visits, said,—' No man shall be more welcome.' And he was no dissembler."—*Hale's Works,* vol. i. p. 90.

### NOTE U.—Page 114.

A writer in the Gentleman's Magazine for 1788, describes " the house of the Lord Chief Justice at Acton, as situated very near the church, and with a fruitful field, grove, and garden, surrounded by a remarkably high, deeply-founded, and long - extended wall."—Vol. lviii. pp. 110, 111. See also Nicholl's Literary Anecdotes, vol. ix. pp. 504, 505.

### NOTE X.—Page 117.

" Because I lived near him, he was pleased to show me the copy of his draft, which was done according to all our sense; but *secretly,* lest the noise of a prepared act should be displeasing to the Parliament. But it was never more called for, and so, I believe, he burnt it."—*Reliq. Baxter,* part iii. p. 35.

A full account of the debates, and alterations agreed upon, is preserved in the same volume, part iii. p. 23, &c.

## NOTE Y.—Page 117.

Dr. Wm. Sberlock was evidently of the number. Some of his remarks, in his Vindication of Ecclesiastical Authority, pp. 185, &c. 8vo. 1685, are indicative of considerable spleen and anger at the attempted comprehension; and betray more than scepticism, as to Baxter's representation of *agreement* upon the subject.

## NOTE Z.—Page 119.

" It is a most certain truth, that things of indifferency in themselves, are easiest digested, and admitted, when they are not imposed, than when they are; the reason is, because it trencheth, as men think, upon their liberty to have indifferent things enjoined, in matters of religion; and because, upon the injunction of such things, men suspect more in them than they see. I am very confident that the use of the Liturgy, and many ceremonies, had obtained with much more ease, if they had *not* been imposed; for men *look* upon things strictly pressed, and things conceived to be necessary by those that impose them; and if they are received, they are *so* received; which, when they are not imposed, they look upon as things not held necessary by them that use them; and they are with more ease digested, when they come under their own dress of indifferency, than when injoined; because then, they are under the prejudice and jealousy of intended innovations, suspicions, and additions to divine worship, without divine warrant."—*Hale, Orig. MS.*

## NOTE AA.—Page 120.

This has been, in part, removed by the repeal of the Test Laws, &c.

Mr. Knox, like many other good men, seems to have satisfied himself with viewing *one side* only, of the great question of ecclesiastical polity : and was either inattentive to, or willingly ignorant of, those facts, which contributed to the renown, others, in proportion as they were conversant with them, acquired, for catholic liberality, and moderation. Who can tell the amount of such influence upon the mind of Paley, by his thorough acquaintance with Lardner's invaluable writings : with the remarks, for instance, of that learned, and impartial man, upon the Council of Nice ? See the Credibility of the Gospel History, chap. 71. Works, vol. iv. pp. 55—68. 8vo. 1827.

### NOTE BB.—Page 122.

Bishop Burnet himself was assailed, by some angry publications on this very account; especially for the remarks he made on the subject, in the New Preface to his Pastoral Care. One part of Mr. Sewell's answer to the Bishop, like the summary given in the foregoing extracts, of the reasons then assigned by opponents, proceeds in a strain exactly similar to Mr. Knox's, and is only less attractive, because less elegant.—*Sewell,* 2d ed. pp. 16, 17. 8vo. 1713.

### NOTE CC.—Page 127.

The title was as follows :—" Un Abridgment des plusieurs Cases et Resolutions del Common Ley, alphabeticalment digest, desouth severall titles per Henry Rolle, Serjeant del Ley, ovesque un Table des general Titles contenus en ceo." 2 vols. fol. 1668. pp. 940 and 836.

### NOTE DD.—Page 130.

" The great men of the law, living in those times, used to say, that this Henry Rolle was a just man, and that Matthew Hale was a good man ; yet the former was by nature penurious, and his wife made him worse. The other was contrary, being wonderfully charitable, and open-handed."—*Wood's Ath. Oxon.* vol. iii. p. 418.

## NOTE EE.—Page 132.

It is greatly to be regretted, that specimens of this correspondence should not be to be found. At the time Mr. Sylvester published the Life and Times of Baxter, expectation was held out, for a considerable volume of letters between that eminent man, and, among other celebrated persons, " the Lord Chief Justice Hale,"—letters polemical, casuistical, and practical, and some monitory and reproving ; but the design failed, for want, it is supposed, of encouragement.—Reliq. Baxter, Pref. to the Reader. Among the Baxter MSS. preserved in Red-cross Street Library, there appear to be no letters of Hale.

## NOTE FF.—Page 135.

The editor of Roger North, On the Study of the Laws, 8vo. p. 32, pointing out the inconsistency, as well as injustice, of the strictures of that lively writer (well styled by the editor of North's Life of Lord Guilford, vol. i. p. 138, an enemy, and a partisan) upon Sir Matthew Hale's character, has instanced, in proof of it, this passage, by comparison with one in the Life of Guilford. Vol. i. p. 124.

## NOTE GG.—Page 135.

A curious manuscript, formerly in the possession of Bennet Langton, Esq., the friend of Dr. Johnson, and in the handwriting of Mr. Langton's great-grandfather, who studied the law under Lord Hale's direction, strikingly exhibits the condescension, and courtesy of the judge's manners; his communicative disposition; and his earnest solicitude to promote useful knowledge. It is as follows :

" Dec. 13, 1672. I was sent to by Mr. Barker, to come to him to my Lord Chief Justice Hale's lodgings, at Serjeant's Inn. I was informed by Mr. Godolphin, about a month ago, that my Lord Chief Justice had declared, at supper, at Mr. Justice Twisden's, that if he could meet with a sober young man, that would entirely addict himself to his lordship's direction, he would take delight to communicate to him, and discourse with him at meals, and at leisure times; and, in three years' time, make him perfect in the practice of the law. I discoursed several times with Mr. Godolphin, of the great advantage that a student would make by his lordship's learned communication, and what influence it would have on a practiser, as well as honour, to be regarded as my lord's friend; and persuaded him to use his interest, and the offers of his friends, to procure his lordship's favour. But his inclinations leading him to travel, and his designs afterwards, to rely upon his interest at court, he had no thoughts to pursue it, but offered to engage friends on my behalf, which I refused, and told him, I would make use of no other person than my worthy friend Mr. Barker, whose acquaintance with my lord I knew, was very particular. After I had often reflected upon the nobleness of my lord's proposition, and the happiness of that person that should be preferred by so learned and pious a man, to whose opinion every court paid such a veneration that he was regarded as the oracle of the law, I made my application to Mr. Barker to intercede with my lord in my behalf, who assented to it with much readiness, as he always had been very obliging to me since I had the honour to be known to him. He made a visit to my lord, and told him that he heard of the declaration my lord made at Mr. Justice Twisden's. My lord said it was true, and he had entertained the same resolution a long time; but, not having met with any body to his purpose, he had discarded those thoughts, which Mr. B. did beg of his lordship to resume, in behalf of a person that he would recommend to him, and would be surety for his industry, and diligent observation of his lordship's directions. My lord then enquired who it was, and he mentioned me. Then he asked how long I had been at the law, of what country I was, and what estate I had ; which he told him, and that I was my father's eldest son. To which he replied, that he might talk no farther of it, for there was no likelihood that I would attend to the study of law as I ought. But Mr. B. gave him assurances that I would ; that his lordship might rely upon his word ; and that I had not taken this resolution without deliberation : that I had often been at Westminster Hall, where I had heard his lordship speak, and had a very great veneration for his lordship, and did earnestly desire this favour ; that my father had lately purchased the seat of the family, which was sold by the elder house, and by that means had run himself into five or six thousand pounds debt.

" ' Well, then,' said my lord, ' I pray bring him to me.'

" Dec. 13. I went to my lord and Mr. B. (for till that time my lord was either busy, or out of town) about four in the afternoon. My lord prayed us to sit, and, after some silence, Mr. B. acquainted my lord, that I was the person on whose behalf he had spoken to his lordship. My lord then said, that he understood that I had a fortune, and, therefore, would not so strictly engage myself in the crabbed study of the law, as was necessary for one that must make his dependence upon it. I told his lordship, that if he pleased to admit me to that favour I heard he designed to such a person he enquired after, that I should be very studious. My lord replied quick, that Mr. B. had given him assurances of it ; that Mr. B. was his worthy friend, with whom he had been acquainted a long time, and that, for his sake, he should be ready to do me any kindness ; for which I humbly gave his lordship thanks, as did, likewise, Mr. B. My lord asked me, how I had passed my time, and what standing I was of. I told him that I was almost six years of the Temple ; that I had travelled into France about two years ago ; since when I had discontinued my studies of the law, applying myself to the reading French books, and some histories. My lord discoursed of the necessity, of a firm, condescension, and courtesy of the judge's manners; his communicative disposition; and his earnest solicitude to promote useful knowledge. It is as follows:

" Dec. 13, 1672. I was sent to by Mr. Barker, to come to him to my Lord Chief Justice Hale's lodgings, at Serjeant's Inn. I was informed by Mr. Godolphin, about a month ago, that my Lord Chief Justice had declared, at supper, at Mr. Justice Twisden's, that if he could meet with a sober young man, that would entirely addict himself to his lordship's direction, he would take delight to communicate to him, and discourse with him at meals, and at leisure times; and, in three years' time, make him perfect in the practice of the law. I discoursed several times with Mr. Godolphin, of the great advantage that a student would make by his lordship's learned communication, and what influence it would have on a practiser, as well as honour, to be regarded as my lord's friend; and persuaded him to use his interest, and the offers of his friends to procure his lordship's favour. But his inclinations leading him to travel, and his designs afterwards, to rely upon his interest at court, he had no thoughts to pursue it, but offered to engage friends on my behalf, which I refused, and told him, I would make use of no other person than my worthy friend Mr. Barker, whose acquaintance with my lord I knew, was very particular. After I had often reflected upon the nobleness of my lord's proposition, and the happiness of that person that should be preferred by so learned and pious a man, to whose opinion every court paid such a veneration that he was regarded as the oracle of the law, I made my application to Mr. Barker to intercede with my lord in my behalf, who assented to it with much readiness, as he always had been very obliging to me since I had the honour to be known to him. He made a visit to my lord, and told him that he

industry, and diligent observation of his lordship's direction. My lord then enquired who it was, and he mentioned me. Then he asked how long I had been at the law, of what country I was, and what estate I had; which he told him, and that I was my father's eldest son. To which he replied that he might talk no farther of it, for there was no likelihood that I would attend to the study of law as I ought. But Mr. B. gave him assurances that I would: that he might rely upon his word; and that I had not made this resolution without deliberation: that I had often been at Westminster Hall, where I had heard his lordship, and had a very great veneration for his lordship, and did earnestly desire this favour; that my father had been persuaded to the seat of the family, which was sold by the same means, and by that means had run himself into so far in debt.

" ' Well, then,' said my lord . . . . . . . . . . . . . .

" Dec. 13. I went to my lord . . . . . . . . . . . . . . my lord was either busy, . . . . . . . . . . . . . afternoon. My lord prayed . . . . . . . . . . . . . Mr. B. acquainted my lord . . . . . . . . . . . . . behalf he had spoken to his . . . . . . . . . . . . . he understood that I had . . . . . . . . . . . . . strictly engage myself in . . . . . . . . . . . . . necessary for one that . . . . . . . . . . . . . told his lordship, that . . . . . . . . . . . . . I heard he designed . . . . . . . . . . . . . should be . . . . . had given . . . . friend, . . . . that, for . . . . for which . . . . Mr. B. . . . . what . . . . years . . . . two years . . . .

uninterrupted prosecution, of that study which any man designed—in the midst of which Mr. Justice Twisden came in, so that his lordship bid us come to him again in two hours after.

"About eight the same evening, we found his lordship alone. After we sat down, my lord bid me tell him what I read in Oxford, what here, and what in France. I told him I read Smith's Log.: Burgersdicius's Nat. Phil.: metaphysics, and moral philosophy; that, in the afternoons I used to read the classic authors; that, at my first coming to the inns of court, I read Littleton, and Doctor and Student, Perkins, my Lord Coke's Institutes, and some cases in his Reports; that, after I went into France, I applied myself to the learning of the language, and reading some French memoirs, as the Life of Mazarine, Memoirs of the D. of Guise, the History of the Academie Fr., and others; that since I came away, I continued to read some French books, as the History of the Turkish Government by ———, the Account of the last Dutch War, the State of Holland, &c.; that I read a great deal in Heylin's Geogr., some of Sir Walter Raleigh, my Lord Bacon of the Advancement of Learning, Tully's Offices, Rushworth's Collections.

"My lord said, that the study of the law was to one of these two ends: first, to fit a man with so much knowledge as will enable him to understand his own estate, and live in some repute among his neighbours in the country; or, secondly, to design the practice of it as an employment to be advantaged by it; and asked which of them was my purpose. I acquainted his lordship, that when I first came to the Temple I did not design to prosecute the study of the law, so as to make advantage by it; but now, by the advice of my father and my uncle, and Dr. Peirse, in whose college I had my education, and received many instances of his great kindness to me, I had formed resolutions to practise it, and, therefore, made my suit to his lordship, for his directions.

"'Well,' said my lord, 'since I see your intentions, I will give what assistance I can.'

"My lord said, that there were two ways of applying one's self to the study of the law : one was to attain the great learning, and knowledge of it, which was to be had in all the old books ; but that did require great time, and would be at least seven years before a man would be fit to make any benefit by it : the other was, by fitting one's self for the practice of the court, by reading the new reports, and the present constitution of the law ; and to this latter my lord advised me, having already passed so much time, a great many of the cases seldom coming in practice, and several of them antiquated.

" In order to which study, his lordship did direct that I should be very exact in Littleton, and after, read carefully my Lord Coke's Littleton, and then his Reports. After which Plowden, Dier, Croke, and Moore. That I should keep constantly to the exercises of the house, and, in term, to Westminster Hall, to the King's Bench, because the young lawyers began their practice there ; that I should associate with studious persons, rather above, than below my standing ; and, after next term, get me a common-place book ; and that I must spoil one book, binding Rolles' Abr. with white paper between the leaves, and according to those titles insert what I did not find there before, according to the preface to that book, which my lord said came from his hands, and that he did obtain of Sir Francis Rolle to suffer it to be printed, to be a platform to the young students. My lord said he would, at any time that I should come to him, shew me the method he used, and direct me, and that if he were busy he would tell me so.

" He said that he studied sixteen hours a day, for the first two years that he came to the inns of court, but almost brought himself to his grave, though he were of a very strong constitution ; and afterwards, reduced himself to eight hours ; but that he would not advise any body to so much ; that he thought six hours a day, with attention and constancy, was sufficient ; that a man must use his body as he would use his horse, and his stomach ; not tire him at once, but rise with an appetite. That his father did order in his will that he should follow the law ; that he came from the university with some aversion for lawyers, and thought them a barbarous sort of people, unfit for any thing but their own trade; but having occasion to speak about business with Serjeant Glanvil, he found him of such prudence and candour, that from that time he altered his apprehensions, and betook himself to the study of the law, and oft told Serjeant Glanvil, that he was the cause of his application to the law.

" That constantly after meals, every one, in his turn, proposed a case, in which every one argued.

" That he took up a resolution, which he punctually observed ever since, that he would never more see a play, having spent all his money on them at Oxford; and having experienced that it was so great an alienation of his mind from his studies, by the recurring of the speeches and actions into his thoughts, as well as the loss of time when he saw them; that he had often disputes with Mr. Selden, who was his great friend, and used to say he found so great refreshment by it; but my lord told him, he had so much knowledge of the inconvenience of them, that he would not see one for a hundred pounds. But he said he was not of Mr. Prynne's judgment (which I minded him of) for he did not think it unlawful, but very fit for gentlemen sometimes, but not for students.

" My lord said, at the beginning of his discourse, that my friends might expect that I should marry, to take off the present debt from the estate, which else would increase, and then there could be no thoughts of a very earnest prosecution of study; to which Mr. B. said, that my father, when he made this purchase that put him into debt, did resolve to sell other land, and by that might either discharge, or lessen it.

" My lord said that his rule for his health, was to be temperate, and keep himself warm. He never made breakfasts, but used, in the morning, to drink a glass of some sort of ale. That he went to bed at nine, and rose between six and seven, allowing himself a good refreshment for his sleep. That the law will admit of no rival, nothing to go even with it; but that sometimes one may, for diversion, read in the Latin historians of England, Hoveden, and Mathew Paris, &c.; but after it is conquered, it will admit of other studies.

" I asked, whether his lordship read the same law in the

afternoon, as he did in the morning. He said no: he read the old books in the morning; and the new in the afternoon, because of fitting himself for conversation. I asked if he kept constantly to one court, which he said he did.

" He said, a little law, a good tongue, and a good memory, would fit a man for the Chancery; and he said it was a golden practice, for the lawyers there, got more money than in all the other courts in Westminster Hall. I told his lordship what my lord chancellor lately said, that he would reduce the practice of the court to another method, and not suffer above one counsel, or two at the most, in one cause.

" My lord said, that 1,000l. a year was a great deal for any common lawyer to get; and Mr. B. said that Mr. Winnington did make 2000l. per year by it. My lord answered, that Mr. W. made great advantage by his city practice, but did not believe he made so much of it. I told his lordship of what Mr. W. had said before the counsel on Wednesday, on the behalf of stage coaches, which were then attempted to be overthrown.

" At our coming away, my lord did reiterate his willingness to direct, and assist me; and I did beg of his lordship, that he would permit me to consult his lordship in the reason of any thing that I was ignorant of, and that his lordship would be pleased to examine me in what I should read, that he might find, in what measure I did apply myself to the execution of his commands; to which he readily assented."—*Miss Seward's Anecdotes*, vol. iv. pp. 409—419.

To the liberality, and kindness of E. H. Barker, Esq. of Thetford, I am indebted for a fragment, in the handwriting of Sir Robert Southwell, which enables me to give the following *additional* counsels. A short account of Sir Robert, in Noble's Continuation of Granger, vol. i. p. 161, notices his having studied the law at Lincoln's Inn; and a letter from him to Lord Hale's grandson has already appeared.[1]

Sir Robert's endorsement upon the document referred to, runs thus: " London, 7th November, 1664. Memorandum,

---

[1] See *ante*, p. 265.

that waiting then upon my Lord Chief Baron Hale, he advised me as within.

"To read the English history from Henry VII. downwards; *that* he commended, and the Annals of Queen Elizabeth, more than my Lord Herbert.

"To read the Pleas of the Crown, and the Jurisdiction of Courts, the statute De Prerogativâ Regis, and Stamford's Commentary thereon. He said, that the king's prerogative is no where, entirely handled; and that with wise design, it being so tender a point; so that all that is of it, is dispersedly up and down in the law books, as occasions in particular cases happened.

"He recommended that Smith's Common-Wealth be read, to know the general constitution of the kingdom, which it does well enough; he observed, that *general* things prepare a man, but it is *particular* knowledge that makes him able.

"He said that I should know the revenue of the king, and what parts of it are more in name, than in fact; that this is learnt from estimates, audits, &c. to be had from the Treasury, &c.

"He advised me to make a common-place book, alphabetically, as Ab, Ac, Ad, &c. first to compute some heads to reduce things to, and then reduce all things to heads, and, if the matter be various, to several heads; and judge well what it does most naturally belong unto; 'and although,' said he, 'you refer things ill at first, yet frequent recourse will make you acquainted with what you have done; you will mend your business every day, and in three or four years grow most dextrous in referring: this will make you quarrel with your first notes; but, though useless to another, they will serve well yourself.'

"'Be sure that your study improve the time you spend in it, which by this exact writing you will do.'

"'You will be perfected in things, although in your common-place book they are more confused; yet to you, not so.'

"'Index your council books, and also write a little extract of the business; the very form of it.'

" ' Read Bodin ; and Tacitus, but be not tied to his wisdom as fit for these times.' "

## NOTE HH.—Page 136.

" Dr. Willis, in his lifetime, wrote his case," says Baxter, " without his name, in an observation in his Pharmaceut, &c. which was shortly printed after his own death, and before his patient's ; but, I dare say it, so crudely, as is no honour to that book."—*Hale's Works*, vol. i. pp. 107, 108.

## NOTE II.—Page 139.

Omnibus Christi fidelibus ad quos præsens Scriptura pervenerit, Matthæus' Hale, miles, capitalis justiciarius Domini Regis, ad placita coram ipso rege tenenda assignatus, salutem in Domino sempiternam : Noveritis me præfatum Matthæum Hale, militem, jam senem factum, et variis corporis mei senilis morbis et infirmitatibus dire laborantem, et adhuc detentum, hâc chartâ mea, resignare et sursum reddere, serenissimo Domino nostro Carolo Secundo, Dei gratiâ Angliæ, Scotiæ, Franciæ, et Hiberniæ Regi, fidei defensori, &c. predictum officium, capitalis justiciarii, ad placita coram ipso rege tenenda, humillime petens, quod hoc scriptum irrotuletur de recordo. In cujus rei testimonium, huic chartæ meæ resignationis, sigillum meum apposui. Datum vicesimo primo die Februarii, anno Regni dicti Domini Regis, nunc vicesimo octavo.

### TRANSLATION.

To all persons in Christ to whom these presents shall come, Matthew Hale, Knight, Chief Justice of our Lord the King, assigned to hold pleas before the King, greeting : Know ye that I, the said Matthew Hale, Knight, having now become advanced in years, and, by reason of my age, being now severely afflicted, with various diseases, and infirmities, and still confined thereby, do, by this instrument, resign, and render up to our most gracious Lord, Charles the Second, by the Grace of God, of England, Scotland, France, and Ireland, King, Defender of the Faith, &c. the said office of Chief Justice; most humbly beseeching, that this deed may be enrolled. In witness whereof, I have set my seal to this deed of my resignation.

Given the 21st day of February, in the twenty-eighth year of the reign of our said Lord the King.—*Works*, vol. i. p. 44.

### NOTE KK.—Page 146.

Mr. Baxter, in his Address to the Reader, prefixed to Gouge's " Surest and Safest Way of Thriving," 8vo. 1676, says: " Experiences are contemptible to none but atheists, who believe not God's providences! I remember that great and excellent person (whose published Contemplations hint the same to the world, though without his consent) hath told me, how the strange providences of God, in laming and disabling his horses, and other impeditions in a journey towards London for worldly advantages, on the Lord's-day, when he was young, did convince him, and engage him ever after to spend the day as he hath since done, and there directed his children to do. God governeth this world, and hath some previous rewards and punishments, stops and helps, though the great and full retribution, be hereafter."

### NOTE LL.—Page 154.

The Sacred Theory of the Earth, by Dr. Thos. Burnet, of the Charter-house, is the volume here intended. Although succeeding philosophers have proved its system untenable, yet, as a mere romance, it is uncommonly well worth reading. The vigour of its conceptions, and the charms of its style, have seldom been equalled, and never, perhaps, surpassed. A full, and able article upon it, appeared in the Retrospective Review, vol. vi. p. 133, &c

## NOTE MM.—Page 156.

Serjeant Runnington, referring to this circumstance, remarks, that the Duke of Sully, who cannot be thought either a credulous or weak man, has noticed it in a very particular manner. Life of Hale, prefixed to the History of Common Law, p. xxvii.

## NOTE NN.—Page 170.

Mr. Sheppard, in his elegant " Thoughts," has, in the section " on the means of maintaining a devotional habit, and spirit, in a life of business," given prominence to the judge's character in this aspect of it.—Pp. 218—222. 8vo. 1829. 5th Edition.

## NOTE OO.—Page 170.

I once asked the late venerable Dr. Abraham Rees, how he managed, amidst his numerous avocations, to achieve so vast a work as the Cyclopædia? He said, it was by rising early.

## NOTE PP.—Page 190.

Baxter, in his Funeral Sermon for Henry Ashurst, Esq. remarks, that " *he* greatly hated backbiting, and obloquy. Speak evil of no man, was a text which he often had in his mouth." And he adds, " I never knew any noted man so free from that vice, as Judge Hale, and Mr. Ashurst." P. 43. 4to. 1681.

## NOTE QQ.—Page 194.

See a very curious, and equally strange volume, entitled, " The Spirit of Detraction conjured, and convicted, in seven

...in Stevius' Reports, fol. 1658; and ...Mr. Evelyn, in his Diary, does the ...vol. i. p. 413, ann. 1819. It is not quite ...our author did not sometimes use the s final himself. His signature to the "Exceptions" delivered into court, on the trial of Love, is so printed.—Trial, *ut supra*, p. 97.

Mr. Malone, in his edition of Dryden's Critical and Miscellaneous Prose Works, vol. iii. p. 156, 8vo. 1800, notices the *s* final, as an inaccurate, but not uncommon, occurrence, both with Dryden, and his contemporaries. Lord Clarendon, for instance, calls Dr. Earle, Bishop of Salisbury, Dr. Earle*s*.


## NOTE XX.—Page 201.

" Thou owest all thou hast to thy Maker, and if thou shouldst give him *all* thou hast, thou givest him but *his own*. 1 Chron. xxix. 14. He calls to thee, but for a *part* of what he hath lent thee, and he is pleased so far to accept thy cheerful obedience herein, as to become thy debtor, even for that which thou owest him. This is thy honour, and this will be thy profit : thou shalt receive thy loan, with advantage. I can safely, and without vanity, say, I have hitherto found this truth exactly fulfilled. In those weeks and years wherein I have thus sowed sparingly, I have, even in temporals, reaped sparingly : and I ever found, when my hand was most liberal, I never lost by it, but found a return a hundred fold more than my expense : and the bread that I have thus cast upon the waters, I found it within a few days. God forbid that I should look upon it as the merit of my charity, for it was his own ; or that I should be, therefore, charitable, because I expected a temporal reward : for I have therein but done my duty, and am therein an unprofitable servant. But I bless God, that hath made good the truth of this, even to my sensible, and frequent experience."—*Hale's Discourse of the Knowledge of God and Ourselves*, pp. 434, 435.


## NOTE YY.—Page 202.

Mr. Wynne, in his valuable edition of Eunomus, vol. iv. p. 8t &c. 12mo. 1785, regards this sentiment, as at variance with Lord Hale's avowed opinion as a judge—on poverty being no plea, in justification of theft. But it seems difficult to perceive the discrepancy. And see the Hist. Plac. Cor. vol. i. pp. 54, 55, and 565.

### NOTE ZZ.—Page 206.

In the elaborate judgment he delivered in the case of Sir Robert Atkyns *v.* Holford Clare, undersheriff of the county of Gloucester, 1 Ventr. p. 399, wherein he differed from "two of his brothers," and because the case related to his own county, and was much to the prejudice of it, would have been glad to have been excused giving his opinion, he openly said,—" I must argue as the law *is,* and not as I wish it; I argue according to my conscience, though somewhat against my desire, and I am sure against my particular interest."

The case just mentioned is preserved in MS. among the Hargrave papers, No. 47, article 3, Catal. *ut supra,* p. 14. Mr. Hargrave, however, alluding to the report of it in Ventris, has written,—" this seems a different report."

### NOTE AAA.—Page 207.

Mr. Joshua Wilson has given prominence to this case in his masterly appeal, "respecting the religious celebration of marriage," 8vo. 1831, pp. 27, 28. And the Rev. author of the Conformist's Pleas, before cited, alludes to it with evident satisfaction, designating our author, in connexion with it, "the honour of all good men." 4th Plea, p. 27, 4to. 1683.

### NOTE BBB.—Page 208.

Dr. Johnson, with his usual penetration, has alluded to this, in one of his notes to Shakspeare.

*Isab.* Shew some pity.
*Ang.* I shew it most of all, when I shew justice;
    For then I pity those, *I do not know.*
        *Measure for Measure,* Act II. Scene 2, Reed's Ed. vol. ii. p 50.

## NOTE CCC.—Page 211.

That excellent man, the Rev. J. Hieron, of Losco, in Derbyshire, mentioning Lord Hale's name, in a letter dated February 15th, 1676, calls him "that upright judge, that scorned to take a bribe; the honour and oracle of the law."— *Life, by Porter*, 4to. 1691, pp. 88, 89.

A Quaker, who, judging from a singular volume, entitled, a Short Account of his "Life," seems to have devoted considerable attention to the judge's writings, and money also, for their distribution; styles him an "eminent pattern of piety, humility, and preacher of righteousness in all his life, and conversation."— *Life of J. Pennyman*, 8vo. 1703, 2d ed. p. 200.

The beneficed minister of the Church of England, who wrote the Conformists' Pleas for the Nonconformists, mentions him as "the renowned Sir Mathew Hale," 2d Plea, 4to. 1682, 2d Edition, the Preface. "The most renowned Sir Mathew Hale, whose sense may be as soon taken as most men's alive, for his wisdom, loyalty, integrity, and impartiality in all acts of judgment."—Ibid. p. 65. The same writer, afterwards styles him "the great Sir Mathew Hale."—*Third Plea*, p. 23, 4to. 1682: and see Fuller's "Worthies," printed in the year 1662, 4to. Ed. 1811, vol. i. p. 381, tit. "Gloucestershire."

## NOTE DDD.—Page 211.

On one of those occasions it was, that he uttered the following sententious judgment:—"Both points are worth trial, and argument at law." The Marquis of Antrim *v.* the Duke of Buckingham, 14 & 15 Chas. 2. January, "in Cancellaria." Cases argued, and decreed in the High Court of Chancery, p. 18. fol. 1707. 2d Ed.

The following extract from the judgment given by Lord Keeper Henley, afterwards Lord Chancellor Northington, in the case of Burgess *v.* Wheate, will apply both to the text connected with this note, and the statements *ante* at pp. 203 —207.

s

" The judgment [by Lord Hale] that I have stated, being an authority in point, great efforts have been made to weaken it. Lord Hale's abilities in Equity a little questioned—that would not bear commenting upon—then, he must be suspected of a little undue compassion, and was determining a general important point, with regard only to the compassionate circumstances of the case.—But this observation is as little warranted, as that of his want of abilities."—*Reports of Cases in Chancery*, from the Orig. MSS. of Lord Chancellor Northington, collected and arranged, by the Hon. Robert Henley Eden [now Lord Henley], vol. i. p. 254. 8vo. 1827.

### NOTE EEE.—Page 212.

Sir Thomas Elyot, in his " Boke named the Governour," gives to the idea intended, the denomination —" Maturitie : " and then adds, " The Grekes, in a proverbe, do express it properly in two words, whiche I can none otherwise interprete in Englysh, but—spede the slowly."—P. 81. 24mo. 1537.

### NOTE FFF.—Page 213.

The celebrated Robert Bolton, in his Funeral Notes upon his Patron, Sir Augustine Nicholls, Knight, Judge of the Common Pleas, mentions as one of his " very special judiciary endowments,"—" Patience to hear the basest ; *both* parties all they could say."— *Works*, p. 153. 4to. 1638.

### NOTE GGG.—Page 215.

The Reverend N. Parkhurst, in his Life of Lady Elizabeth Brooke, notices the conduct of our " worthy Judge" towards the Nonconformists, in illustration of that practised by her ladyship.—12mo. 1684. p. 72.

### NOTE HHH.—Page 217.

He thought that " in several particular churches, or conventions of Christians, there may be several forms of government; differing forms of ordination; differing ceremonies: and yet, nevertheless, as long as they continue in unity in *fundamentals* of faith, and Christ's institutions, with other churches, the *unity* of the church visible is not thereby broken, much less that of the invisible."—*Hale, Orig. MS.*

### NOTE III.—Page 217.

" Many ceremonies might be useful to draw over an ignorant or unconverted people, but they will be found of less use and less value, in a knowing people; and such are, at this day, even the very English laity; among whom thousands will be found, that can reason the point of ceremonies, their usefulness, or uselessness, as well as many divines; men that will tell them, they are not so well agreeing with the simplicity and spirituality of the gospel; nor will they be easily beaten from that hold by arguments, policy, or antiquity."—*Hale, Orig. MS.*

### NOTE KKK.—Page 217.

" The Lord," he writes, in a manuscript ' concerning the christian religion, its own excellency, amiableness, and purity, and admirable congruity to the perfection of the human nature,' —"the Lord be merciful to us, such hath been the malice, and subtlety of the devil, such the villany and corruption of mankind, that they have formed devices, by additions and sophistications, of their own contriving; by lies and fictions; by false doctrines, and corrupt interpretations; by pretended revelations, and feigned miracles; by corrupt glosses, and devised canons; and a world of such trash, fathered, and hung upon this pure and excellent institution, to prostitute it to the base and ugly designs, and ends of a pack of ambitious, proud, vain-glorious, covetous men; whereby that glorious gospel, that was given from heaven to bring, and conduct men *to* heaven, is, by these artifices, made the engine and device for men that pretend to it, to acquire wealth, domination, and power in the earth; to the extreme dishonour of the glorious God; to the contempt of our Saviour Christ; to the indignity of the gospel; and the shaking of the truth of all true religion, unless the same Almighty God interpose his own power and goodness, to prevent, or remedy it."—*Hale, Orig. MS.*

### NOTE LLL.—Page 218.

Baxter, in his " Second True Defence of the meer Non-conformists against the Untrue Accounts, Reasonings, and History of Dr. Edward Stillingfleet, Dean of St. Paul's," &c. 4to. 1681. says, at chapter xv. which contains some notes on the book called the Lively Picture of Dr. Lud. Moulin, and his Repentance, subscribed by Dr. Simon Patrick, Dean of Peterborough, and Dr. Gilb. Burnet,—" You seem to vindicate the book called the Friendly Debate; I shall, shortly, further tell you of somewhat in it to be repented of. And if partiality made not repentance a very difficult work, you would have no need of a monitor. But you may think me partial, though I acknowledge your civilities to me; I can shew you a manuscript of one both impartial and judicious, even the late Judge Hale, expressing so great a dislike of that Debate, and the Ecclesiastical Policy, as tending to the injury of religion itself, that he wisheth the authors would openly profess, that they write for themselves, and no more so abusively pretend, it is for religion."— Pp. 187, 188.

### NOTE MMM.—Page 218.

Hale's Works, vol. i. pp. 291, 296, 297. As a "note" to the latter of these pages, Mr. Baxter, in his edition of that discourse, says,—" His," Lord Hale's, " preference of epis-copacy before all other governments, was his real judgment.

But it was its essentials, and not all the additionals, that he meant. For, to my knowledge, he would have been glad of the primitive model of Bishop Usher, who was his much-valued friend."—4to. 1684. Preface to the Reader.

### NOTE NNN.—Page 224.

" At this day we have no warrant at all for giving credit to any predictions as prophetical, but those that are contained in the sacred Scriptures; for though it must be agreed, that there was a time, both under the Old and New Testaments, wherein there *were* prophetical spirits, yet they were for that extraordinary end, of giving a seal to the truth of the holy word, which is to be now, our only standing prophecy; as, likewise, was that of miracles, and tongues. But now that the testament is sealed, we have no warrant, either to expect, or believe such extraordinary revelations."—*Hale, Orig. MS.*

Again he writes,—" When a prophecy is clothed in obscure, and dark expressions, it becomes us, with patience and sobriety, to expect the interpretation of it by the *event*, and not too curiously to determine concerning it, or to make our own fancies the interpreters of it; yet, sometimes, it pleaseth God to make the very prophecy, though obscure, and the strong persuasion of persons of the meaning of it, the instrument to fulfil it. It is reported of Vespasian, that the prophecy of Christ touching the destruction of Jerusalem, made him the more confident, and industrious, in effecting it; and I have reason to conjecture, that the very prophecies touching the fall of Antichrist, and the conversion of the Jews, will be an instrument in the hands of God, exciting the minds, and spirits of men, to the effecting of both."—*Ibid.*

### NOTE OOO.—Page 224.

Thus he writes in his Treatise on Policy :—" It is most certain, that the best of men are subject to errors, and mistakes. The Fathers were excellent men; gave great attention to the christian religion; and deserve great esteem among all Christians; but we deny the privilege of infallibility, to any since the times of Christ, and his apostles."—*Hale, Orig. MS.*

### NOTE PPP.—Page 229.

Dr. Johnson, in his Rambler, has noticed this circumstance, in illustration of an author's pride, when, sometimes concealing his name,—Works, vol. iv. p. 82. 12mo. 1816.

### NOTE QQQ.—Page 230.

My late venerated friend, the Rev. Robert Hall, describing Dr. Ryland, beautifully observed, that "he was seldom known to speak of his religious joys, or sorrows: his devotional feelings were too deep, and too sacred, to suffer themselves to evaporate in ordinary conversation. His religion appeared in its fruits; in gentleness, humility, and benevolence," &c.—*Hall's Works*, vol. i. p. 392. A fine passage, on the same topic, occurs in Lord Hale's Letter of Advice, pp. 80, 81.

### NOTE RRR.—Page 236.

Mr. Hargrave has some conclusive remarks, upon this part of the same "rash censurer's" assertions, in his very elaborate Preface to Hale's Jurisdiction of the Lords, p. lxxvii. 4to. 1796.

### NOTE SSS.—Page 240.

In the Preface to the Treatise on the Knowledge of God and Ourselves, Bishop Burnet's narrative is, in connexion with this subject, said, "very unadvisedly and improperly," to bear the name of Sir Matthew's "Life." Mr. Stephens, who intended to have written it (see the Works, vol. i. p. 92), was, no doubt, the author of the "Preface."

## NOTE TTT.—Page 242.

The Rev. R. B. Hone, in his Lives of Eminent Christians, has noticed some of their excellencies, p. 122. Life of Dr. Hammond.

## NOTE UUU.—Page 242.

See a Model for the maintaining of Students of choice Abilities, at the University, and principally in order to the Ministry; with Epistles and Recommendations; and an Account of the Settlement, and Practice of it in the Universities, from the Doctors there, &c. 4to. 1658. London.

## NOTE XXX.—Page 244.

" I was a better Grecian in the sixteenth year, than in the sixty-sixth year of my life. My application to another study and profession, rendered my skill in that language of little use to me, and so I wore it out by degrees."—*Primit. Orig.* Address to the Reader.

## NOTE YYY.—Page 245.

Bishop Beveridge was not a poet; but whenever, was there a finer eulogium pronounced upon music, than in his " Private Thoughts "—" Concerning my words?"—Resolution v. 12mo. 1710. Pp. 161, 162.

## NOTE ZZZ.—Page 245.

To one part, however, of the worship he refers to, he had a strong *objection;* and the notice of it, by so wise and good a man, may have its use. Thus he writes :—

" Some part of the service that is *sung,* methinks is better, and more suitable, to be *said,* than sung. It hath a kind of incongruity in it, and to me abates the value, and use of the matter itself. Possibly, praises and thanksgivings, and the Psalms of David, which, for the most part, are such, may be conveniently *sung ;* but to sing with music—' Lord have mercy upon us, miserable sinners ;' or, ' Lord have mercy upon us, and incline our hearts to keep this law ; ' and such like; carries a kind of incongruity, and, to me, an indecency, in it. The tones, too, seem very affected ; and, to me, offensive. I could, with more intention of mind, follow the repetition of the Lord's Prayer, according to our usual speech and pronunciation, than follow it after that uncouth, and, I am sure, unnecessary tone, and pronunciation, wherein it is used in cathedrals, and when men do not understand, what reason there is for such a singularity ; and understand not what is the meaning or use of it, as I profess I do not; it troubles, and distracts them in that business, wherein they should be freest from perturbation.—— *Hale, Orig. MS.*

## NOTE AAAA.—Page 246.

Lilly styles him, " that monster of ingratitude, my quondam taylor, John Gadbury."—*Life and Times,* p. 86. 8vo. 1822.

## NOTE BBBB.—Page 250.

Dr. Henry more generally styles Lord Hale, " a learned author ; " in one place he asserts, that there is the redounding of no small commendation to him, for his industry and dexterity, and special sagacity, in making, and improving hydrostatical experiments ; and he expressly imputes it to modesty, that he entitles his second book, " Difficiles Nugæ."— Remarks, *ut supra,* p. 188.

## NOTE CCCC.—Page 252.

It would be easy, by extracts, to shew, how beneficially the belief in question operated upon Dr. More himself, and how deeply he was impressed with a conviction of its utility to others : but it shall suffice, to refer merely to his " Remarks," upon Lord Hale's Discourses, on the Gravitation, and Non-gravitation of Fluid Bodies. 12mo. 1676. pp. 191, 192, where, in a " Lucretian strain of confidence," he justifies the sentiment in the Text, as an " ancient Platonic, or rather Pythagoric opinion."

## NOTE DDDD.—Page 252.

In the Biographie Universelle, Ancienne et Moderne, almost the smallest space possible is allotted to Lord Hale : the writer says, however, " Versé dans presque toutes les sciences humaines, il l'était surtout profondément dans la jurisprudence, et dans la théologie."—Vol. xix. p. 325.

## NOTE EEEE.—Page 255.

This MS. consisting of two volumes, was presented by Francis Hargrave, Esq. to the Rev. Dr. Parr, and deposited by him in the Library of Emmanuel College, Cambridge. See Bibl. Parriana, p. 538. In the works of Dr. Parr, vol. viii. p. 38, a letter is inserted from Mr. Hargrave, partly upon Lord Hale's " Tentamina concerning the Soul," in which a desire is expressed, of knowing how the Doctor was struck with the manner, in which so abstruse a subject was treated. Unfortunately no reply is printed.

The Rev. T. S. Hughes obtained permission from the Society of Emmanuel, to publish the MS. in question, but the design was objected to, it should seem, by Dr. Parr. See Dr. Parr's Works, vol. viii. p. 196.

Mr. Dyer states, that the MS. is not in Sir Matthew's own hand-writing : that it was written in 1673, but that the copy was made in 1692, the original having been lent to Sir Robert Southwell, for the purpose, by Matthew Hale, Esq. Lincoln's

Inn, the judge's grandson.—Privileges of the University of
Cambridge, vol. i. p. 622.

In a biographical memoir of Jeremy Taylor, prefixed to his
selections from the Bishop's works, Mr. Hughes has given a
brief specimen of the MS. Vol. i. p. lxiv.

### NOTE FFFF.—Page 255.

See the Hargrave Collection in the British Museum, No.
485, where it appears with the following title, " A Treatise of
the Nature of Lawes in General, and touching the Law of
Nature." Fol. Catal. p. 131. And in Bibl. Harl. 7159, Plut.
xxxiii. E, in the British Museum, is a MS. entitled, "Some
Chapters touching the Laws of Nature, by the late Ld. Ch. J.
Hale, and copied from his own writing, lent to Sir Robert
Southwell, by his grandson, Matthew Hale, Esq. 1693, and
copied from the same, August 19, 1696."

### NOTE GGGG.—Page 256.

See Hale's Jurisdiction of the Lords' House, Pref. ccxii.;
and also the Hargrave Collection in the British Museum, No.
490, Article 7.

In the British Museum, Bibl. Harl. 4666–69, Plut. xlv. B,
are papers attributed to Lord Hale, " concerning the succession
to the crown of England."

### NOTE HHHH.—Page 256.

See Hale's Jurisdiction of the Lords' House, Pref. p. ccxiii.
And see the Hargrave Collection, No. 94, Catal. p. 25. The
title runs thus : " Copy of a Treatise, by Lord Ch. Justice
Hale, intitled, Prærogativa Regis : with Marginal Notes, in Mr.
Hargrave's hand-writing." At the beginning is a table of the
chapters into which the work is divided. At the end, are
the following papers : 1. The Titles in Sir Matthew Hale's

Commonplace Book, in Lincoln's Inn Library. 2. An Account of Three Manuscript Volumes, of Lord Hale, on the King's Prerogative. 3. An Extract from Ld. Ch. Jus. Hale's Volume conceived to be what Bishop Burnet, in his list of his Lordship's Manuscripts, entitles, "Incepta de Juribus Coronæ." Folio, on paper.

In a separate paper, at the end, it is said, "There are three manuscript volumes of Lord Hale, on the King's Prerogative, all in folio."

"1. The first is, chiefly, a rough collection of materials for the subject, without any title : but, from being the most imperfect of the three volumes, seems to be what, in the list of MSS. of Lord Hale, in Bishop Burnet's Life of him, is entitled, *Incepta de Juribus Coronæ.*

"2. The second is entitled, by Lord Hale, *Preparatory Notes touching the Rights of the Crown.* This appears digested into the form of a treatise ; and contains fourteen chapters, which, from the number of subjects in each, appears to comprehend, in a general way, a rough draft of a very great part of his Lordship's design.

"3. The third has the semblance of being Lord Hale's latest attempt on the subject. It is entitled, at the beginning, *Prærogativa Regis.* It contains thirteen chapters. But this volume, in consequence of allotting fewer subjects to each chapter than the *Preparatory Notes,* doth not extend nearly so far in the execution of Lord Hale's design, as the last mentioned volume. So far, however, as it goes, it is more full, copious, and complete ; and, consequently, seems entitled to be considered as of higher authority. This is the volume from which the extract relative to Regencies, has been made ; though at first, by mistake, I styled the volume, *Incepta de Juribus Coronæ.*

"Besides the three volumes before mentioned, there is an analysis, or syllabus, of the whole of the designed work, in Lord Hale's own hand-writing ; and by this it appears, that he had gone as far in the division of the work into chapters, as No. 51. This proves, that the design was of immense extent ; for, notwithstanding his having gone so far in his chapters, the latter part of the analysis, being almost one-fourth of it, stands unchaptered, and, from its contents, seems as if it would have required, at least, twenty chapters more. F. H. 6 Dec^r- 1788."

Mr. Hargrave, in Co. Lit. 70, b., mentions a MS. by Sir M. Hale, entitled, Jura Coronæ, and he gives an extract in the Collection of Tracts, Pref. p. xxx. &c.

And see Bridgman's Legal Bibliography, p. 147. An extract from the Prerogativa Regis, appeared in the Jurist for July, 1832, p. 251.

## NOTE IIII.—Page 256.

See Hale's Jurisdiction of the Lords' House, Pref. p. ccxvii. In the Hargrave Collection, No. 95, Catal. p. 26, it appears with the following title : " Lord Chief Justice Hale's Preparatory Notes, touching Parliamentary Proceedings." Folio, on paper. At "the end are some memoranda to the work, in Mr. Hargrave's hand-writing ; and also a fair copy of two chapters of the work. Folio, on paper." In the same collection, No. 492, Catal. p. 134, is preserved, The "Discourse, or History, concerning the Power of Judicature in the King's Council, and in Parliament. By Lord Chief Justice Hale. Copied from the original, in his own hand-writing, (imperfect.) Folio." For an account of this manuscript, see Hale's Jurisdiction, p. ccxvii. There is a MS. in the British Museum, Bibl. Harl. 1698. Pt. xliii. c., on " Judicature in Parliament," but it seems doubtful, whether it is Lord Hale's.

## NOTE KKKK.—Page 256.

Mr. Hargrave, in his preface to the volume thus referred to, notices two other MSS. of Lord Hale's, having relation to the same subject, communicated to him by John Blagden Hale, Esq. The one entitled, a "Discourse, or History, concerning the Power of Judicature in the King's Council, and in Parliament." The other, entitled, "Preparatory Notes, touching Parliamentary Proceedings." Preface, pp. 1. ccxv. ccxvii.

### NOTE LLLL.—Page 256.

In the Hargrave Collection, No. 137, Catal. p. 36, it bears the following title : " A Treatise, by Lord Chief Justice Hale, on the Admiralty Jurisdiction. Folio, on paper." Opposite the beginning, Mr. Hargrave says, " Some part of this book, at least, written after 1669. Prynne's Animadversion on 4th Institute, which was published in that year, being seemingly referred to." P. 155.

### NOTE MMMM.—Page 256.

In the Hargrave Collection, No. 98, Article 1, Catal. p. 26, it appears thus : " A Narrative Legall, and Historicall, touchinge the Customes : in the hand-writing of Lord Ch. Jus. Hale. Fol. 1."

Mr. Hargrave has written at the beginning, thus : " Recd. as a present, from Mr. Beardsworth, F. H. The hand-writing is Lord Hale's, as I conclude, from a comparison with various MSS. known to be Lord Hale's, which I have seen." F. H.

" I am clear that the hand-writing is Lord Hale's." F. H.

### NOTE NNNN.—Page 256.

Now printed. In the Hargrave Collection, No. 97, Catal. p. 26, the manuscript is preserved, with the following title, " A Folio Volume on paper ; containing a Treatise in English, De Jure Maris, et Brachiorum ejusdem." It has a table of contents at the beginning, and a few alphabetical references, in Mr. Hardinge's handwriting, at the end.

A note in Mr. Hargrave's hand, says, " This Treatise is cited as a MS. by Lord Hale, in Parker's Reports, p. 69."

### NOTE OOOO.—Page 256.

In the Hargrave Collection, in the British Museum, this forms Article 13, of No. 494 ; and Mr. Hargrave has noticed it, as copied from one of Mr. Jekyll's three volumes of copies of various MSS. of Lord Hale.

The title given to it in Mr. Hargrave's Catal. is, " A Scheme of the Laws of England, drawn by Sir M. Hale, entitled, Schema Monumentorum Legum Angliæ." fol. 299. Catal. p. 135.

There is in the British Museum Bibl. Lansdown, 632, P. L. LXXVII. G. a MS. entitled, "Hale on the Laws of England." It thus commences : " Extracts from a MS. of Sir Matthew Hale, Ch. J. of England, by J. Anstis, Esq. in one of his MS. volumes." N. d. 3. p. 507, &c.

## NOTE PPPP.—Page 257.

This was entitled, " Reflections by the Lord Chief Justice Hale, on Mr. Hobbs' Dialogue of the Law ; " and at the time Mr. Hargrave published the Collection of Tracts, already cited, it had fallen into his possession. He notices it as a performance, though unfinished, which contains both a very pointed refutation, and a very severe reprehension of Mr. Hobbs, for his arbitrary notions concerning the extent of the king's prerogatives. " In general," says Mr. Hargrave; " Lord Hale is the most dispassionate of all writers, upon our law, and constitution." But he saw the pernicious tendency of Mr. Hobbs's doctrine, in so strong a point of view, that in this instance, Lord Hale appears to have been scarce able to restrain his indignation.—*Collection of Tracts*, Pref. p. xxii.

In the Hargrave Collection, No. 96, Catalogue, p. 26, it is thus entitled: " Reflections on Mr. Hobbs his Dialogue of the Law, by the Lord Chief Justice Hale, copied from the original, which was lent to Sir Robert Southwell, by his grandson, about November, 1690." Folio, on paper. Bound with this volume, is another copy of the " Reflections," differently arranged : also, an extract from one of Lord Hale's MSS. " touching the particulars that would be fit to be reformed ; and first, concerning the books of the law, both statute law, and common law."

The Orig. MS. on Hobbs, is at Cottles.

An extract from it, is given in the Report of the case of Impositions, on an information in the Exchequer, by the Attorney General, against Mr. John Bates, Merchant, 4 James I. 1606—1610. State Trials, by Howell, vol. ii. p. 379.

### NOTE QQQQ.—Page 290.

The publisher of the volume entitled, Magnetismus magnus, conjectured to be Mr. Stephens, says, in the preface to that work, expressly alluding to this "Tract of Humility," that Sir M. Hale wrote it on *his* motion, not long before his last sickness, pp. ii. iii.

### NOTE RRRR.—Page 290.

Dr. Parr, after bestowing high commendation upon this " very picture" of Hale himself, adds,—" Upon every account of matter, style, and spirit, it is a work which deserves to be read every year, by every light of the Church, and every sage of the Law, in Christendom."—*Works*, vol. iv. pp. 167, 168.

### NOTE SSSS.—Page 294.

In one of his Manuscripts, touching the Law of Nature, Sir Matthew thus expresses himself:—" Since words and phrases, are but a sort of institution, chosen or agreed upon, to signify things or notions, I shall take the liberty to be master of my words; and use such as I think fit, and sufficient, to be the image of my thoughts, without being solicitous of using those modes, or obliging myself to the strict rules, or artificial terms, now, or formerly, in fashion among many learned men."— *Orig. MS.*

### NOTE TTTT.—Page 295.

The passage given in the text, (as are some other paragraphs from the beautiful discourse of which it forms a part,) is introduced into a scarce sermon, by Timothy Rogers, M. A. on the death, and in pursuance of the will, of Mr. Anthony Dunwell. The title is,—" Fall not out by the way ; or a persuasion to a friendly correspondence between the Conformists and Nonconformists," 12mo. 1692 ; and there are few sermons better worthy of universal regard. It is characterised, throughout, by the same spirit of judgment, wisdom, and love, which dwelt in Lord Hale.

I must be allowed to refer here, with a desire that every reader, whether Churchman or Dissenter, may peruse it, to a discourse, lately published by my beloved, and honoured friend, the Rev. J. Pye Smith, D. D.—" On the Temper to be cultivated by Christians of different Denominations, towards each other." Annexed to it, is a Letter, addressed by the learned preacher, to the Rev. S. Lee, D. D. &c. Regius Professor of Hebrew, in the University of Cambridge ; and whatever difference of opinion may be cherished, with respect to some portions of the epistle, there can be none as to the courteousness, the candour, and the holy feelings, of the writer.

## NOTE UUUU.—Page 303.

It may be as well to state, that the remarks contained in the 5th vol. of the Christian Observer, p. 567, were not noticed, until after those in the text were written. Had it, however, been otherwise, those last mentioned, would not have appeared to the writer the less necessary. The critique, referred to, in that justly admired periodical, was the more gratifying, because of the assent given in an earlier volume (the 4th, p. 38,) to the Bishop of Salisbury's *general* commendation of Hale's " Contemplations," in his Easter Catechism.

Citations, in support of the strictures to which this note is prefixed, might easily be adduced, and even accumulated. But as that would be beside the design more immediately in view, a reference to " an attempt to explain, and establish the doctrine of justification by faith *only*, in Ten Sermons, upon the Nature and Effects of Faith, by James Thomas O'Brien, D. D. Fellow of Trinity College, and Archbishop King's Lecturer in Divinity, in the University of Dublin," 8vo. 1833, shall satisfy. The cardinal truths of the gospel, especially that in question, are there, not merely advocated with great learning, and courageous wisdom, but set forth, also, in their genuine, practical, and inevitable efficacy. A finer illustration than that volume presents, can scarcely be imagined, of the accuracy of the late very Reverend Dean of Carlisle, when he declared his belief, that "the doctrine of justification by faith, as stated in the eleventh, twelfth, and thirteenth Articles of "the Church of England," is the *very corner-stone* of the whole system of the first Reformers. "It was the doctrine," he said, "both of Luther, and Calvin, and of Philip Melancthon ; and lastly, it was the doctrine of the whole college of Apostles."—*Dr. Isaac Milner's Sermons*, vol. i. p. 24.

## NOTE XXXX.—Page 309.

No notice need, perhaps, have been taken of what is objectionable in Lord Hale's writings, had it not been that the matters pointed out as erroneous, are of VITAL IMPORTANCE : or had it not, at least, been true, that, in such matters, no error can be innocent. But his Lordship has so forcibly expressed himself upon this very subject, as to supersede the necessity for apologetical observations. His remarks, it is thought, more than justify the strictures which have been submitted.

"Possibly there may be an innocent error in Philosophy, or in Mathematics; but it is not possible, there should be an innocent ERROR in any matter, especially dogmatical, in RELIGION. For, first, the matter and business of Religion, is more consequential to mankind, than other sciences; therefore, all errors in *this* are, at least, dangerous. Secondly, every error admitted in Religion, doth bring a prejudice to another *truth*, and the credit of it; for if one may be an error, and yet admitted for a truth, why not another; and thus every error doth, in some degree, shake, and disgrace, and bring into suspicion undoubted truths? Thirdly, It opens a way to admit all *kinds* of errors in Religion, to be tolerable and innocent; for one may hold that adoration of saints is an error, but an innocent one; and another may hold the like of *justification by* works an error, but an innocent error; and another may hold the like for adoration of images; and so it will be endless. Certainly, that which reflects upon the honour of God, cannot be an innocent error; and such are *all* errors in matters of religion; they abuse the truth of God, and obtrude a lie upon the world, as that of the divine truth."—*Hale, Orig. MS.*

### NOTE YYYY.—Page 310.

"Some works have escaped total destruction, but yet have had reason to lament the fate of orphans, exposed to the frauds of unfaithful guardians. How *Hale* would have borne the mutilations, which his Pleas of the Crown have suffered from the editor, they who knew his character will easily conceive."—*The Idler.* Dr. Johnson's Works, vol. vii. pp. 212, 213.

### NOTE ZZZZ.—Page 311.

Lord Erskine continually styles him "the great judge;" or, "the great Hale"—"the great and benevolent Hale;" or, "the venerable Hale."—Speeches, passim.

The name of Lord Erskine having been so often mentioned in the present volume, the insertion of a letter here, in my possession, in his Lordship's own hand, on the subject of his decrees as Chancellor, may not be thought intrusive. In various aspects it is an interesting document; and not having, it is believed, been printed, it may be fairly associated with the object of his admiration.

" Sir,

" Your letter was sent to me from Sussex yesterday. I certainly was appointed Chancellor, under the administration under which Mr. Fox was Secretary of State, in 1806, and could have been Chancellor under no administration, in which he had not a part ; nor would have accepted, without him, any office whatsoever. I believe *that* administration was said, by all the *blockheads*, to be made up of all the *talents* in the country.

" But you have certainly lost your bett on the subject of my decrees. *None of which,* but one, was appealed against, except one upon a branch of Mr. Thelusson's will ; *but it was* AFFIRMED, without a dissentient voice, on the motion of Lord Eldon, then, and now, Lord Chancellor. If you think I was no lawyer, you may continue to think so. It is plain you are no lawyer yourself; but I wish every man to retain his own opinions, though at the cost of three dozen of port.

" Your humble servant,

" Mr. ————. " ERSKINE."

" To save you from spending your money upon betts, you are sure to lose—remember, that no man can be a great advocate who is no lawyer. The thing is impossible."

## NOTE AAAAA.—Page 316.

An instance of this occurs in reference to that difficult passage, Luke xxii. 42. See the Family Expositor, *in loc.* where Dr. Doddridge quotes Lord Hale's " Contemplations," and prefers the sense *there* given, to the solution offered by the judicious Hooker.

## NOTE BBBBB.—Page 318.

The author of the Preface to the Discourse, by Lord Hale, on the Knowledge of God, bears the following testimony :—" I am persuaded, that as much time as he spent, and pains as he took, in the study and practice of the law, and business of a not ordinary Judge, but Chief Baron, and Chief Justice; that the time he employed, and the pains he took (if I may call that pains which afforded so much pleasure, and satisfaction to him), in these [theological] studies, and for that purpose, would be found to *exceed* them."

### NOTE CCCCC.—Page 320.

See President Edwards's Dissertation concerning the End for which God created the World; Works, vol. i. p. 443, and particularly Dr. E. Williams's Note, ibid. p. 533; the Enquiry into the Freedom of the Will, ibid. p. 145, or part 1, sect. 4; also part 3, sect. 4, and the Note at p. 278; likewise Dr. Pye Smith's Sermon on "The Divine Glory displayed in the Permission of Sin." 8vo. 1803.

One short extract must be added to the above references, from the pages of a beautiful, living writer. It is closely allied to the subject; and should it only be the means of inducing acquaintance with the volume from which it is taken, and some other devout, and exquisite productions from the same pen, the design, in the selection, will be fully answered.

" Let me now, with the honest wish, that you should attain substantial peace, not ' such as the world giveth,' once more recall to view, the sum, and essence of this ' gospel.' It has been represented as a free, gratuitous, and entire remission of sins, granted through the amazing mediation of that Lord of glory, who gave his life a ransom : becoming thus a demonstration of all moral perfections in God, and a creative power, to reawaken them in man : far more than a mere pardon, or reprieve from penal justice—rather a justification, or honourable release ; an act of full oblivion, which instates offenders in the same enjoyment of Divine favour, as if their progenitor had never fallen ; as if they, themselves, had never renewed, and multiplied his fall : nay, which seals to them in reversion, for the sake, and as the chosen reward, of the Great Restorer, a *sublimer happiness* than they could have enjoyed, unfallen ; sublimer, if only for that love of *gratitude*—boundless and eternal *gratitude,* which is its best constituent ; which begins, when first we look, with the eye of faith, on Him whom we 'have pierced,' and can terminate only, when He shall cease ' *to be* GLORIFIED *in his saints, and admired in all them that believe.* ' "—*Essays designed to afford Christian Encouragement and Consolation. By John Sheppard.* Pp. 33, 34. 8vo. 1833.

### NOTE DDDDD.—PAGE 322.

The wisdom of that celebrated enactment, 29 Charles II. c. 3, was not only often applauded by Lord Kenyon, and some other Judges, but attributed, generally, to Sir Matthew Hale. Our author's title to that honour is, however, doubtful. See the preface to the valuable Treatise on the Statute of Frauds, by W. Roberts, Esq.

The Hon. Daines Barrington thought it great injustice to the memory of Hale, to say, that he was the person who drew it—Observations on the more Ancient Statutes, p. 196. 4to. 1775.

### NOTE EEEEE.—PAGE 323.

Lord Chief Justice Willes, delivering judgment, in the case of Smith d. Dormer, *v.* Parkhurst, on a writ of error, in the House of Lords, after laying down certain rules, with respect to the construction of deeds, added,—" These maxims are founded upon the *greatest* authority, Coke, Plowden, and Lord Chief Justice Hale." 3 Atk. p. 136.

Hale and Coke are classed well together, by Mr. Hallam, in reference to the law of Treason. See the Constit. Hist. vol. ii. p. 507.

### NOTE FFFFF.—PAGE 324.

Mr. Mallet, in his Life of Lord Bacon, says, in contrast with the universality of that great man's genius, that Lord Coke could be nothing more than a lawyer."—P. 47. 8vo. 1740.

### NOTE GGGGG.—Page 324.

In the case of Omichund and Barker, *ante*, p. 323, Lord Chief Justice Willes, having alluded to the New Testament in reference to the Jews, as put by the great oracle upon a footing with stigmatized and infamous persons; added, with studied quaintness, " Coke is a very great lawyer, but our Saviour and St. Peter are, in this respect, much better authorities, than a person possessed with such *narrow* notions."

### NOTE HHHHH.—Page 324.

The king used to say, " He was like a cat; throw him which way you would, he would light on his feet."

" He was often observed to insult upon misery, and to lose a life sooner than a jest, when he sat upon the tribunal of justice."—Howell's Dodona's Grove, pp. 85, 86. 12mo. 1645.

There is an interesting chapter in D'Israeli's Second Series of the Curiosities of Literature, on "Coke's Style and Conduct," vol. i. p. 313; and another on his " Domestic History," ib. p. 289.

### NOTE IIIII.— Page 326.

He called the Duke of Buckingham, " our Saviour."— 1 Clarendon, 6; Herbert, 210. Sir Henry Wotton calls this, exalting the Duke's allegiance, with blasphemy.—Reliq. Wotton, p. 62. 12mo. 1651.

### NOTE KKKKK.—Page 327.

The ambiguity thus apparent in the Will, as to the first Lady Hale, may be thus explained :—A tomb was erected at Alderley, to her memory, but her remains were deposited at Acton.—Information from Mr. Hale.

## NOTE LLLLL.—Page 343.

This legacy was laid out by Mr. Baxter, in the "greatest Cambridge Bible;" which, says he, "waiting for my own death, I gave to Sir William Ellis, who laid out about ten pounds to put it into a more curious cover; and he keeps it for a monument in his honour."—Reliq. Baxter, Part iii. p. 181. Before it, Baxter prefixed the judge's picture.—Reliq. Baxter, Part iii. p. 181; and the following sketch of his character :—

" Sir Matthew Hale, that unwearied student, that prudent man, that solid philosopher, that famous lawyer, that pillar and basis of justice, (who would not have done an unjust act for any worldly price, or motive,) the ornament of his Majesty's government, and honour of England, the highest faculty of the soul of Westminster Hall, and pattern to all the reverend and honourable judges; that godly, serious, practical Christian, the lover of goodness, and all good men; a lamenter of the clergy's selfishness, and unfaithfulness, and discord, and the sad divisions following hereupon; an earnest desirer of their reformation, concord, and the church's peace, and of a reformed Act of Uniformity, as the best, and necessary means thereto; that great contemner of the riches, pomp, and vanity of the world; that pattern of honest plainness, and humility, who, while he fled from the honours that pursued him, was yet Lord Chief Justice of the King's Bench, after his long being Lord Chief Baron of the Exchequer; living and dying, entering on, using, and voluntarily surrendering his place of judicature, with the most universal love, and honour, and praise, that ever did English subject in this age, or any that just history doth acquaint with, &c. &c. &c. This man, so wise, so good, so great, bequeathing me, in his testament, forty shillings, merely as a testimony of his respect and love, I thought this book, the Testament of Christ, the meetest purchase by that price, to remain in memorial of the faithful love which he bore, and long expressed, to his inferior, and unworthy, but honouring friend, who thought to have been with Christ before him, and waited for the day of his perfect conjunction with the spirits of the just made perfect."—*Additional Notes, Hale's Works*, vol. i. pp. 113, 114.

### NOTE MMMMM.—Page 348.

Mr. Stephens, in the Preface to his Discourse of the Knowledge of God and Ourselves, 8vo. 1688, says, the Judge " changed his mind."

Bishop Burnet notices the same thing, and explains the matter, that the Judge's " worthy executors, and his hopeful grandchildren, may not conclude themselves to be under an indispensable obligation, of depriving the publick of his excellent writings."—*Life*, pp. 185—187. 12mo. 1682.

### NOTE NNNNN.—Page 349.

In 1697, a folio volume was published, under the title of, Catalogi Librorum Manuscriptorum Angliæ et Hiberniæ, in unum Collecti cum Indice Alphabetico.

That volume contains a full account of the manuscripts preserved in the library of Lincoln's Inn; and the department in question bears the following title :—

LIBRORUM
MANUSCRIPTORUM
HOSPITII LINCOLNIENSIS
CATALOGUS.
ISTORUM AUTEM PLEROSQUE, HONORABILI SOCIETATI
TESTAMENTO DONAVIT, PRÆSTANTISSIMUS ANTECESSOR ET
GENERE OMNI DOCTRINÆ EXCELLENS,
MATTH: HALES MILES,
SUPREMUS ANGLIÆ JUSTITIARUS :
CONTINET AUTEM CODICES CXCII.
HUNC QUOQUE CATALOGUM DEBEMUS FAVORI, AC STUDIO,
REVERENDI VIRI D. PHIL. STUBBS COLL. WADHAMENSIS SOCII.

*FINIS.*

R. CLAY, PRINTER, BREAD-STREET HILL.

# Im The Story
## personalised classic books

JANE
IN
WONDERLAND

LEWIS
CARROLL

"Beautiful gift.. lovely finish.
My Niece loves it, so precious!"

Helen R Brumfieldon

☆☆☆☆☆

**UNIQUE GIFT**

FOR KIDS, PARTNERS
AND FRIENDS

## Timeless books such as:

### Kids

Alice in Wonderland · The Jungle Book · The Wonderful Wizard of Oz
Peter and Wendy · Robin Hood · The Prince and The Pauper
The Railway Children · Treasure Island · A Christmas Carol

### Adults

Romeo and Juliet · Dracula

**Highly** Customizable

**Change** Books Title

**Replace** Character's Name in your

**Upload** Photo (for inside page)

**Add** Inscriptions

## Visit
# Im The Story .com
### and order yours today!